TAOS MODERNS

TAOS MODERNS

ART OF THE NEW

David L. Witt

Foreword by Gerald Nordland

Photography by Michael O'Shaughnessy

David L. Witt

RED CRANE BOOKS

Santa Fe

First Edition

Manufactured in Hong Kong

Cover and text design by Karen Olsen, Webb Design, Taos

Cover painting by Edward Corbett

Cover photograph by Michael O'Shaughnessy

Photograph Acknowledgments:

Two important writer/photographers of Taos, Mildred Tolbert and Regina Cooke, were responsible for taking the black-and-white illustrations in this book, or were directly responsible for the preservation of the images. Between them, they gave thousands of prints and negatives to the Harwood Foundation Museum archives. Their documentation of the 1950s in Taos is a resource of incalculable value. Thanks to the Harwood Foundation for allowing inclusion of these photographs in this book.

Thanks to various private collectors and to the following institutions and persons for allowing the photography of their paintings.

The Albuquerque Museum, Albuquerque, New Mexico: Plate 37

The Harwood Foundation of the University of New Mexico, Taos, New Mexico: Plates 1, 2, 3, 4, 5, 12, 13, 24, 35, 36, 42, 45, 46, 47, 48, 49, 50, 51, 52

Taos Municipal Schools, Taos, New Mexico: Plate 30

The University of New Mexico Art Museum, Albuquerque, New Mexico: Plates 10, 44

Helen M. Derbyshire: Plate 25

Ted Egri: Plates 32, 33

Beatrice Mandelman Ribak: Plates 15, 16, 17, 18, 19, 20, 21, 22

Robert Sonora: Plate 26

Witt, David L., 1951-
Taos moderns: art of the new / David L. Witt; foreword by Gerald Nordland; color photography by Michael O'Shaughnessy. — 1st ed.
p. cm.
Includes bibliographical references and index.
ISBN 1-878610-16-3 (cloth) — ISBN 1-878610-17-1 (paper)
1. Art, American—New Mexico—Taos. 2. Art, Modern—20th century—New Mexico—Taos. 3. Artists—New Mexico—Taos—Biography.
I. Title.
N6535.T3W58 1992 92-10213
759.189'53—dc20 CIP

Red Crane Books
826 Camino de Monte Rey
Santa Fe, New Mexico 87501

For the people of the valley.

CONTENTS

FOREWORD

This book makes a welcome contribution to our knowledge of the art life of Taos in our century and more specifically the 1940s, 1950s, and 1960s. David Witt has brought much needed attention to a remarkable group of artists who came to be known as "The Taos Moderns," and he has assembled a valuable photo documentation of their work, which has been unknown or unavailable for too long. From among the hundreds of artists who visited or lived in Taos in this period, Witt spotlights fourteen who came primarily in their mature years and, in response to the land and the community, elected to stay and produce their art in the relative isolation of the high desert. These artists came from New York, San Francisco, or elsewhere—on a whim, at the casual suggestion of friends, or because of an eye-catching photo. Few knew anything about New Mexico, but they liked the look of the land, the quality of light, and the fact that it wasn't like home. Their responses to living in the community were immediate and positive. Although essentially nonfigurative artists, unconcerned with specific subject matter, they all spoke fondly of the impact of their early impressions of the land, its impressive gorges, great distances, continually changing light, colors, and skies. They shared an immediate respect for the native peoples and their history, perhaps intuiting a mystical correspondence with the Indian's world-view.

The Taos Moderns are contrasted with their precursors, the successful Taos Society of Artists, a group which embodied a concern for romantic landscape and native Indian subject matter imbued with sentiment and nostalgia. The Moderns focused on motif and the manner in which an artwork is developed; they had great respect for the teachings of European modern art as received through the work of Kandinsky, Miró, Mondrian, Hofmann, and Albers.

The Taos Society group was older, content with its proprietary views of place and history. Most of them felt the Moderns were practicing "weird distortions" relating to cubism and expressionism, and seemed to be inadequately trained amateurs. In their turn, the Moderns felt the Taos Society members were repeating the same paintings without growing. It was a classic conflict in which a group of outsider have-nots strove to create their new vision while challenging their established elders, as each generation must.

The early visits to Taos of New York's "Ash Can painters" and Stieglitz circle masters like Marsden Hartley, John Marin, and the soon-to-be-naturalized Georgia O'Keeffe are outlined. The roles of important regional art figures like Emil Bisttram and Raymond Jonson are described. With a growing tourist industry, an expanding market for American painting, and colonizing expeditions by Taos galleries into Texas and California, aesthetic and financial scrutiny came to be focused on the rival camps. Important exhibitions put the national reputation of these groups into new aesthetic balance. "Taos Painting: Yesterday and Today," staged by the Colorado Springs Fine Arts Center in 1952, provided the earliest usage of the name "Taos Moderns," and other presentations followed at the Jonson Gallery of the University of New Mexico in Albuquerque.

Witt provides a brief overview of the history of the region's private art galleries as well as their impact on artists' loyalties. The national juried annuals organized by the University of Illinois—"Contemporary American Painting and Sculpture"—began to feature the Taos Moderns to the disadvantage of the rival group. A brief but important account of the development of community groups such as the Harwood Foundation, the Helene Wurlitzer Foundation, and artists' cooperative galleries further clarifies the depth of support these artists received from local art organizations.

Witt's sensitive analysis of the Moderns' art and the welcome illustrations of the little-known work of the period serve to reestablish reputations and to legitimize the contribution which the Moderns made to our cultural history. Andrew Dasburg (1887–1979) met Picasso and Matisse in Paris and discovered Cézanne for himself by 1909. His personal vision is demonstrated through landscape-inspired compositions which balance originality and tradition. His participation in the Armory Show (1913) and the Forum Exhibition (1916) places him, as a modernist pioneer, with Max Weber, Marsden Hartley, and Stanton Macdonald Wright.

Tom Benrimo (1887–1958) was already an established nonfigurative painter when he built a career as a teacher at the Pratt Institute and as an illustrator in New York in the 1920s and 1930s. In Taos he recast his painting manner, utilizing surrealist elements in one body of work and flat-patterned, post-cubist color compositions in another. Witt reveals that László Moholy-Nagy so admired Benrimo's work and teaching that he invited Benrimo to succeed him as director of "The New Bauhaus" in Chicago.

Cady Wells's (1904–1954) brief career is represented by a powerful, dark composition that suggests the energy and boldness of Hartley. Ted Egri (b. 1913) came to Taos in 1950 as a painter but turned with success to innovative multiple-figure sculptures. John DePuy (b. 1927) studied in New York with Hans Hofmann and retains the bold flatness and surface awareness characteristic of the master. Robert D. Ray (b. 1924) arrived in 1954 and came to utilize landscape metaphors with modernist simplifications and subtlety. Oli Sihvonen (1921–1991) studied at Black Mountain College with Albers, came to Taos in 1949, and began working in a large-scale color-field manner unparalleled in Taos art. Earl Stroh (b. 1924) wanted to come West to the University of New Mexico and after a summer in Taos (1947), he settled in and developed the abstract landscape poetry which has inspired his work.

Louise Ganthiers (1907–1982) came to Taos in 1950 and painted from local subjects, achieving recognition with works like the heavily impastoed *Buffalo Dancer* (reproduced here). Her later paintings reveal a lyrical color sense. Agnes Martin (b. 1912) first came to Taos as a student in 1947. She returned in the 1950s as a young professional and later, as a well-recognized professional, settled in Cuba, New Mexico. Her work from the 1950s in Taos was an intense effort of self-discovery, investigating her own perceptions, overcoming resistances, exploring consciousness, patiently seeking revelation. Martin had learned how to look at paintings, and now she taught herself to construct abstract compositions with shapes, colors, and space, without egoistic expressivity. The examples of her work which Witt illustrates have rarely been seen outside of private collections, and the body of work from which they were drawn has been destroyed by the artist. The illustrations enhance our knowledge of this most poetic and personal contributor to the movement called minimalism.

Louis Ribak (1903–1979) and his wife Beatrice Mandelman came to Taos in 1944 from successful careers in New York. Ribak founded the Taos Valley Art School in 1947 and served the GI generation importantly. Mandelman had studied in Paris with Léger. The two were accomplished painters, broadly experienced, aware of current directions in abstraction, and quick to explore possibilities in a painterly fashion but without dogma. The Taos Valley Art School provided a brief but important center for scores of students to investigate the arts under Ribak's compassionate guidance at a crucial moment in their and our country's artistic development.

Edward Corbett (1919–1971) had taught for five years alongside Clyfford Still, Mark Rothko, Clay Spohn, and Richard Diebenkorn at the California School of Fine Arts (CSFA) in San Francisco. He came to Taos for the summers of 1948–1950 and settled there in 1951, following a managerial/aesthetic coup at CSFA. Diebenkorn was pursuing an M.F.A. at Albuquerque (1950–1952), and Spohn had relocated his studio in Taos. Corbett sought refuge at Ribak's school on the GI Bill and was later awarded the Rosenberg Fellowship of the San Francisco Art Association. Corbett had been a painter of mysterious dark canvases in experimental media, but he quickly found his way to pastel, charcoal, chalk, and pencil in a poetic body of work that is simultaneously abstract and reflective of the light and nature of the northern desert. While organizing "15 Americans" for New York's Museum of Modern Art, Dorothy Miller visited Diebenkorn's studio at the University of New Mexico. She saw Diebenkorn's vigorous new canvases (one is reproduced here in color) and followed his advice to seek out Corbett in Taos. The resultant exhibition and catalog (spring 1952), which featured, among other northeasterners, Baziotes, Pollock, Rothko, Still, and Tomlin, also launched the national career of one unknown westerner—Ed Corbett, with his poetic pastels and chalks.

Clay Spohn (1898–1977) was a witty, worldly San Franciscan, who embodied the most extreme, iconoclastic, and dadaistic spirit of the CSFA. He had the temerity to question abstract expressionism and the moral leadership of Still and Rothko. Spohn was so thoroughly antiestablishment that despite his unusual plastic sensitivity and his obvious gift for painting, he was unable to deal successfully with the commercial art world. He remains the elusive and incomprehensible eminence of the glory years of the CSFA.

David Witt's thoughtful and soundly researched study reestablishes an exciting generation of artists for contemporary readers. Until this book, serious students have known these artists only partially, as individuals committed to freedom and to the fulfillment of their talents. Now we can begin to see the Moderns in their Taos context (with all its pluses and minuses). We can begin to appreciate the full dimensionality of the courage and dedication that was required to evolve a fresh and communicative vision within the modernist language.

As individuals, the Taos Moderns have had an impact on the national sensibility, setting themselves apart in the exploration of internal responses to the great themes and ideas of their time. As a social group, they exhibited together, argued, praised, and fulminated—inspired by example, spirit, and unpretentious tenacity. *Taos Moderns* will serve to generate new studies of these fascinating individuals who did so much to further the evolution of the modern spirit in our American Southwest.

Gerald Nordland

PREFACE

In a conversation with Beatrice Mandelman on December 23, 1982, she described herself to me as being "the first of the second generation of artists in Taos." By reason of age or temperament, she insisted that the artists who had come to Taos before the Second World War were out of a different mold from those who came during or afterward. (She and her husband Louis Ribak moved to Taos in 1944.) That interview began my years of research into a fascinating and little known aspect of American art history, the story of the Taos Moderns.

In this book, I have included the words of art critics and have quoted the artists to help explain their intentions. I interviewed most of the Taos Moderns still living; the artists, as primary sources, were essential to the writing.

Many of my colleagues were kind enough to review the manuscript and make important suggestions. Wesley Rusnell, curator at the Roswell Museum and Art Center, and a painter in Taos during the 1960s, brought considerable focus to the work, identifying the need to make the book more than just a collection of artists' anecdotes. He gave me great insight into the artists through analysis of their work and personalities.

The text was edited for content by Earl Stroh, who generously brought to it fifty years of experience as an artist and art historian. He more than lived up to his reputation as the toughest, most perceptive, and most knowledgeable critic in the Southwest.

By believing in the project, the staff of Red Crane Books and their outside editor, Suzan Campbell, gave the Taos Moderns their first chance to have a book of their own.

I am grateful to you all.

CHRONOLOGY

1939 Thomas and Dorothy Benrimo move to Taos.
The La Fonda Gallery opens.

1944 Louis Ribak and Beatrice Mandelman move to Taos.

1945 The Blue Door Gallery opens.
Cady Wells makes the first of several visits to paint at a studio owned by Rebecca James.
Clay Spohn visits Taos.

1946 La Galeria Escondida opens.

1947 *Taos and Its Artists,* by Mabel Dodge Luhan, is published.
Charles Stewart moves to Taos.
Agnes Martin and Earl Stroh study art at the University of New Mexico Summer Field School of Art.
Louis Ribak opens his Taos Valley Art School.
Edward Corbett visits Taos.

1948 Cliff and Barbara Harmon move to Taos.
Earl Stroh moves to Taos for study with Andrew Dasburg.

1949 John DePuy visits Taos.
Oli Sihvonen comes to Taos to attend Ribak's art school.

1950 Ted and Kit Egri and Louise Ganthiers move to Taos.
La Galeria Escondida artists are given a group show in Lubbock, Texas.

1951 Edward Corbett, Clay Spohn, and Arthur Jacobson move to Taos.
The Ruins Gallery opens, showing the work of Egri, Ganthiers, Mandelman, Spohn, Jacobson, Ribak, and others.

1952 The Colorado Springs Fine Arts Center exhibits "Taos Painting, Yesterday and Today" in which twenty-one Taos modernist painters are included.
The Taos Art Association is established.
John DePuy and Agnes Martin move to Taos.
Joseph Glasco lives part-time in Taos.
Edward Corbett is included in the "15 Americans" exhibit at New York's Museum of Modern Art.

1953 Louis Ribak, Beatrice Mandelman, and Agnes Martin show at Gallery Ribak for the summer. Ribak closes the Taos Valley Art School.
The Stables Gallery opens.

1954 Robert D. Ray moves to Taos.
Leona Kahl is hired as director of the Stables Gallery.
Cady Wells dies.

David Hare and Ibram Lassow spend the summer in Taos.
The Helene Wurlitzer Foundation is established.

1955 *Pioneer Artists of Taos*, by Laura Bickerstaff, is published.
Last summer of the University of New Mexico's Summer Field School of Art in Taos.

1956 "The Taos Moderns" exhibit opens at Raymond Jonson's gallery at the University of New Mexico in Albuquerque. The Museum of New Mexico in Santa Fe exhibits thirty-two artists in its exhibit "The Taos Moderns."
Oli Sihvonen moves to Taos.

1957 "2d Annual Exhibition of Taos Moderns," featuring thirty artists, opens at the Museum of New Mexico.

1958 Thomas Benrimo dies.
"3d Annual Exhibition of Taos Moderns," featuring seventeen artists, opens at the Museum of New Mexico.

1959 "Taos Now" exhibit of fifteen Taos Moderns opens at the Esther Robles Gallery in Los Angeles.
"Taos Moderns," featuring seventeen artists, opens at the Museum of New Mexico.

1960 "Taos Moderns '60," featuring sixteen artists, opens at the Museum of New Mexico.

1962 Mabel Dodge Luhan dies.

1963 "Art and the Atom" exhibit, featuring eight Taos Moderns, opens at Los Alamos Scientific Laboratory.

1964 Patrocinio Barela dies.

1966 "Group 7," a show of Taos Moderns opens at the Jonson Gallery at the University of New Mexico.

1971 Edward Corbett dies.

1973 "Modern Painting in Taos: The 40's and 50's—A Selection," opens at the Stables Gallery featuring thirty-five artists.

1976 Emil Bisttram dies.

1977 Clay Spohn dies.

1979 Louis Ribak and Andrew Dasburg die.

1982 Louise Ganthiers dies.

1984 *Modernist Painting in New Mexico 1913-1935,* by Sharyn Rohlfsen Udall, is published.

1985 "Taos Modernist Art of the 1950s," featuring nineteen artists, opens at the Harwood Foundation in Taos.

1986 "Art in New Mexico 1900–1945: Paths to Taos and Santa Fe," a major traveling exhibition organized by the National Museum of American Art, opens in Washington, D.C.; it includes work by Adams, Benrimo, Bisttram, Dasburg, Hartley, Lockwood, O'Keeffe, and Wells.
The New Mexico Art History Conference holds its first annual meeting in Taos; Wesley Rusnell gives a paper on Edward Corbett and Clay Spohn.

1991 Oli Sihvonen dies.

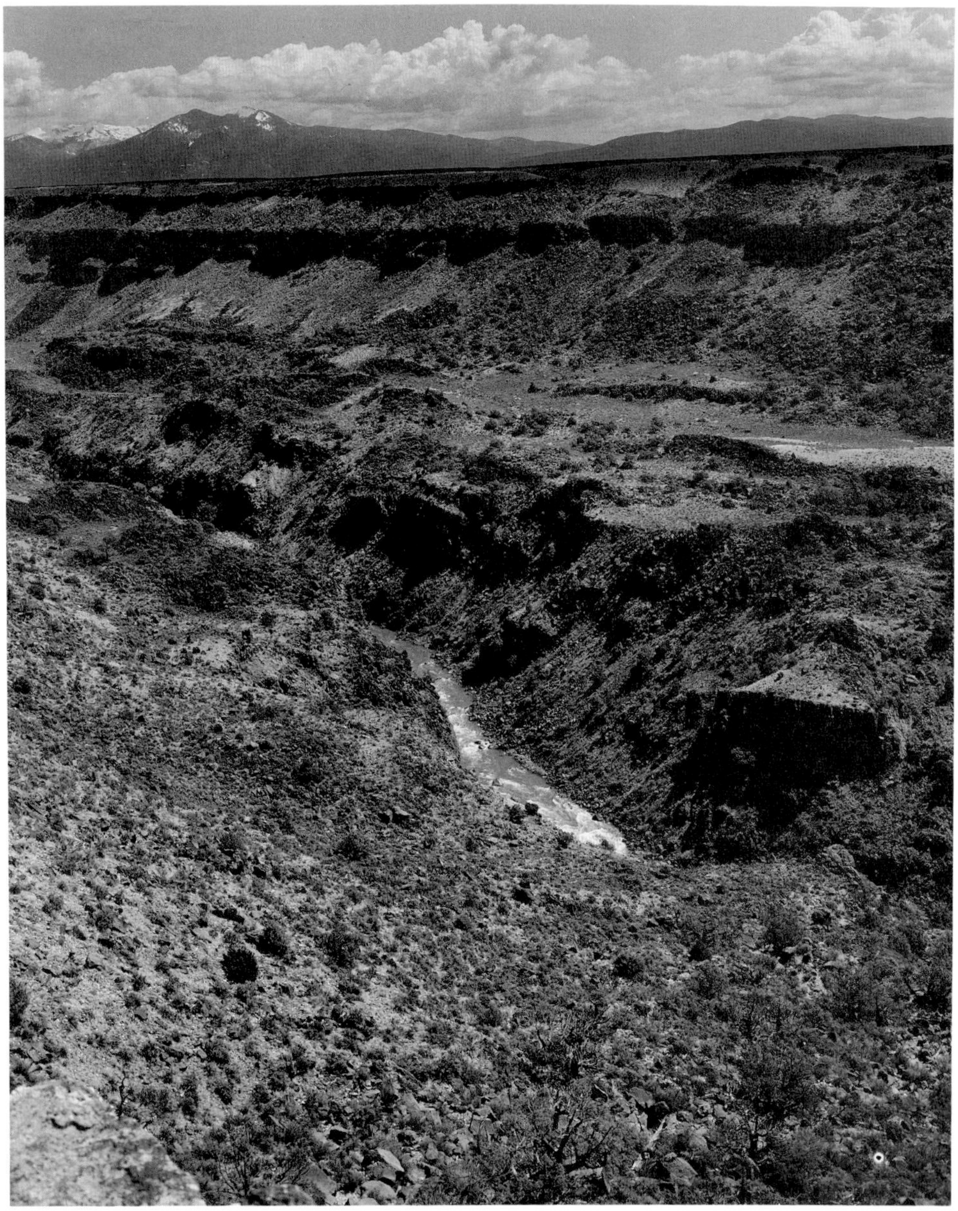

PART ONE:

The Time and the Place

Taos Valley. Photographer: Michael O'Shaughnessy

Vital life signs of the Santa Fe and Taos colonies began to deteriorate during the 1930s; for all intents and purposes by 1942 both artistic communities had expired.[1]

—Arrell Morgan Gibson, 1983

In the American art world of the late 1940s and early 1950s, most of the modernist artists were centered in New York, San Francisco, a scattering of university art departments—and Taos, New Mexico. During that period, the Taos art community underwent dramatic change when new painters arrived who did not accept the artistic conservatism for which Taos had been known. When the famed art community turned from academic western scene art to another kind which freely abstracted from nature, irritated observers pronounced the death of the "art colony." Unquestionably, an era had passed.

The new artists scarcely thought of themselves as a group, but they shared time and place and in their exhibitions called themselves Taos Moderns. They believed that art must be about the "new," that it must make fresh statements compared to what had been said before. The Taos Moderns were like a new bright spot beneath the heavy shadow of the old imposing cliff of the academics.

This study focuses on those artists who created a substantial body of work in Taos between the mid-1940s and the early 1960s. Sixty or more artists who identified themselves as modernists, or as being influenced by modernism in art, lived in Taos during this period. A representative group of them are featured in this book.

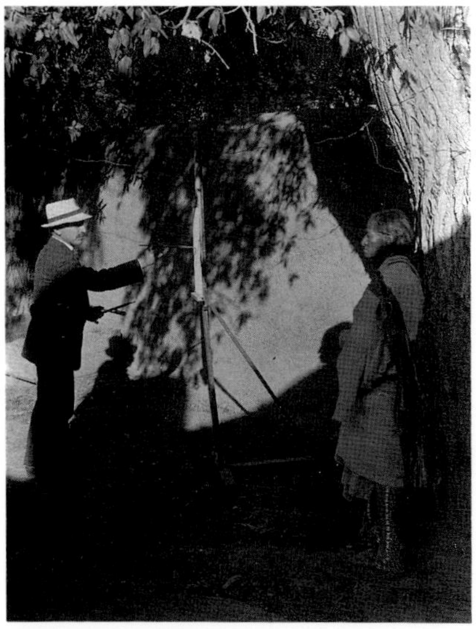

ILL. 1
Bert Phillips painting a model just across from his studio, outside the wall of Arthur Manby's house. ca. 1920. Photographer: unknown

Andrew Dasburg first came to Taos in 1918 and, in a sense, had two careers as an artist in Taos. In the first, he painted in a style influenced by Paul Cézanne. Then during the late 1930s and early 1940s, he practically retired from painting due to illness. When he returned to art in the mid-1940s, his work achieved new dimensions in its geometric interpretations of the Taos Valley.

Cady Wells was another artist who started over on an art career. In the 1930s, he had been caught up in the excitement which watercolorist John Marin had brought to the New Mexico art community. After the Second World War, Wells returned to Taos from time to time, working out new directions in abstraction.

Thomas Benrimo had also experimented with modern art before 1920, but he, too, experienced a long hiatus from fine art, making his living from commercial art instead. He moved to Taos in 1939 and by the mid-1940s began to develop the glorious work of his late period, influenced by surrealism.

Louis Ribak had established a successful career before he moved to Taos in 1944. He left his New York home to explore the unknown West, which he loved from the beginning. He was to become a mentor to many younger artists who gathered in Taos.

Beatrice Mandelman moved to New Mexico with Ribak and in the 1940s was one of the most progressive artists in the state. She worked with full abstraction at a time when most artists were not daring enough to do so and has continued to paint through six decades while living in Taos.

Earl Stroh came to Taos in 1947 as a student at the University of New Mexico (UNM) Summer Field School of Art. He formed lifelong friendships with Dasburg and Benrimo as he made his way through a decade of studies in France and New Mexico, becoming a superb painter and an excellent art historian.

Agnes Martin also attended the 1947 UNM Summer Field School of Art in Taos. When she returned in the early 1950s, she exhibited matchless determination to make it as an artist. Her success in combining minimalist and abstract expressionist sensibilities led to her international reputation in the art world.

Oli Sihvonen first came to Taos in 1949, left, returned for much of the 1950s, then moved yet again in the 1960s, this time to New York. He brought to Taos the influence of Josef Albers from that other little known outpost of modernist sensibility, the progressive Black Mountain College in North Carolina.

Ted Egri came to Taos from New York in 1950, determined to become a painter. He brought with him a piece of wood, which he later carved. Before long Egri found sculpture to be his true passion. He literally brought a new dimension to an art community which had always concentrated on painting.

Louise Ganthiers also arrived in 1950, escaping a mundane career in the East Coast textile industry for the chance of making it as an artist in the West. Like many of the Taos Moderns, she endured difficult economic circumstances just for the opportunity to paint.

Clay Spohn had been a prominent avant-garde figure in the San

Francisco art world before moving to Taos in 1951. Although he rejected the label of abstract expressionist, clearly he was just that, teaching and developing his art at the same time as Mark Rothko and Clyfford Still. His name should be included among those who pioneered this style.

Edward Corbett moved to Taos in 1951 and was, like Spohn, a transplant from San Francisco. Unlike the other Taos Moderns, Corbett had grown up at least partly in the Southwest and perhaps had visited Taos years before he moved there. He also was one of the first generation abstract expressionists.

John DePuy came to Taos in 1952, following studies with Hans Hofmann in New York. He brought to his painting the sensitivity of a naturalist who was equally at home exploring trackless desert, experimenting in the art studio, or vandalizing billboards north of Taos with Edward Abbey.

Robert D. Ray arrived in Taos in 1954. A native of Denver, the experience of mountains was not novel to him. The serene colors, and the delicacy and harshness of the landscape which coexist in the fabled light of the Taos Valley, have inspired his career.

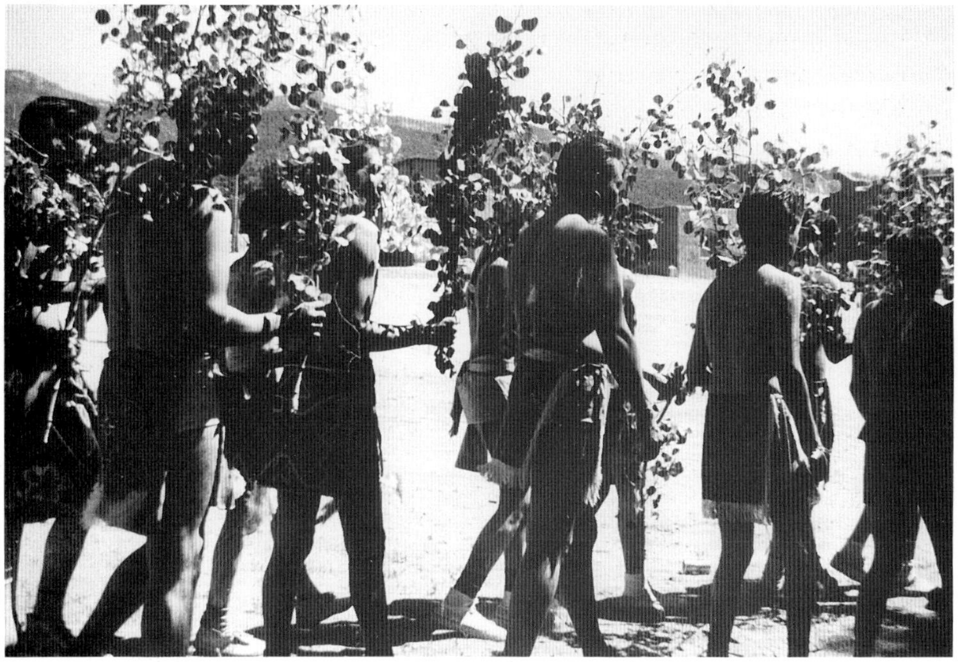

ILL. 2
Corn Dance at Picuris Pueblo. ca. 1952. Photographer: Mildred Tolbert

These fourteen artists, and the scores of others who visited or resided in Taos, brought to the art community a dedication to the new which has characterized modernism in art during the past hundred years. Modern art, which includes artists from Édouard Manet to Robert Motherwell, encompasses such a variety of styles as to nearly defy definition. It may be thought of as art which forces us to see life in a new way. The Taos Moderns were—and are—part of the grand continuum in modern thinking. They brought to Taos both the oriental-influenced art of San Francisco and the high-energy art of New York. They acknowledged the modernist innovations of cubism, surrealism, expressionism, and related European movements. They were in tune with their time, not removed from it, and they utterly changed the face of art in Taos.

Equally, Taos changed them. Whatever their backgrounds, the artists found that the past lingers in the long-memoried Taos Valley. More than ten centuries of history by settled peoples had accumulated by the 1820s when American fur trappers entered New Mexico for discovery and exploitation. In the nineteenth century, Taos included among its residents such heroic men as Antonio José Martinez, the most important New Mexican religious and political leader of his time, and Kit Carson, the Anglo-American fur trapper, explorer, and military officer. The story of their lives created a legacy which was part history, part legend. Fascination with such individuals and with the Southwest environment led Bert Phillips and Ernest Blumenschein, the artists credited with founding the Taos art colony, to seek what in their time had become idealized wilderness. Anglo-American artists who moved to northern New Mexico between 1898 and the First World War did so to escape the industrialism, wars, and general ugliness of modern life. They were also searching for romantic subject matter to transfer onto canvas.

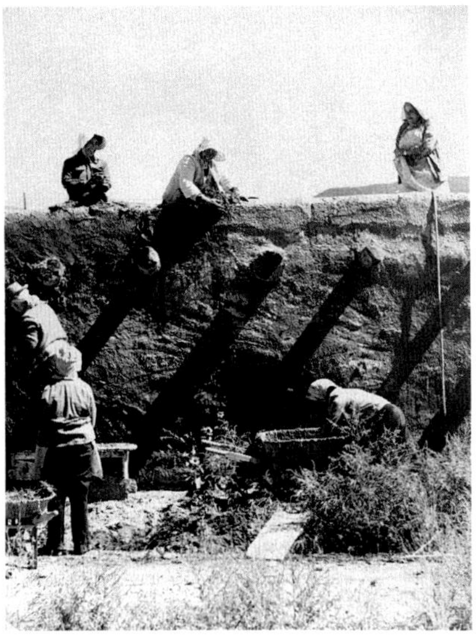

ILL. 3
Hispanic enjarradoras *at work plastering a wall somewhere in Taos or Ranchos de Taos. ca. 1952. Photographer: Mildred Tolbert*

The artists drew their imagery from both dramatic landscapes and exotic cultures. The Hispanic farmers formed a society whose religious, economic, and linguistic traits derived from medieval Spain. The ancient Taos Pueblo provided the artists with symbolic, spiritually-based contact with the land. The early immigrant artists painted up a storm of images of Taos Pueblo, Taos Mountain, and the Taos Indians—their greatest inspirations and their bestsellers. These Taos representational painters were academic romanticists who combined a romantic aesthetic (idyllic, sentimental, and exotic) with their classical academic training at the École des Beaux-Arts and Académie Julien in Paris (or the equivalent schools in New York and Munich).

A number of these painters banded together to form the Taos Society of Artists, a marketing organization active between 1915 and 1927. Their diverse imagery included the "noble savages" of Bert Phillips, the stark-lit landscapes of Walter Ufer, and the mildly cubist elements in the canyon depictions of Ernest Blumenschein. They held in common the need for a refuge where they could continue to be romantics, free of the influences and distractions of the outside world. The imagery they created favored the idyllic and ignored social ills. And their romanticism proved emotionally satisfying as well as financially profitable. The academic romanticism of the Taos Society has fluctuated in popularity, but the art market hungers for bits of Americana. More than a generation after the deaths of the last Taos Society members, the images they created continue to define what most people think of as Taos art.

While scholars are beginning to recognize that many of the finest painters who lived in Taos never belonged to the Taos Society, this view has been long in coming. Popular writing about Taos has emphasized amusing anecdotes about the artists or their romantic legacy. The danger here is that writing about New Mexico which places sole emphasis "upon *what* was painted at the expense of how it was painted results in an unintentional reinforcement of the stereotype that regional art colonies produce only regional art."[2] This illustrative, "regionalist" imagery has proven so strong that the work of moderns who painted in Taos before World War II has been largely ignored outside the Southwest.

Resident painters who worked in a modernist vein in Taos before 1940 include Emil J. Bisttram, Ward Lockwood, and Howard Cook. These Taos artists (along with Dasburg and Wells) established a modernist tradition, albeit one which was always overshadowed by the imagery of the Taos Society. At the same time, however, they were more closely aligned with the earlier generation of Taos painters than with the Taos Moderns because they arrived in the community fifteen years or more before the group which called itself the Taos Moderns.

Patrocinio Barela, a woodcarver who worked in Taos between 1931 and 1964, created sculpture of stunning originality which has been almost entirely overlooked. Barela transformed the Hispanic tradition of the *santero,* or saint maker, by moving from literal depictions to highly conceptual abstractions expressing deep emotion. Sometimes his subjects are religious, but more often they convey the hard struggle of the individual in the world and conflict and alienation within families. His work can be thought of as the best of primitivism or, viewed somewhat differently, as the finest of self-taught modernism, since his organization of space is highly sophisticated. He would not have considered himself to be one of the Taos Moderns since they were all Anglo immigrants, but the Taos Moderns greatly admired his sculpture. He showed his work beside theirs in La Galeria Escondida, the most important commercial gallery for the Taos Moderns.

Three important visitors to Taos were Marsden Hartley (June to October 1918), John Marin (summers of 1929 and 1930), and Georgia O'Keeffe (first visited in 1929). Hartley created a handful of paintings with New Mexico subject matter while he sojourned in the state and a number of weird New Mexico landscape reminiscences after he left. He was

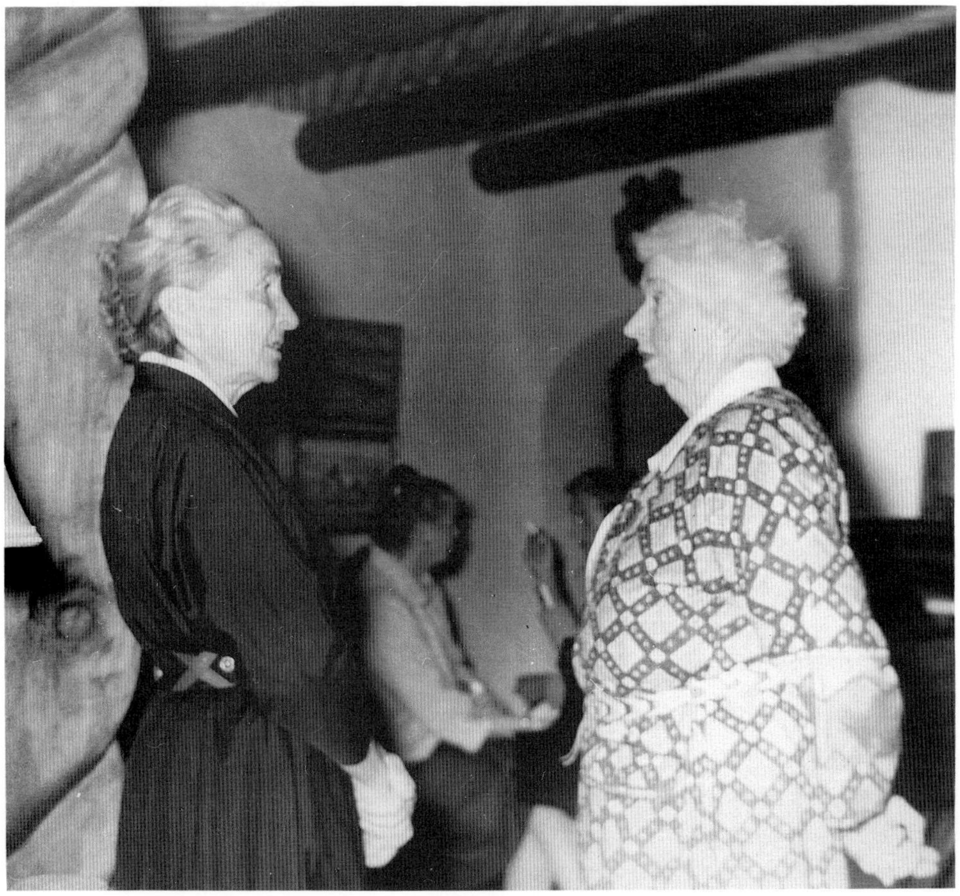

ILL. 4
Georgia O'Keeffe and Dorothy Brett confront each other at Brett's birthday party at Claude Anderson's house just north of Taos. Woman in the background is Tinka Fechin, former wife of the painter Nicolai Fechin. ca. 1959. Photographer: Regina Cooke

recognized by the Taos Moderns as a major American artist but had no important influence on them. Marin's watercolor landscapes created great excitement in New Mexico in the 1930s. The Taos painters of that time knew a world-class artist when they saw one; several of them adapted his dynamic brushwork methods and formal compositional elements to their own work. Marin had some stylistic influence on the work of the Taos Moderns. Artists such as Earl Stroh and Cady Wells incorporated the lessons learned from the older artist into their own artistic development.

For O'Keeffe, New Mexico was not a side trip but a life passion. In May of 1929 she painted at a studio owned by socialite Mabel Dodge Luhan and stayed through the beginning of August. She returned to Taos for the summer of 1930, and later in that year her New Mexico paintings began to sell in New York. Another trip to New Mexico in 1931, and part-time residency in the Abiquiú area (now an hour west of Taos, much longer back then) from 1934, led her to become a permanent resident of the state in 1949. From the 1930s through the 1950s she made occasional social visits to Dorothy Brett, a painter, and to other friends in Taos.

During the years she worked in New Mexico, O'Keeffe painted flowers, bones, and red hills standing dramatically in stark desert light. Among her most enduring scenes are crosses contrasted against foreboding skies. Painted in Taos during the summer of 1929, these works have become indelible images of the Southwest. Writing about one of these paintings in 1976 she said:

> ***One evening when I was living in Taos we walked back of the morada toward a cross in the hills. I was told that it was a Penitente cross but that meant little to me at the time. The cross was large enough to crucify a man, with two small crosses—one on either side. It was in the late light and the cross stood out—dark against the evening sky. If I turned a little to the left away from the cross, I saw the Taos mountain—a beautiful shape. I painted the cross against the mountain although I never saw it that way. I painted it with a red sky and I painted it with a blue sky and stars.***[3]

There is still a cross on that site behind the old Penitente chapel near Mabel Dodge Luhan's house. Lands belonging to the Taos Pueblo spread out behind it for unbroken miles leading to Taos Mountain. The juxtaposition of cross to sky and land is today as powerful an image as it ever was.

O'Keeffe's vision of the Southwest had no direct impact on the Taos Moderns of the 1950s. The new artists who began arriving in Taos during and after World War II brought with them no previous awareness of the earlier brief flourishing of modernism in New Mexico. They did not associate artists such as Marin and Hartley with New Mexico. In any event, the stylistic lineage of the Taos Moderns can be traced through (among others) the early European moderns, Joan Miró, Wassily Kandinsky, Josef Albers, and Piet Mondrian, and the abstract expressionists, including Clyfford Still, Hans Hofmann, and Mark Rothko.

Furthermore, few of the new arrivals to Taos had heard of the Taos Society. And more striking, most of them had never heard of Taos at all! They came to New Mexico on the recommendation of friends and colleagues, or purely by chance, intending to pass through on the way to somewhere else.

The history of the Taos Moderns has been obscured not only by the perception of Taos as a center of regional, illustrative art but also by the curious chance that the era of the Taos Moderns came about independently of all that had passed before. They came to Taos separately, but together they ended up creating the most important period in the history of the Taos art community.

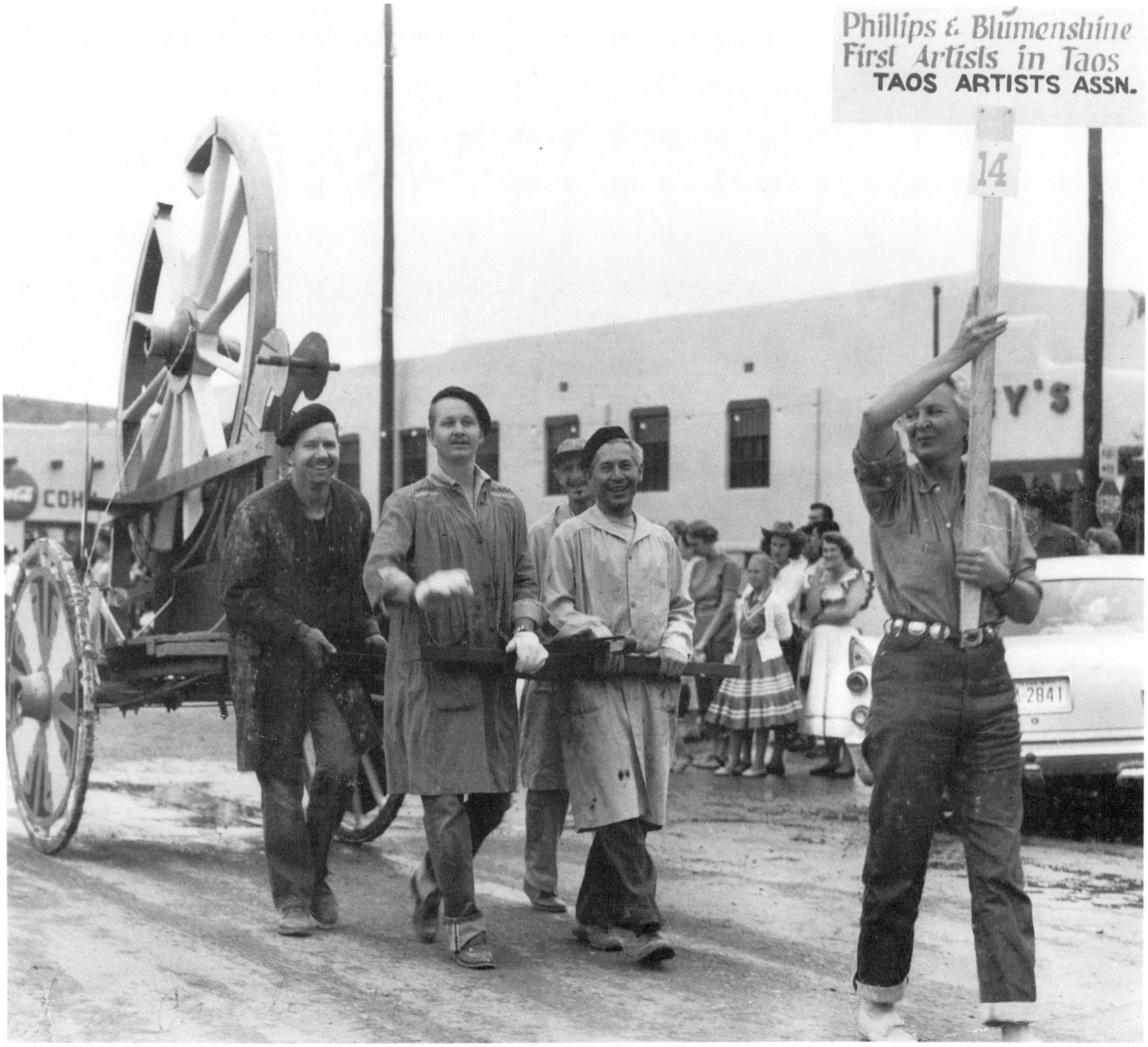
Phillips & Blumenshine
First Artists in Taos
TAOS ARTISTS ASSN.
14

PART TWO:

The Newcomers and the Aspen Painters

Charles Stewart (second from left) and Ted Egri (third from left) in early 1950s Taos parade. Photographer: Martin Shaffer

I personally prefer art that has a [sic] *objective subject matter. But I can't say to anyone who paints non-objectively that he is wrong. It is still experimental. Maybe something good will come out of it.*[1]

—Leon Gaspard, one of the early Taos academic romanticists, commenting on modern art, and possibly on the Taos Moderns, ca. 1963

They were commercial illustrators, they were never artists. . . . I don't think serious art historians pay any attention to them.[2]

—Earl Stroh, one of the Taos Moderns, commenting on the Taos academic romanticists, January 1985

Taos is multilayered, something like the seven hells and thirteen heavens of the ancient Maya. The particular layer with which one happens to identify depends on both ethnic identity and the time when one arrived in Taos, whether by birth or immigration. Older generations continue to see the "old" Taos while younger ones discover the "new" Taos, which they in turn take and keep as their own through subsequent years. Many of the academic romanticists lived to advanced age and saw the end of their conservative era. Because of economic changes engendered by the Second World War, the growing fear of communism, and the old age and impending deaths of the early artists, their reality was doomed, whatever the separate fate of their artistic creations. Within the many-layered site of Taos (the art scene was but one aspect of the larger community), the academic romanticists and the moderns coexisted but with different perceptions of the place they inhabited. They each saw art as religion, but their interpretations of that religion varied greatly; they felt they had nothing in common.

The elders bristled at hearing their art pronounced dead by the newcomers and at being labeled "aspen painters" (which in the view of their modernist critics amounted to the same thing). Yet, despite their differences, the artists of both groups found inspiration from the same sources—the American West and the unique physical and cultural environment of Taos. The pretty curves of the land seduced most of the early artists into concentrating on the surface while many of the later ones probed into its structure to find meaning, but it was the same land, the same catalyst which moved them despite the differing pictorial results. Like theological disputes between Catholics and Protestants, Sunnis and Shi'ites, the bitterest disputes in art grow from comparative differences, not from utter ones.

Because the Moderns held no preconceived notions of Taos imagery, they felt no sense of oneness with the earlier imagery of the art community. For them, Taos could be their own discovery.[3] The rivalry between artist factions was little more than a microcosmic reflection of the larger art world. It was made interesting because of the relative importance of art to Taos compared to larger places, where the art scene was more diluted within the general bigness.

Representational art, declared passé by critics in the early 1950s, continued to be favored by art buyers who came to Taos. Reacting to the rivalry and to the economic privations suffered by the Moderns, poet and newspaper columnist Spud Johnson offered suggestions for artist population control:

> ***It might be quite simply arranged to stage an armed conflict between the Abstractionists and the Realists, another intro-mural struggle between the Non-Objectivists and the Surrealists; and even a suicide pact among the Old-Timers, leaving the field uninterruptedly open to the young Avante-Garde.[4]***

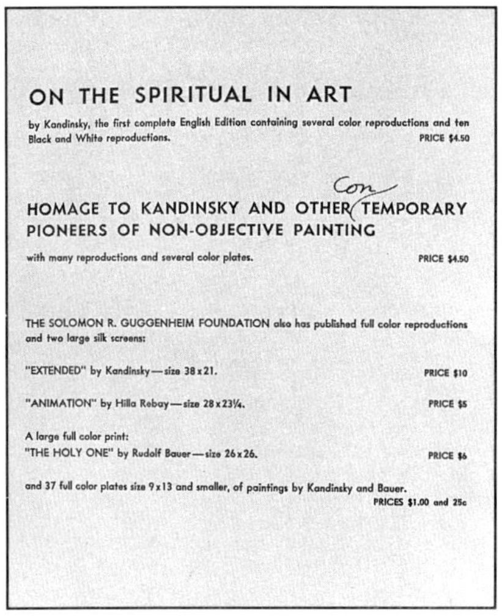
ON THE SPIRITUAL IN ART

by Kandinsky, the first complete English Edition containing several color reproductions and ten Black and White reproductions. PRICE $4.50

Con
HOMAGE TO KANDINSKY AND OTHER TEMPORARY PIONEERS OF NON-OBJECTIVE PAINTING

with many reproductions and several color plates. PRICE $4.50

THE SOLOMON R. GUGGENHEIM FOUNDATION also has published full color reproductions and two large silk screens:

"EXTENDED" by Kandinsky—size 38 x 21. PRICE $10

"ANIMATION" by Hilla Rebay—size 28 x 23¼. PRICE $5

A large full color print:
"THE HOLY ONE" by Rudolf Bauer—size 26 x 26. PRICE $6

and 37 full color plates size 9 x 13 and smaller, of paintings by Kandinsky and Bauer. PRICES $1.00 and 25c

ILL. 5
Temporary Art? An advertising flyer from the Guggenheim Foundation with a correction written in by Emil Bisttram. However, it may be true that pioneers can only be temporary.

Johnson's humorous view recognized (even while poking fun at) the obvious generational differences between the artists.

The history of the Taos Moderns is one characterized by the artists' striving for recognition from museums and commercial art galleries amidst a struggle for economic survival. Like western mining towns, western art colonies also have seen their share of boom and bust cycles.

The founding dates of the first commercial art galleries in Taos are uncertain, but there were probably two operating by 1933. Native Taoseña Maggie Gusdorf acted as artists' agent at the Don Fernando Hotel before it burned down that year. Emil Bisttram ran the Heptagon Gallery in one or two locations before giving up near the end of the decade. And in 1939, the Karavas brothers founded the La Fonda Gallery at their hotel of the same name.

By 1947, six places in Taos exhibited art: the La Fonda, the Blue Door, and La Galeria Escondida, all galleries showing the work of several artists; the Harwood Foundation, open to all Taos artists; and two other galleries

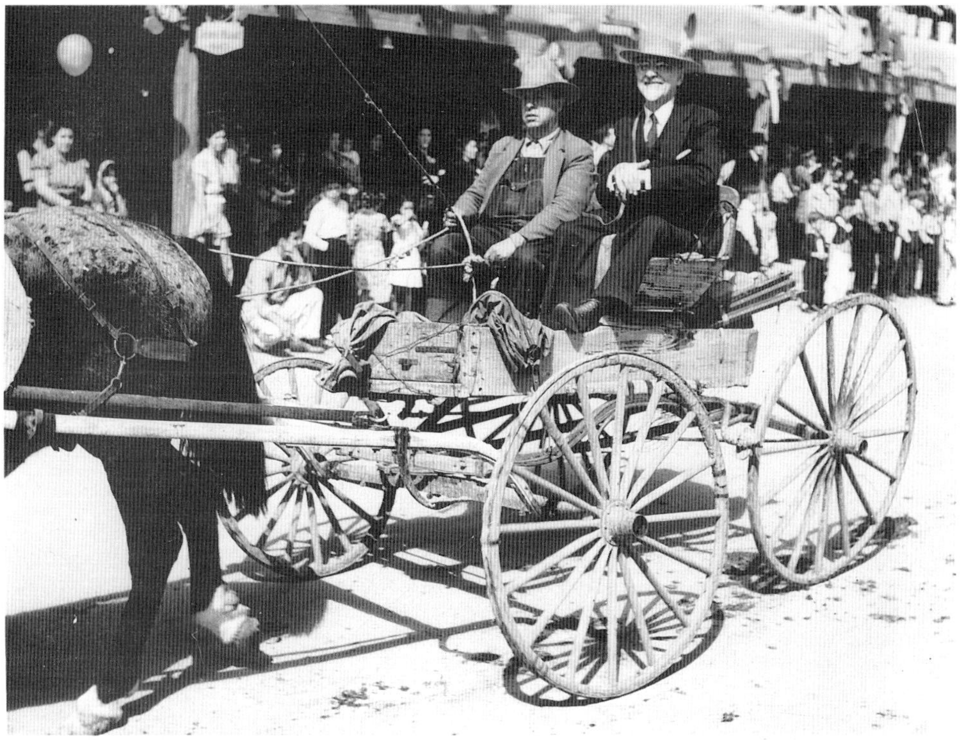

ILL. 6
Joseph Sharp, whose "discovery" of Taos in the nineteenth century helped lead to the founding of the Taos art colony, is featured in a parade on Taos Plaza at the fiesta of San Geronimo. September 1940. Photographer: unknown

that showed the work of their artist-owners. Mabel Dodge Luhan, a writer and long-term resident who was also Taos's greatest publicist, kept a keen eye on the art scene; that year she wrote the first book on Taos artists. In a newspaper review of seven artists showing at the Blue Door, Luhan described them as modern and, having introduced a term which may have been unfamiliar to many Taoseños, she offered a definition: "Perhaps it is describable as unique and individual vision joined to the ability to express experience."[5] Clearly, postwar modernism was becoming established in the community. A few blocks away, an exhibition at the Harwood Foundation featured art produced at the UNM Summer Field School of Art in Taos. Longtime resident artists Andrew Dasburg and Ernest Blumenschein gave critiques of the students' work. A local newspaper took particular note of two artists who would become outstanding Taos Moderns: "Among the more advanced students, Agnes Martin and Earl Stroh have turned out some excellent work."[6]

That summer the Taos newspaper announced that the number of resident and visiting artists had grown to an all-time high, and that the Blue Door's "open door policy of exhibiting paintings of anyone spending the season or living here" began to be questioned. Nan Sheets, an artist and writer, reported in the newspaper the *Taoseno* that the Blue Door continued to take on any artists who cared to show, leaving it "entirely up to the client to make his own decision as to the merits of the work." As a result, the Blue Door contained a hodgepodge of styles. The more sophisticated La Fonda Gallery did not leave sales to chance and as a result sold 105 "pictures" between July 1 and mid-August. Under Taos Society artist Bert Phillips's influence, the gallery took a selective view, limiting who could show. Phillips, the senior member of the art community by virtue of having founded it nearly forty-nine years earlier, probably carried considerable weight in determining gallery policies.

Sheets accurately reported Phillips's condescending opinion, which was the prevailing view of the academic romanticists toward the modernist "newcomers":

> *He says he is not against exhibiting painting by any extremely modern artist if his work shows that he has a background of study and recognition. However, he says that to hang the work of rank amateurs along with the paintings of sincere recognized artists is not conducive to the sale of any picture shown. Mr. Phillips would be classified as a realistic painter, but says he would have no difficulty in painting abstraction if he cared to do so.*[7]

She also quoted Phillips as saying that "any true artist . . . need not resort to distortion or abstraction."[8]

Oscar Berninghaus, another of the old Taos Society members, complained to Ted Egri that the old-timers were being pushed out.[9] The old-timers felt this way because the Taos Moderns believed that the "distortions" being painted in Taos were not their paintings, but those supposedly realistic works of the academic romanticists. At the same time, the younger artists felt that the older ones wanted to close off their commercial opportunities. In reality, it was the academic-romanticist image associated with Taos and the kind of art buyer that image attracted which determined the bulk of art sales in Taos. The majority of buyers just didn't like modernist "distortions." As a result of what they saw as their commitment to artistic integrity, most of the Taos Moderns lived in poverty. They consoled themselves by claiming moral victory—that of aesthetic virtue defeating the urge to satisfy the desires of the marketplace.

The *Wall Street Journal* covered the Taos art business scene of 1956, noting the existence of an art sales depression for many of the artists. At that time there were eighteen commercial galleries in Taos, in addition to sixty studios of the most serious artists and an artist population reported to number two hundred ten, of whom one hundred were said to be "professional."[10] The 300,000 Taos visitors in 1955 were reported to have purchased $150,000 worth of "paintings" (presumably also including prints, drawings, and sculpture) and about an equal amount of native arts and crafts. The old-timers sold their work for the highest prices; representational painting accounted for at least ninety percent of all art dollar sales. Even assuming that the Taos Moderns also sold their work outside of Taos, it is apparent that as a group they were not financially prosperous on the basis of art sales.

The conservative and modern groups found their antagonisms for each other fueled by this grim competition. "The aspen painters just paint the same picture over and over again," Eulalia Emetaz complained to the *Wall Street Journal*. Her La Galeria Escondida handled modernist art almost exclusively and had never grossed more than $18,000 in a year.[11] Ted Egri, Louise Ganthiers, Clay Spohn, and almost all of the other Taos Moderns left the area from time to time to take commissions, to teach, or to do just about anything which would make it possible for them to return to Taos.

If they did not prosper financially, because of La Galeria Escondida the Moderns did at least begin to garner recognition. The gallery was so named because it was hidden in the back of the Taos Book Shop when both fledgling businesses opened in the summer of 1946. Eulalia Emetaz had been in New Mexico by 1929 and, following a divorce in the 1940s, persuaded her mother to provide the initial financing for the gallery operation. Emetaz had heard that the Blue Door did $36,000 in business in its first few months of operation, indicating that commercial galleries could prove lucrative in the Taos market. La Galeria Escondida featured modernist art from the start, making it one of the first postwar galleries outside of New York to do so. Nearly all of the Taos Moderns showed there at one time or another. The venture became successful enough to move to a new location just south of Taos Plaza for the 1948 season.[12] In order to further encourage sales, throughout the 1950s Emetaz traveled to Arizona and California in the winter to sell artists' work since the Taos tourist season was then strictly summer-based.

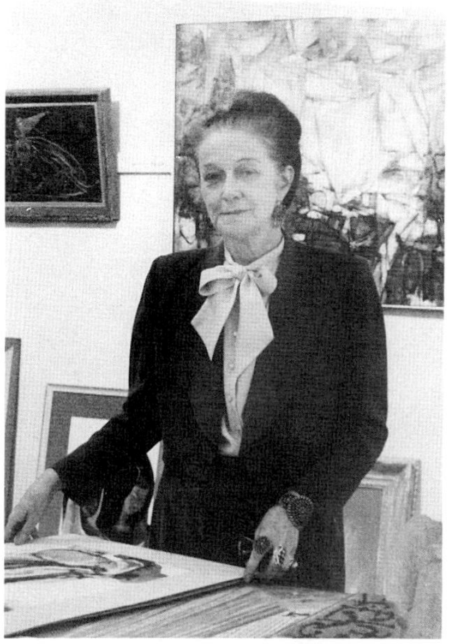

ILL. 7
Leone Kahl, director of the Stables Gallery. ca. 1955. Photographer: Mildred Tolbert

Complementing Emetaz's efforts were those of two other women dealers. Leone Kahl, representing the Stables Gallery (after its founding in 1953), pursued winter sales in Texas. Jane Hyatt worked year-round at the La Fonda Gallery on the Plaza. All three art dealers played critical roles in keeping the art community financially alive during the 1950s.

In addition, Emetaz arranged the first show that included the Taos Moderns in a venue outside of Taos, putting together an exhibition of La Galeria Escondida artists at Lubbock's Texas Technical College in 1950. The content of the show is unknown, but its artists included Ted Egri, Earl Stroh, Louise Ganthiers, Louis Ribak, Ward Lockwood, and Andrew Dasburg.[13]

A magazine article led to a second and more important exhibition that gave significant notice to the Taos Moderns. Writing for *Atlantic Monthly* in 1951, Mitchell Wilder, director of the Colorado Springs Fine Arts Center, considered the art of Taos and pronounced it dead.[14] He did not know of the Taos Moderns, or, knowing of them, he simply dismissed them. Understandably, the Taos Moderns were outraged. Beatrice Mandelman was particularly angered. She was one of the most progressive artists in a region dominated by conservative old-timers who could not bring themselves to acknowledge that women could be serious artists. Knowing that Ted Egri, her fellow former New Yorker, would prove to be an activist, Mandelman persuaded him to take action. Egri recalled the event:

> ***So I wrote a letter to Mitch Wilder and asked him to give us a show up in Colorado Springs Fine Arts Center to prove that he was wrong about his assertions. He was very sensitive to my telling him that people here were sort of offended by what he had said. He went ahead and quickly wrote a letter to me and said, "Yes, by all means, please let's talk about a show." However, skeptical that the basis for a show actually existed, he insisted on combining moderns with old timers.***[15]

The show's curator, Fred Bartlett, met Egri in Colorado Springs in November 1951 to conclude arrangements for an exhibit to open the following March. Bartlett then traveled to Taos in January to collaborate with Egri in selecting works to be included in the show. Of the thirty pieces chosen, nine were by members of the old Taos Society, three were by the 1930s moderns, and the balance were by the Taos Moderns. Bartlett understood the changes occurring in Taos. After giving artists of both conservative and modern ilk credit for "their desire to record the truth," he wrote in the exhibit catalog of the Moderns, "It must be said that there is little in the work of most contemporary painters of this region today which sets them apart from that produced in any locality."

In recognizing the connection between the Taos Moderns and the rest of the art world, he suggested that they were an integral part of it. He may also have been the first person to record that the academic romanticists' era had given way to modernism: "The local landscape, the local color, is still present and gives a flavor of locality, but the basic precept has changed." The Colorado show established an identity for the Taos Moderns through a rite of passage which confirmed that the Taos art community now belonged to them as much as to the old-timers.[16]

Recognition also came from even farther away. Beginning in 1948 and continuing into the 1960s, the College of Fine and Applied Arts at the University of Illinois at Urbana produced one of the most significant exhibit series in the country.[17] Under the leadership of C.V. Donovan and Allen S. Weller, who were on the jury of selection, the "Contemporary American Painting and Sculpture" shows chronicled the development of postwar art. Each year a three-person jury traveled extensively around the country looking for the best work being produced in America. Donovan, particularly, had an affinity for Taos and traveled to the art community several times. His visits to artists' studios, in part directed by Emetaz, led to a number of invitations.[18] In the seven exhibitions at the University of Illinois held between 1951 and 1961, the work of fourteen Taos artists made twenty-eight appearances (see Appendix A).

Many of the nationally prominent artists showing in the Urbana series had at one time or another been in Taos. Leon Kroll, John Marin, Maurice Sterne, Stuart Davis, and Georgia O'Keeffe had visited in earlier decades.

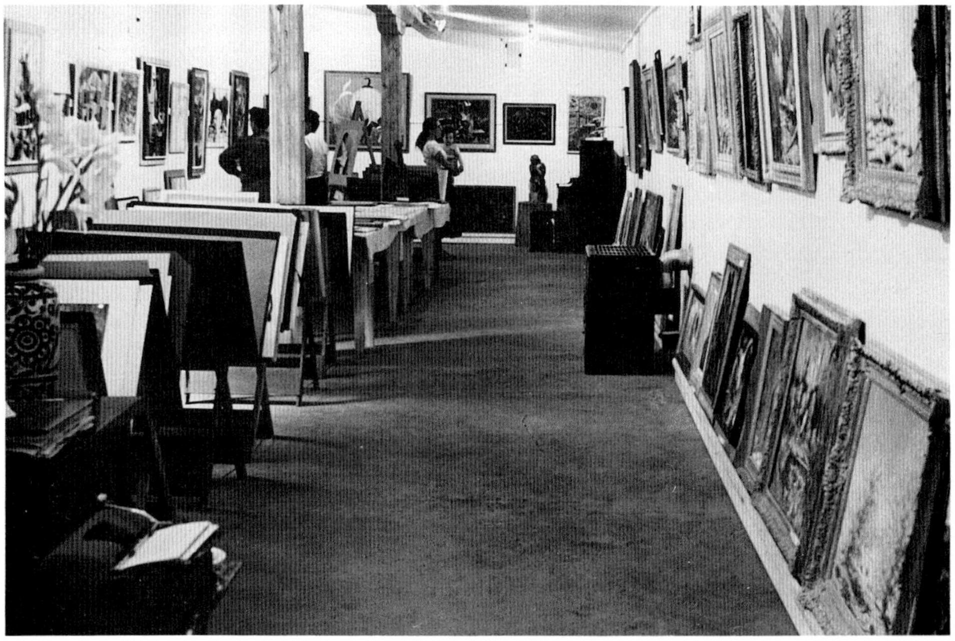

ILL.8
The Stables Gallery of the Taos Art Association was located in a cramped space where the visitor could casually browse through stacks and piles of artwork. ca. 1955. Photographer: Mildred Tolbert

Joseph Glasco, David Hare, Ad Reinhardt, Mark Rothko, and Richard Diebenkorn made appearances in the 1950s. Others included in the shows would later move to Taos. Despite its distance from the major modernist centers of San Francisco and New York, Taos maintained important ties to the postwar modernist movement nationally.

In June of the same year that Taos artists joined the Urbana series, a number of Taos Moderns banded together to create the Ruins Group of Ranchos of Taos. Like the later Stables Gallery, this gallery was named for the kind of building it inhabited. The artists were described in a brochure issued by a Los Angeles artists' representative that depicted Taos as being the home of traditional landscape painters but stated that Taos also

> *had become the home of modern artists who, though not so literal in their work, are revitalizing the human and spiritual scene around them . . . national and international art trends are apparent in their work.*[19]

In his weekly column, "The Horsefly," Spud Johnson wrote about the gallery in an essay which had otherwise been devoted to the subject of churches:

> *Since Art is a religion of Taos, we might also comment on the modest new sanctuary of this devout denomination—a sort of Ranchos mission started by a dissident group from the mother church of Our Lady of Sorrow, Eulalia [Emetaz of La Galeria Escondida]. We refer to "The Ruins," a charming outpost of the local colony aimed at snatching the incoming tourist before he has seen a single "sight" or wasted his substance on post-cards and curios. This new and pleasantly informal establishment is entered through a most decrepit patio. The first thing which meets the visitor's eye is a tiny and tumbling wooden shed, obviously a Chic Sales, and which we did not personally investigate; but for all we know it may also be hung with paintings of a less sacred nature.*[20]

The artists who Johnson thought had left Eulalia and La Galeria Escondida for the Ruins Group continued to show with her as well, a fine point he corrected in his next newspaper column.

In May of 1952, another writer expressed opinions which affected the Taos Moderns. In *Art Digest*, Joan Evans reported that an April exhibit of modernist art in Albuquerque had brought criticism from conservative artists at an open forum on art at the University of New Mexico. She wrote that Richard Diebenkorn and others had been called upon to defend the art exhibit; Evans also took the opportunity to compare the art scene in Albuquerque to those in Santa Fe and Taos:

> *Slowly the artistic center of gravity in New Mexico is shifting from her mountains to her mesas; from the established colonies of Taos and Santa Fe to a spirited, sometimes garish boomtown, Albuquerque. This city . . . is the scene of an exciting spiritual renaissance in New Mexican art.*[21]

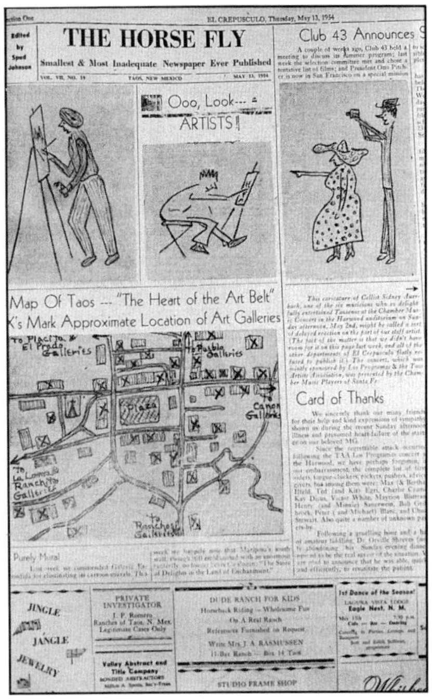

ILL. 9
Taos art galleries as seen by artist and writer Spud Johnson, and published in El Crepusculo, *at the beginning of the summer tourist season in 1954.*

As proof, she listed the names of several artists then residing in Albuquerque. Like the similar pronouncement the previous year in *Atlantic Monthly*, this relegation of Taos to the past moved the Taos Moderns to reply. The letter's confusing punctuation and general rambling, and its refusal to acknowledge Santa Fe as significant in the New Mexico art world must have amused some readers. It also gained a degree of homespun charm by first claiming that the list of modernist painters is "far too lengthy to mention" then going on to name many of them anyway. At the same time that the artists' response was interesting as a defense of Taos, it was also important because it showed that the Taos Moderns were connected to the larger art world. Despite occasional petty defensiveness, the letter sent by the artists gives considerable insight into the thinking of that time: they recognized themselves as being a part of the larger American art world. Published in the August issue of *Art Digest* in the letters column under the heading "Taos Artists Take Exception" and signed "Marjorie Rogoway (for a group of Taos Artists)," it was also reprinted in full in the Taos newspaper *El Crepusculo,* where it was signed merely, "Taos Artists."

Accepting academic romanticist images of Taos as *solely* representing the art of Taos had led Wilder in 1951, Evans in 1952, and Gibson as late as 1983 to claim that the Taos art community had died out by the 1940s. Even when the modernists were acknowledged, critics could still be vicious. The death of Thomas Benrimo in May 1958 caused writer Martin Tucker to reflect on the nature of Taos:

> *In this little village where painting is almost a residential disease, the factions have grown so complex . . . that the observer is reminded of the tangled skeins of intrigue and cabal in exotic places like Hong Kong and Macao.*[22]

For Tucker, the problem was the growing number of "dilettante" artists. He did recognize the Moderns, whom he referred to as the "left-bank group . . . generally acknowledged to be headed by two Greenwich Village painters who happen to be married to each other, Louis Ribak and Beatrice Mandelman." In his view, the day of the serious painter was about over since so many painters approached painting as if it were just like any other job:

> *But in the process of conforming to a tourist-infected economy and Foundation-sponsored art, they have lost their enthusiasm. . . . The Taos artist—beset on all sides by phony bohemianism, indifferent residents, pretentious intellectuals, greedy innkeepers, a host of well-heeled sycophants, and hangers-on, and a dearth of dedicated painters—has good reason to fear he may be seeing the end of an era.*[23]

Tucker found *his* Taos being replaced by someone else's Taos and, like many before him, found that loss difficult to bear.

Museum curator and former Taos painter Wesley Rusnell considered this form of nostalgia and suggested the image of a large speeding truck on a New Mexico highway. In its windy wake, the grasses wave wildly as if in frantic signaling, demanding, "Wait! Slow down!" But the thing which has passed moves on, leaving no more than a powerful memory: the thing and its time are gone. For the Taos Moderns, the memory which most haunts them is the Stables Gallery, an artists' cooperative created in the 1950s and abolished, to their dismay, in the 1980s (see Appendix B).

The Stables is the quintessential symbol of the Taos Moderns' era. In a time when there were few galleries in Taos and the academic romanticists dominated what few commercial opportunities did exist, the Taos Moderns felt that some mechanism was needed to bring a greater sense of community to all Taos artists. On October 10, 1952, twenty-eight artists met at the Harwood Foundation to consider forming an artists' organization. A second meeting, on October 17, marked the formal beginning of the Taos Artists' Association (TAA). (They replaced "Artists'" with "Art" at the 1962 annual meeting.) By the following week, the organization had elected officers and in November embarked upon its planned program of weekly sketch classes with other activities soon to follow.[24] Seven months later, the TAA contemplated the ambitious act of creating what would become the Stables Gallery.[25]

At about the same time that the TAA was formed, another group, the Kit Carson Memorial Park Committee, entered into negotiations with Helen Williams of the philanthropic Taos Foundation to discuss the fate of the Thorne House. It was once owned by real estate developer Arthur R. Manby, who lost his head there in 1929, resulting in one of New Mexico's most famous unsolved murder cases. The committee hoped to convince the state legislature to purchase the property and create a historical museum there to complement Kit Carson State Park. They succeeded, but the governor vetoed the bill, and the project fell through during the 1953 legislative session. Less than a month later, TAA artists voted unanimously to buy the property for $45,000 and then incorporated to manage it. In those days, all things seemed possible. They planned to use the house, which faced the highway, as a meeting place and historical museum and the old stable in the back as a cooperative gallery. Substantial support was solicited and received from a community which had been highly disappointed by its failure to receive state funding for a museum. To head off any complaint from commercial gallery owners, Emil Bisttram assured them that "such a set-up would in no way interfere with the other existing galleries, but would, in fact, help them," a prediction which came true.[26]

The property was purchased, and by July the museum and a sketch group facility were opened. Expectations of success ran high. Winnie Berninghaus (widow of Taos Society artist Oscar Berninghaus), who helped organize the new museum, promoted it, believing that the cooperation required by such an undertaking would generate a spirit of unity in Taos. The TAA organizers had ambitions of making the Thorne House cultural center into a nationally prominent gallery and museum. The postwar enthusiasm of America's ability to do anything was still strong in Taos, where the art community would soon reach its greatest moment of creative power.

As in any new relationship where there is nothing but anticipation, and no history of unfulfillment to ponder, the September 13, 1953, opening exhibition of the TAA's Stables Gallery was judged a success. Kit Egri, a writer and the wife of Ted Egri, wrote of the event, "The TAA policy of drawing all schools of painting together was justified by the harmony of the paintings on the wall." Even antimodernist Bert Phillips was reported by *El Crepusculo* to have said, "This is the finest gallery in town."[27]

Looking back on the history of the Stables from the perspective of the 1980s, Beatrice Mandelman reminisced:

> ***The artists had the opportunity to show what they wanted to show at what time they wanted to show it, and they were in control. One had a chance to move ahead in one's work without the stamp of the dollar. In the [commercial] gallery you're the victim of the gallery dealer's taste and you have to comply with that. Whereas, at the Stables, you had a chance to show what you wanted to show—and no one could judge, which was really freedom for the artist.***[28]

In the beginning, any member artist could show at the Stables, and anyone could be a member. However, the artists almost immediately realized, as had the Museum of New Mexico in Santa Fe a few years earlier, that an "open-door" policy was an artistic disaster since the tiny display space could not handle the work of nearly as many as desired to show. Ultimately, membership was restricted to Taos residents elected by the existing members. Each artist could show one painting, and for a small fee could show a second, giving Taos one showplace where visitors could see a cross section of all the kinds of art produced in the community. An art buyer could purchase a work directly from the Stables, but it was common for someone to first learn of an artist through the Stables and then go to that artist's commercial gallery or private studio to see a larger selection of work. This arrangement cut into profits, but the gallery survived. On its extremely crowded walls and floors, with paintings often crunched together and stacked in windrows, the Stables succeeded in its goal to expose the work of Taos artists. On the gallery's first anniversary, a news story went out on a national wire service that "peace" had come to the various art factions in Taos.[29] That was not entirely true.

Seventeen conservative artists maintained their allegiance to the La Fonda Gallery, at least in part because of concerns about showing next to "distortions." The gallery at the La Fonda enjoyed greater prestige, and the older artists rightly feared their work and reputations would be lost in the crowded Stables. Phillips, perhaps in his role of senior member of the art colony, finally underwent a change of heart, and joined the Stables.[30]

In 1954, another new arts institution, the Helene Wurlitzer Foundation, also became important to the Taos Moderns. Its purpose was twofold: to encourage creative work in art, literature, and music and to be of benefit to those who might otherwise be unable to complete their work. In its earliest days, assistance from the foundation to creative people included cash grants, residencies, or both.

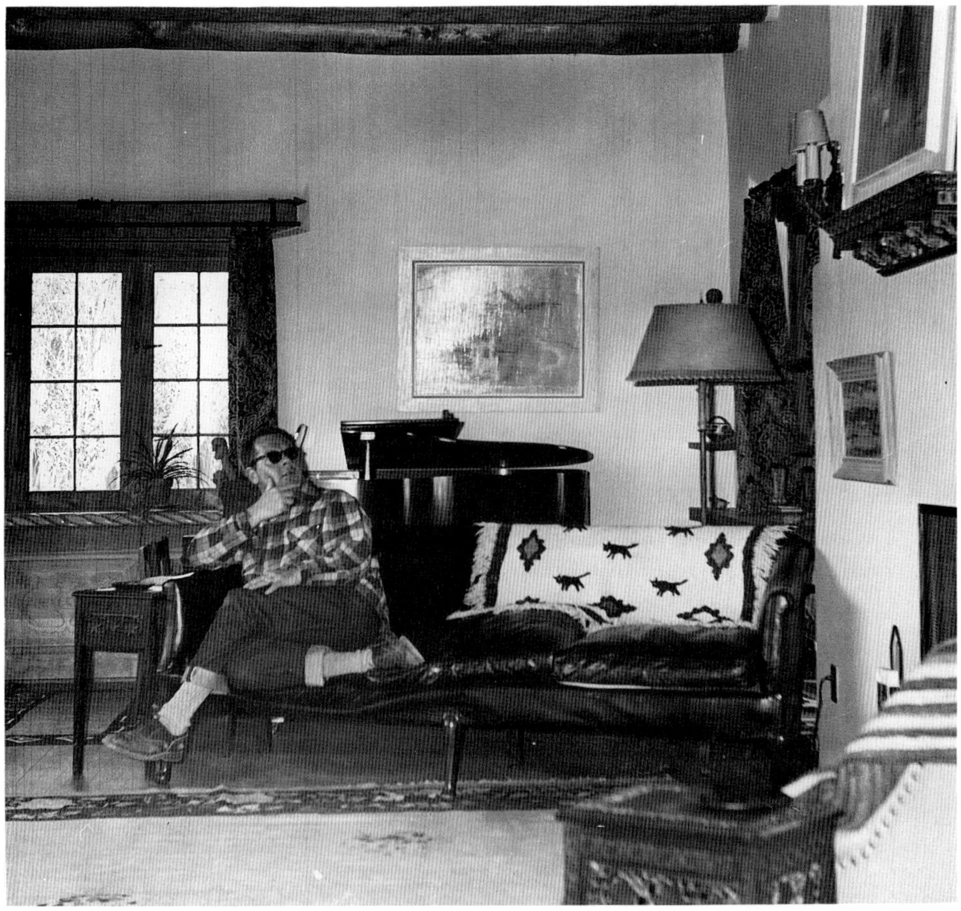

ILL. 10
Dr. Henry Sauerwein, director of the Wurlitzer Foundation, in the sala of the main house. ca. 1956. Photographer: Regina Cooke

The Wurlitzer represented a new concept in Taos. At other colonies, such as Yaddo and McDowell in the East, artists lived together. At the Wurlitzer, they lived alone in individual adobe buildings, surrounding themselves with whatever degree of isolation they desired. Nothing was asked of them in return. The foundation maintained a balance among the kinds of arts represented (primarily painting, writing, and music) and also the types of residents invited, in order to assure a geographic and ethnic diversity—almost certainly an uncommon policy in the 1950s.

Mrs. Wurlitzer, the organization's founder, had married into the family of musical instrument makers. She never achieved a lifelong desire to be an artist, but her support of the arts made her a significant figure in Taos almost from the time of her arrival in 1945. She had an affinity for the West, for although educated in Germany and in Cincinnati, Wurlitzer had grown up in Salt Lake City, Denver, and Socorro, New Mexico. In Taos she met Henry Sauerwein, a literary scholar, who also first visited the community that same year. They discovered that their families had been friends in the East, and the two of them continued that tradition. In 1951, Sauerwein (who had his Ph.D. by then) moved to Taos and took a job with the Harwood Foundation driving its bookmobile, which traveled to forty-three communities outside of Taos. He took books and movies (powered by a gas generator in the truck) to people throughout the area in all varieties of inclement weather on unpaved New Mexican roads. That challenging task ended after Wurlitzer asked him to help design and then run the Wurlitzer Foundation. He served as its de facto manager while she lived and as its director after her death. Of the hundreds of artists aided by the Wurlitzer Foundation over the years, a number of them were Taos Moderns, including Robert D. Ray, Agnes Martin, Oli Sihvonen, and Clay Spohn.[31]

Institutional support for the Taos Moderns also began to develop in Albuquerque and in Santa Fe. Raymond Jonson, a painter who took part in the early days of American modernism, and later became an art professor at the University of New Mexico, ran a small gallery on the university campus where he showed the Taos Moderns in individual and group shows beginning in the 1950s and continuing into the next decade. The first exhibit to be titled "Taos Moderns" was also the first appearance of that term in print. The show opened at Jonson's gallery on February 26, 1956, and was noted in both the *Albuquerque Journal* and the *Santa Fe New Mexican.*

Taos artists frequently formed a plurality and sometimes a majority of the juried and invitational exhibits held at the Museum of Fine Arts in Santa Fe between 1951 and 1961. The composition of the Taos contingent changed over that period from a majority of academic romanticists to a majority of Taos Moderns. Beginning in 1956, and continuing annually through 1960, the Taos Moderns were given their own special autumn invitational at the museum. The first such exhibit included thirty-two artists.

This recognition by the Museum of Fine Arts and other museums finally led to greater acceptance of Taos Moderns by collectors. Marvin W. Buckels, for example, began collecting art for Denver's Midland Federal Savings (which later became Bank West) in 1964. Motivated in part by a study that suggested this savings and loan corporation primarily attracted elderly customers, Buckels envisioned attracting younger clients by developing a new corporate image based in part on displays of modern art at its branch offices. Consequently, he built one of the largest and most outstanding corporate art collections in the West. He purchased many works from the Taos Moderns and in so doing formed the most significant collection of their work.[32]

In addition to the social and economic aspects of Taos in the postwar era, brief mention must be made of the political climate, especially situations arising from the cold war with the Soviet Union. In 1948, Eulalia Emetaz invited presidential candidate Henry A. Wallace to speak on the Taos Plaza. This event sent tremors of fear through the conservative business community and seems to have been the beginning in Taos of the years-long paranoia known as the McCarthy era, which gripped other regions of the country even more tightly. In northern New Mexico, there was ongoing tension concerning the socialistic nature of the rural electric cooperative, and a flaring of passions over the proposed showing of a neo-fascist propaganda film to school children in the late 1950s. Reactionary forces made modern art the subject of congressional hearings as early as the late 1940s when it was labeled as a communist plot against America.

A few years later, two businessmen compiled a list of "subversive" Taos artists and gave it to the FBI. This list came to the attention of the artists by chance when artist Cliff Harmon and a modern dancer friend stopped by the Albuquerque FBI office to report the interstate theft of the friend's car. An agent told them they were on a list of communist sympathizers and then produced it for them to see. The list was a roster of the Taos Moderns. These forces of subversion with their smocks and berets must have alarmed the FBI, which perceived something more threatening than turpentine fumes in Taos.[33]

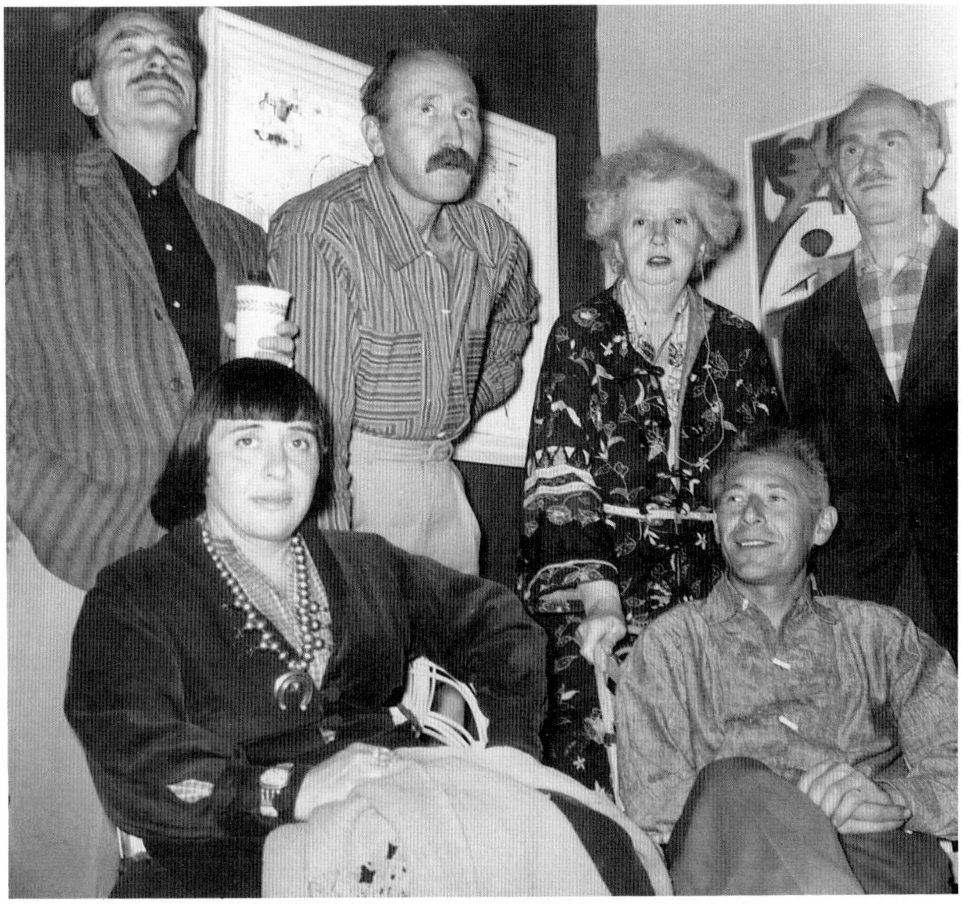

ILL. 11
Members of the Ruins Group pose for a group portrait, possibly at the Ruins Gallery in Ranchos de Taos. From left to right, Louis Ribak, Beatrice Mandelman, Alfred Rogoway, Dorothy Brett, Ted Egri, and Clay Spohn. ca. 1952. Photographer: Regina Cooke

Harmon, trained in Bauhaus design at North Carolina's Black Mountain College, found that his work, and perhaps his politics, were too radical for Jane Hyatt (or perhaps for the conservative gallery artist-members) at the La Fonda Gallery. She asked him to withdraw his work. Harmon later commented on FBI tactics of the time:

> ***Their practice in those days was to go around and ask businessmen if there was anything suspicious going on in every town in the country. They used businessmen because they meet people all the time. [Thomas] Lewis accused Bisttram of being a communist. Bisttram finally got fed up with it and threatened to sue him if he didn't stop doing this. It scared the heck out of Lewis, as I remember, and he had a mild heart attack and went back to Texas for awhile.***[34]

The politically liberal Moderns reacted to the right-wing hysteria in one of two ways: by eschewing political activism or by speaking up and risking being labeled a "commie." This insulting name-calling in Taos was as frequently motivated by personal animosities as by political conviction. In one of the more serious incidents, a government undercover agent posing as an art student enrolled in Louis Ribak's GI Bill-supported Taos Valley Art School, apparently to keep an eye on Ribak and the Taos Moderns who attended his school. Ted Egri and John DePuy, who were close to the situation, claimed that the government mole was placed there to gather information which could be used to close down the school; and soon thereafter the school did close. Beatrice Mandelman said that the school closed because Ribak grew tired of teaching.[35] It may also be true that Ribak ran out of students, most of them having exhausted their GI Bill education benefits.

The Taos Moderns give contradictory views about the significance of political events in Taos during the McCarthy era—so much so that determining the effect these events had on their lives is difficult. But whether motivated by personal or political issues, rightist harassment of artists was an undeniable part of that period. It is a tribute to the Taos Moderns and their commitment to art that attempts to intimidate them failed. A more salient factor than ideology in art community disputes, however, may be the general contrariness of artists (or of Taoseños, for that matter), arising at least in part at that time from economic conditions. In Taos, conspiracy is a weaker force than anarchy.

After consideration is given to art history, economics, and politics, the strongest force of all influencing artists of Taos is the land itself. Almost every immigrant Taoseño can recall when he or she first drove up from the Rio Grande gorge to overlook the Taos Valley. From that place, you can see the beauty of gorge depths riving the mesas on the west and the looming Sangre de Cristo mountain range encircling the valley on its other three sides. Most artists who had this experience and then remained for a summer or a lifetime have developed a personal, indelible creation myth of Taos. Their personal myths closely resemble American Indian mythology of emergence from a "lower world" to a "higher" one, referring both to spiritual development and to change in time and place. In Taos, the striking similarity between Indian world-view and artist world-view is perhaps no coincidence. The metaphor of the emergence myth fits with the physical properties of the Taos Valley.

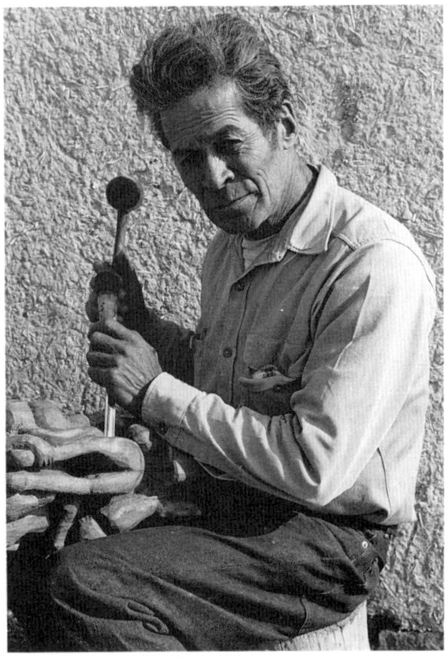

ILL. 12
Patrocinio Barela working on a wood carving. ca. 1954. Photographer: Mildred Tolbert

The cañons leading into the valley are like birth canals out of which immigrants emerge or are reborn into the world of Taos. The art community has always been more a nurturing place than an innovative one, a better place for mature artists than for beginners. Both the land and the indigenous cultures suggest this nurturing: the ancient Pueblo culture is a permanent, "timeless" feature; until recently both Pueblo and Hispanic cultures have been largely agrarian; mysticism among all the cultures represented in Taos is more prominent than hard-edge urban thinking; even the mountains are rounded, feminine forms.

These features suggest what traditionally has been thought of as feminine rather than masculine energy. In these attributes the academic romanticists found imagery ideally suited to their needs. Most of them perceived a quality of changelessness in the Taos Valley, and most of them interpreted this literally, altering their artistic styles only marginally over decades. Most of the Taos Moderns, who equated lack of change with artistic death, saw the same environment as symbolic of continual rebirth, with the result that the artwork they completed in 1964 bore little relationship to works created in 1954 or in 1944.

For Taos artists, the West is not only a big land—big enough to encompass wildly differing interpretations of its numinous qualities—but one which, in its unavoidable emphasis on isolation, draws loners—those who prefer to live outside mass society and those who require relatively uninterrupted working conditions. As a result, there has never been a "Taos School." For those who needed to be part of the Group, the Scene, the Movement, or the School, for those, Taos was not the place. Artists seeking the gregarious life do not move to the great independent isolation of the rural interior-West.

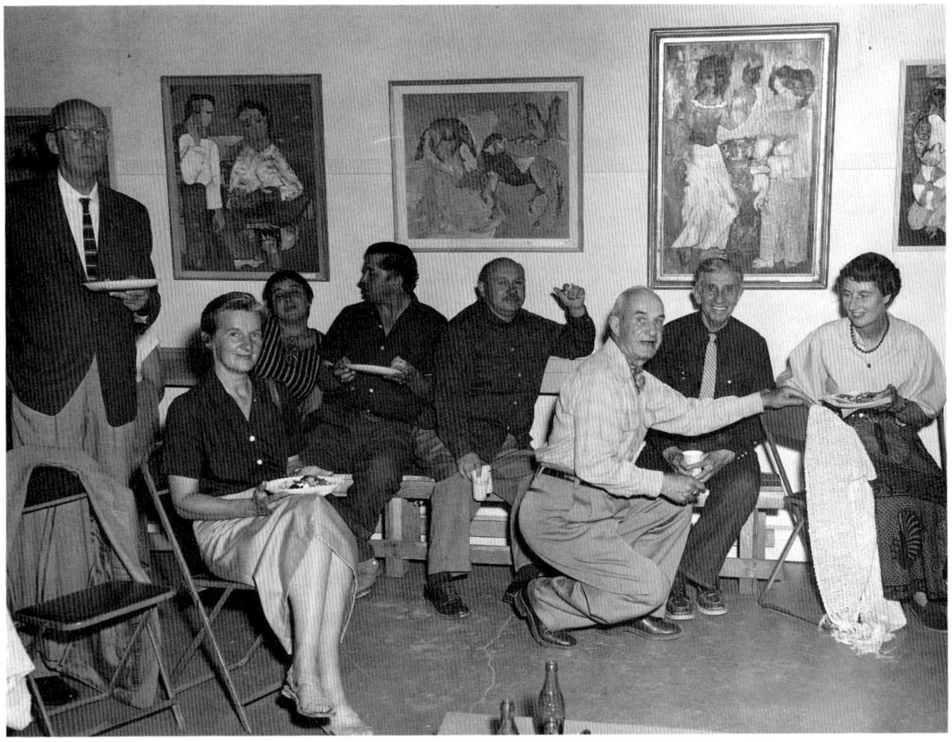

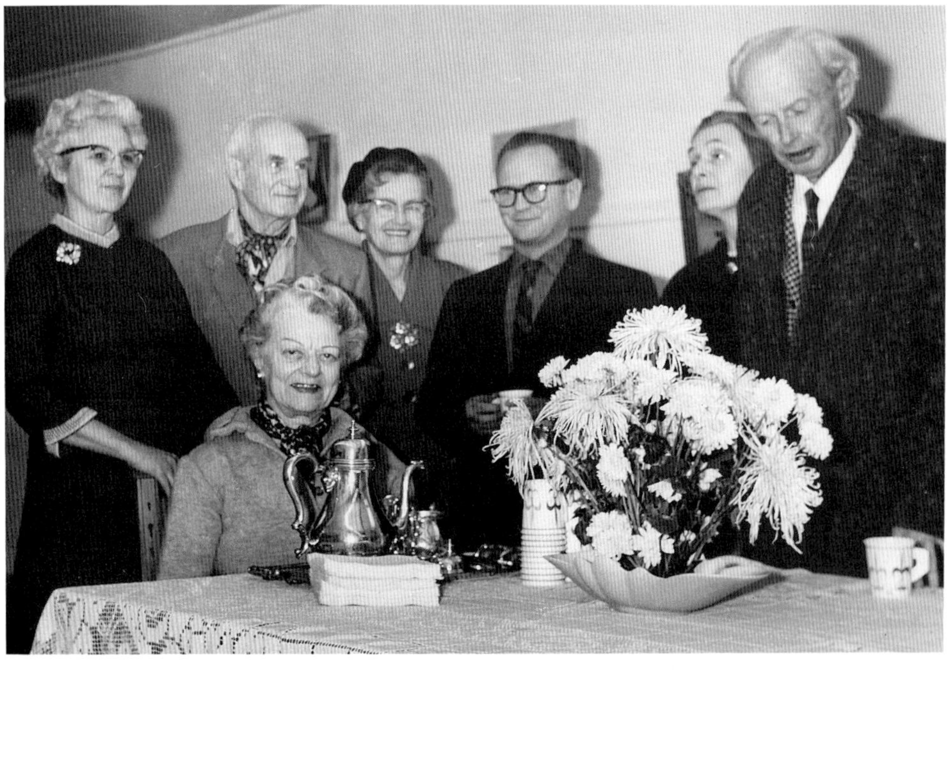

PART THREE:

The Artists

(TOP)
Gallery opening of works by Alfred Rogoway, l to r: Doel Reed, Louise Ganthiers, Beatrice Mandelman, William Heaton, Michael Klein, Emil Bisttram, Thomas Benrimo, Gene Kloss. ca. 1956. Photographer: Martin Shaffer

(BOTTOM)
At the Stables Gallery, standing l to r: Alice Farrell, Emil Bisttram, Ila McAfee, Earl Stroh, Leone Kahl, Andrew Dasburg; seated: Mayrion Bisttram. ca. 1960. Photographer: Regina Cooke

I thought it was important for us to recognize that points of view on [the] quality of art change from time to time and the actual character of art reflects the time in which the art is done.[1]

—Ted Egri, February 1985

In their search for artistic truth, the Taos Moderns portrayed the essence of New Mexico in new ways. Art which abstractly expressed deeply felt responses to, and interpretations of, the environment required an imagery different from that which worked for earlier generations. Distillation of form, line, and color could not remain literal or anecdotal. The Moderns correctly saw that art must continually sweep onward to new forms, often at the expense of old definitions. Art which stays most alive is that which outruns language's ability to invent terms to categorize it. If it is difficult to subject contemporary art to so-called objective critical tests, then we must admit that in the postwar era the values by which we judge nearly everything (including art) are more elusive—or at least less agreed upon—than in earlier times. In an attempt to judge, we must use reasoned vision which seeks in art originality, intensity, technical competence, and, in a specific work, an internal coupling of form and content, even if they may mesh in unexpected ways.

The Taos Moderns intended to be different. Taos after 1944 was not the same kind of place it had been in 1904. The artistic integrity of the Taos Moderns made it impossible for them to repeat the painting formulas of earlier Taos artists. These artists were not just people fresh out of art school—many were World War II veterans straight out of hell. They were mature, seasoned, and able to pursue their own paths, no matter how difficult or lonely.

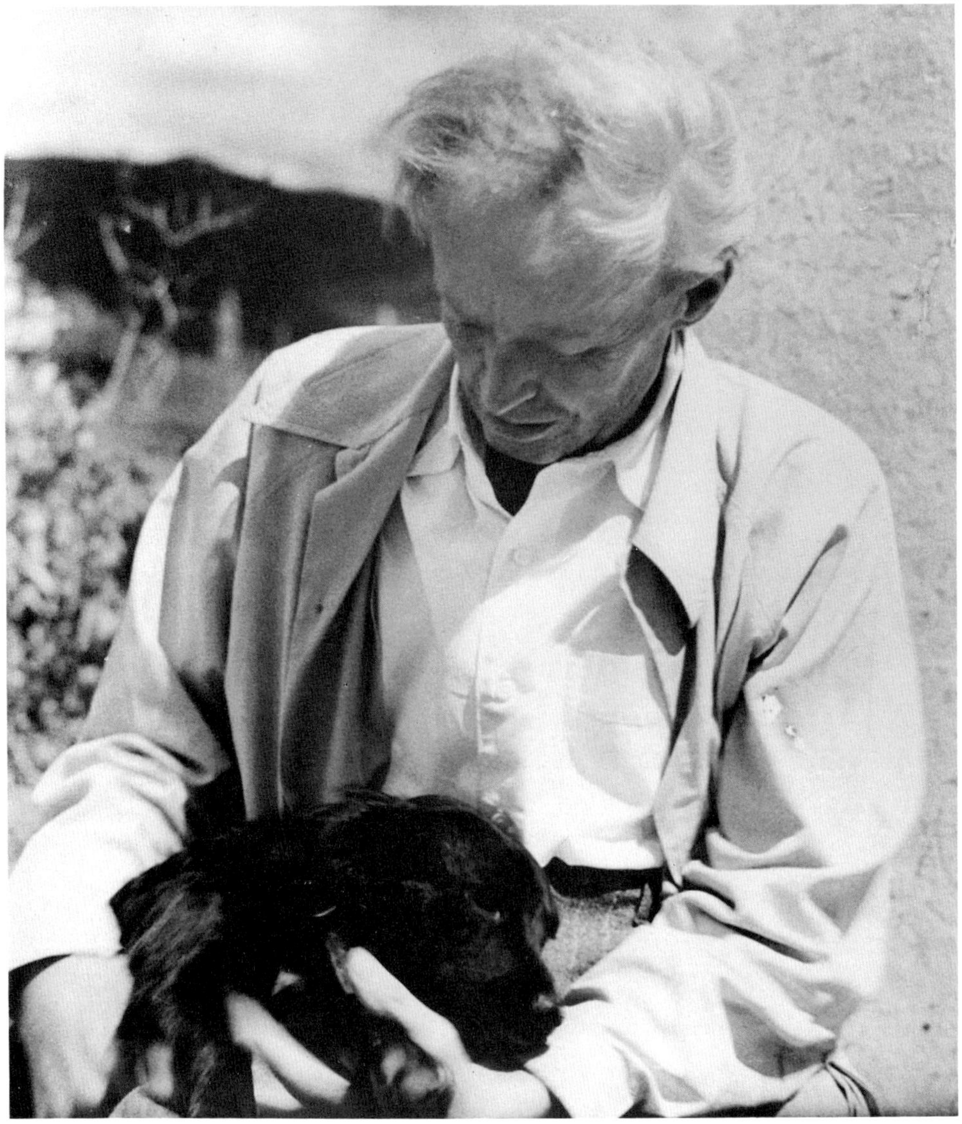

ILL. 13
Andrew Dasburg, probably at his home in Talpa, just south of Taos. ca. 1952. Photographer: Mildred Tolbert

ANDREW DASBURG (1887–1979), first visited Taos in 1918.

> ***The exhibition was well received, and showed very definitely what a powerful painter Andrew is and what a great creative force he has.***[2]
>
> —Jerry Bywaters, April 1957

> ***I really taught people to see: a sort of evangelist for modernism, because of my experience of seeing Matisse paint for most of an hour.***[3]
>
> —Andrew Dasburg, Winter 1975

Not only did Dasburg meet Henri Matisse, but he also discovered the work of Cézanne in Paris and became one of the first American artists to grasp the possibilities of modernism. So powerfully did he convey the message of modern painting that he became a leader of the Woodstock art colony before the First World War. Dasburg recalled the genesis of his abstraction painting, speaking of his experiments in synchromism, the first modernist *ism* created by Americans in Europe:

> *It was about 1912 when I thought of the possibility of making a painting that could exist as a thing in itself without reference to a subject beyond its general color and configuration of movements, allowing the form to evolve out of these two primary impulses—avoiding all illusional values as much as possible in the hope of making an object existing in an environment of objects and not as a pointer to something seen elsewhere.*[4]

Dasburg's work was included in the important 1913 modernist New York exhibitions at the Macdowell Club, in the famous Armory Show, and in the 1916 "Forum Exhibition of Modern American Painters." He became a member of the group of artists which formed around photographer and modern art promoter Alfred Stieglitz in New York. In 1923, Dasburg enhanced his reputation in the art world by writing an important article on the rise of cubism for *The Arts* magazine. No other artist would move to Taos having already achieved such a significant presence in the American art world.

Howard Cook, Dasburg's student in New York and later a Taos artist, wrote about Dasburg's time at the Art Students League:

> *I can remember enrolling in this latter class at the League, a class which was exploratory in nature, having in succession as teachers Andrew Dasburg, Max Weber, and Eugene Speicher. The whole art world was in a state of ferment. . . . For at that time the academic world . . . exercised much more powerful control. The artist friends of Dasburg, being rebels, aroused much controversy among my friends and fellow students as we gathered in the corridors. . . .*[5]

During the 1920s, when Dasburg divided his time between New York and New Mexico, he painted landscapes and still life inspired by Cézanne. He moved permanently to Taos in the 1930s but soon contracted Addison's disease, which left him too weak to produce much artwork.[6] By 1947, he recovered sufficiently to resume his career and join the new Moderns to become part of the postwar creative explosion. As he had done throughout his long career, Dasburg once more gave active encouragement and private critiques to advanced art students such as Earl Stroh. He became greatly admired and respected by the Taos Moderns who, if they did not know his place in American art history before coming to Taos, soon learned of it. But Dasburg was also open to inspiration. Edward Corbett's startling white abstractions (almost entirely white with a few dark fissures of paint cutting through) influenced both Dasburg and Benrimo to create their own essays in white.[7]

Dasburg's gradual return to painting and drawing led to the period of his finest work, from the late 1940s to the early 1960s. Just as Cézanne examined Mont Sainte-Victoire over many years, Dasburg studied the Taos Valley until he could convey its underlying geometry with an intimate precision attained by no other Taos artist. In his drawing, he looked beyond the smooth, feminine form of hills and rounded mountains to reveal the skeleton beneath with supreme economy of line. This process of reduction, of elimination of the extraneous to reveal the essential, is an important basis for much modern painting. In work such as *White Morning* (1963), thought to be Dasburg's last completed oil painting, he depicts the geometry of Taos, its valley, buildings, and suggestion of mountains, each along its own plane. He painted the Taos Valley not as a mass of dead geometric blocks but as a vital, living thing. In the land's visual rhythm he found harmony coming out of contrasts, an artistic perception of nature and time and also an artistic attitude which defined much of the art of that era.

Late in life, Dasburg was honored with museum shows in Dallas, Los Angeles, Albuquerque, and New York. Although *Newsweek* and *Art News* noted his continuing survival, these publications did not emphasize his continuing artistic genius. It is because of work such as the pastel *Llano Spring* (1953), with its cubist forms of buildings which became part of the land itself, that Dasburg stands out as a master of serious modern painting.

In an address to art students at UNM's Taos Summer Field School of Art in 1953, Dasburg spoke of how an artist should approach the process of creation:

> ***What is a work of art if not elevation of spirit? Something that in its best instances has the power to instill with a heightened awareness of life—both its joy and enigma. Be the theme lyrical or tragic, a great work of art is always more profound and at the same time simpler than the verbiage with which we obscure in trying to describe it. Someone is always introducing the word "problem" to replace joy, a sense of play, and mystery which is the fertile soil of art. The only problem that confronts the artist beyond his daily bread is to rid his mind of cobwebs of confused thought and to throw away the crutches of theory. Work is the mother of craft which cannot be earned as an end itself but only as servant to a guiding vision. A purpose to be achieved.***[8]

When Dasburg died in 1979, he was the last surviving artist of the Armory Show, and thus the last direct link to the earliest days of American modernism.

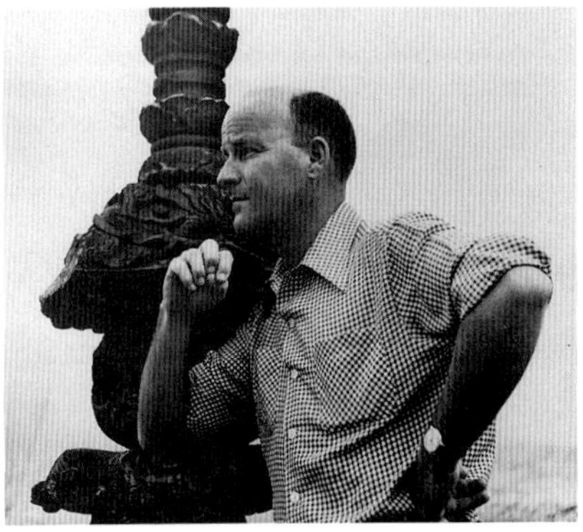

ILL. 14
Cady Wells. ca. 1948. Photographer: unknown

CADY WELLS (1904–1954), first visited Taos in 1932.

> ***Perhaps it is to those who do not live too long that the gift is given of fully savoring every moment.***[9]
>
> —E. Boyd, 1956

In his watercolor painting, Cady Wells, like his teacher Dasburg, sought to capture the geometry of the land, combining his interest in landform structure with a Marin-like boldness. A sense of rapidity often appears in Wells's semi-abstract landscapes—particularly the early ones. Slashed with rains of line, the paintings are as much a map of the land's movement as of the land's form. His cuneiform-like abstractions hold all the mystery of ancient Sumerian tablets, like a language still recognizable but not exactly remembered. Such traits led Georgia O'Keeffe on more than one occasion to state that Wells (along with herself!) was one of the two or three finest painters in the Southwest. He assimilated the lessons of Dasburg and later went through a period where the work of Georges Rouault and Paul Klee influenced his work.

Wells never was a permanent resident, but he continued to visit and work in Taos after World War II, staying at a studio owned by Taos artist Rebecca James. By the late 1940s he worked in thick, full-bodied watercolor, putting down on paper a more sensual texture than in previous work to achieve fuller definitions of space. He enlarged the closely worked details in his landscapes until they developed into his late abstractions such as *Brown Barranca 54* (ca. 1952).

Wells learned the use of colored inks from Benrimo, utilizing them for dramatic effect. Influenced by the stained glass windows at Chartres Cathedral, Wells set his work in ink within a "framework of translucence and dark contrast."[10] One critic understood the artist's intent exactly when he noted that Wells was ornamenting "his patterns and intervals as though they were richly complex tapestries."[11]

Wells seemed to be finding an important new direction in his work after 1952, but he did not live long enough to fulfill its potential. It is a tragedy that Wells did not have a few more decades to explore such a promising direction.

THOMAS BENRIMO (1887–1958), moved to Taos in 1939.

> ***The flowing quality of design which Tom Benrimo subtly employs suggests a penetrating musical quality.***[12]
>
> **—Allen S. Weller, 1952**

In an art community known for its reclusive artists, Thomas Benrimo stood out exceptionally by his absence from the art scene in his first Taos years. He lived in Taos for over twelve years before sharing his work with the public for the first time in a group exhibit at the La Fonda.[13]

Benrimo moved to Taos on the strength of the Art Director Medal for Color Illustration award, an honor that included a $5,000 prize. He left New York's Pratt Institute, where he had taught such courses as "Applied Surrealism" for commercial artists. A painter whose roots went back to the early days of American modernism, he now had the means to make the transition back into fine art, an area he had abandoned in order to support his tubercular mother and brother through commercial art.[14]

His first artistic project in Taos, done in partnership with his wife, Dorothy, a fine jeweler, was converting an old adobe ruin into a stately house. In his early Taos painting, he attempted to regain a position staked out more than twenty years before in New York. Little of his work from that period remains, but it is clear that the Armory Show deeply impressed him; he painted abstractions by 1918, if not before.

His Taos work included subject matter suggested by ancient Roman and Etruscan art and Greek vase painting and was influenced by cubism. His facility for painting detail exceeded that of most artists, and his studies of modernist painting during his teaching career made him one of the best informed artists in the country. His teaching notes reveal a brilliant mind which welded together the many currents of modernism to make them understandable to his students. Benrimo's reputation was such that László Moholy-Nagy, an artist and founder of the New Bauhaus art school in Chicago, invited him to become the school's director in the 1940s. But, by that time Benrimo had decided to devote the remainder of his life to painting.

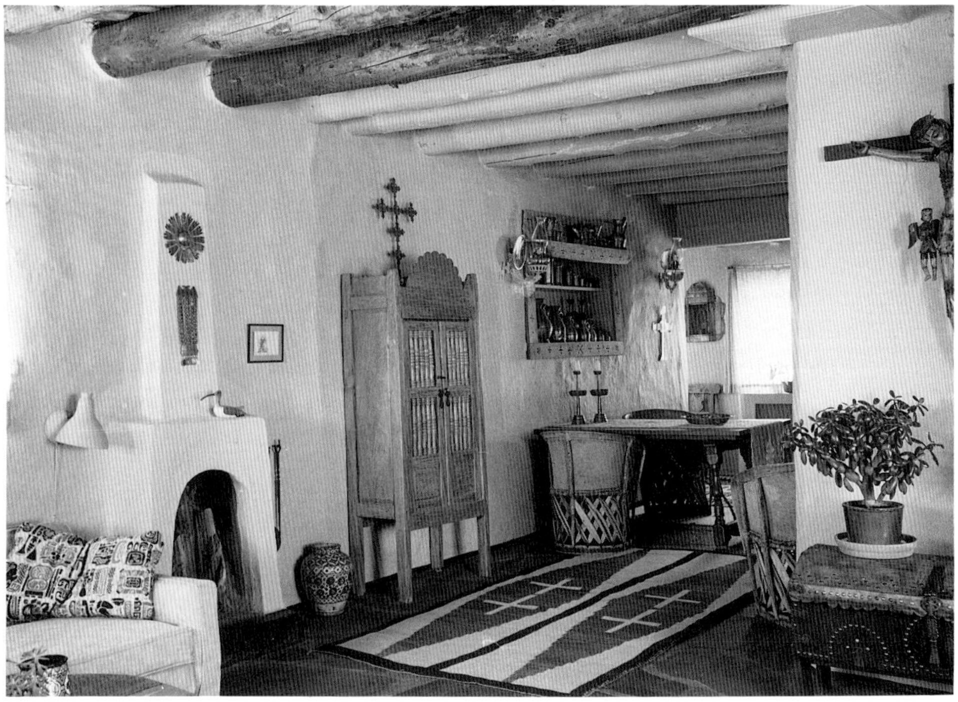

ILL. 15
Interior of Thomas and Dorothy Benrimo's house. ca. 1959. Photographer: Mildred Tolbert

During the war years, he concentrated on finely crafted surrealistic paintings. A major oil of 1946, *The Hollow Men*, combines his interests in architecture and the surreal. Here he balances figurative and abstract elements, clearly favoring the latter. The painting expresses strong emotion in an allusion to the poetry of T. S. Eliot—the dark side of humanity, all in a spider's web of chilling connections, the unpleasant aspects of the human condition. *The Hollow Men* contains passages of exquisite detail, sensuous lines, and color which would become the fully developed subjects of later paintings. In the 1950s, Benrimo combined surrealism and strong structural form with lyrically tragic and passionate themes.[15] The bone structure and line-systems from *The Hollow Men* are sometimes quoted in late work such as *White Moon Number Two* (ca. 1954).

Benrimo's work achieved national exposure when one of his paintings was included in the 1951 "Contemporary American Painting and Sculpture" exhibit at the University of Illinois. Asked to comment on his work for the catalog, he took the most conservative course by quoting someone else's words: "Feeling and form are all; and that man is most an artist who fuses those two into an indivisible one."[16]

LOUIS RIBAK (1903–1979), moved to Taos in 1944.

> ***In his first show in eight years he reports from Mexico and the Southwest with added strength and color. There is new freedom with emphasis on forms as such rather than on objects visioned in market still-lifes. An Indian dance and "Conquistador" in expressionist vein with strongly silhouetted figures are vigorous and vivid.***[17]
>
> —*New York Times*, May 1954

Beginning with work that was included in the 1934 "Venice Biennial" art exhibition (an important European show), and continuing with his social realist painting of that decade, Louis Ribak captured the vibrant images of urban life with considerable power. He appeared to be making an important career for himself when, in 1944, he chose to abandon New York. So complete was this break that New York art dealer Harry Salpeter was able to write in the spring of 1954, "It gives me great pleasure to be able to present the first exhibition in eight years of the work of the well known American painter, Louis Ribak."[18] An eight-year stretch between shows was a long one for an up-and-coming painter.

Various reasons have been suggested by his wife Beatrice Mandelman, by other artists, and by Ribak himself for the move: his health, John Sloan's suggestion that he move to Santa Fe (where Sloan, a New York artist, had been a summer visitor for decades), and general disenchantment with New York.[19] All of those were probably contributing factors, but, since there was a good deal of wanderlust in him, perhaps he just needed a change:

> ***Something entirely unsuspected gripped Ribak in the Southwest and he was never able to disenthrall himself from the heady solemnity of the landscape, its beauty or emotive potential.***[20]

Ribak's approach to art shifted from a modern figurative style to full abstraction during his Taos years. Much of his early Taos work consists of semi-abstract landscapes, artistically descended from the paintings of American artist Albert P. Ryder in whose work there is a *living* aspect to the environment in which humankind is not isolated, but is instead an intimate part. Ribak seems to have brought this concept with him from New York but, under the powerful influence of contact with New Mexico's Indian pueblos, it was dramatically reinforced, expanded, and adapted to the changed circumstances of his life. In the first Taos paintings of Indians, there remains a feeling of packed closeness left over from his artistic approach in New York. However, Ribak later abandoned tight city scenes for the vastness of the American West (and of Mexico), which turned out to be a more natural subject matter for an artist who had a predilection for the dramatic. He had to change to meet the demands of the new environment. Beatrice Mandelman said, "We had to start all over again. We spent the first couple of years painting the landscape" as a means of coming to understand the West.[21]

Highly respected by his peers, Ribak was looked up to by the Taos Moderns as "an elder *compadre*," a role model. In 1947, he opened

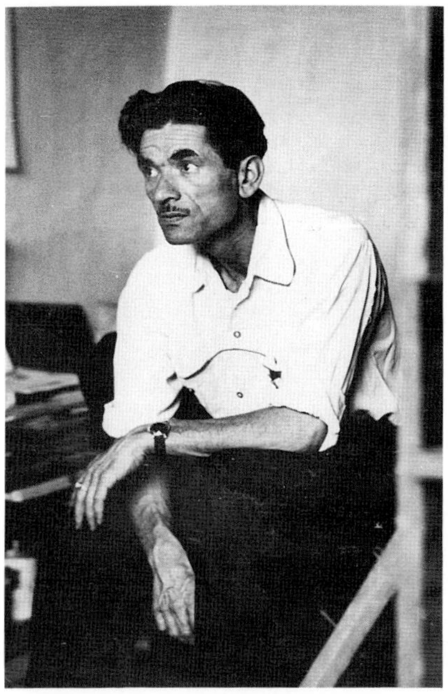

ILL. 16
Louis Ribak posing in the La Loma Plaza studio of the late Taos artist Herbert Dunton. ca. 1948. (La Loma Plaza is the oldest neighborhood in what is now the Town of Taos, established around 1797.) Photographer: Mildred Tolbert

the Taos Valley Art School for returning veterans who used their GI Bill benefits to pay tuition and living expenses. In addition to attracting beginners, mature artists who needed no training used the stipend to enable them to continue painting and drawing.

Unlike Emil Bisttram, who attempted to overwhelm his art students with his own personal formulas, Ribak, like Dasburg, offered no ideology to his students: "I'm not truly anything. I'm against everything. Damned abstract[ionist]s, realists, illustrators. . . ."[22] He condemned taking any single approach—it would lead to academicism, an art of deadness, whether abstraction or representational.

In the mid-1950s, Mandelman and Ribak sojourned in New York for a time then returned to Taos.[23] Ribak was well acquainted with the work of the abstract expressionists and knew artists of the New York School. From that time, Ribak developed the lyrical abstract expressionism which would occupy much of his subsequent career. *Movement No. I and Movement No. II* are examples. The flowing calligraphy, which is evident in much of his work, comes out of decades of landscape drawings. His abstract painting seems not to have come from cubism so much as out of his own preoccupation with working directly from nature, with rocks and cliffs and the relationships and proportions of natural forms.

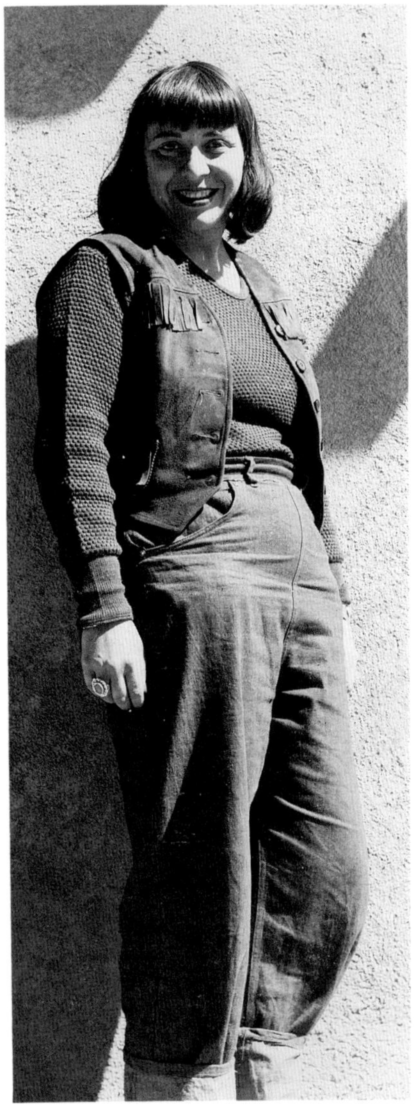

ILL. 17
Beatrice Mandelman. ca. 1955. Photographer: Mildred Tolbert

BEATRICE MANDELMAN, moved to Taos in 1944.

> ***The complexity of the abstractions, the simplicity of color, the structures painted within the large canvases were highly organized. They had a child-like elegance to them, a transparency and depth that held me spellbound. There were open areas of white out of which colors, her shapes and forms seemed to explode, like prisms through the very surface rather than merely refracting light onto the surface.***[24]
>
> —Ed Sasek, 1982

In 1944, there were few Moderns in Taos, and all of them were considerably older than Beatrice Mandelman. The young woman was an anomaly in an art community still characterized by elderly, male, "old-hat" painters. Mandelman painted semi-abstractly even before she came to Taos. Abstracted forms showed up in her work more and more frequently until for the most part she dropped the use of identifiable subject matter near the end of the 1940s. Mandelman created complex forms with sophisticated application of simple colors—earthy grays and yellows in early work, later replaced by bold colors, a reference to Matisse. Her forms owe some of their boldness to Fernand Léger, with whom she studied in Paris from 1948 to 1949.

The progression of her work over five decades in Taos shows the development of what she sees as an artistic "language or vocabulary," an exploration of repeated forms examined in great depth, a decades-long meditation on a theme with a continual simplification of its elements, though not of its concepts. The forms in *Winter* (1954) chart a course taken in her later paintings, which become increasingly stark and more daring in attempting to define space.

While her paintings make no direct analogies to the land, her purpose is to express in artistic language her emotional feelings for the land and to convey what living in this region means to her. Although New Mexico has served as an inspiration for her work, the interpretation in paint has been more universal. Mandelman has made use of planar, sometimes elliptical areas of clear color without the presence of line, making the work feel open, de-emphasizing divisions. In other works, there are linear elements which serve as edges or as a flexible grid through which color zones appear, particularly in the early paintings, painted in close values.

Many of the forms in Mandelman's vocabulary resemble the geometric patterns seen in the basketry, textiles, and painted pottery of Southwest Indians. While her art does not refer directly to Native American cultures any more than it does to landscape, it is not surprising that artists from different cultures reacting strongly to the same environment would reach similar artistic conclusions.[25]

EARL STROH (born 1924), first lived in Taos in 1947.

> ***For me, his pictures are essentially spacial, not as an illusion of depth arrived at by means of traditional perspective but by the total divisions of the surface of his pictures according to the imagery he had in mind. There is no vanishing point, only a horizontal and diagonal interplay of tones.[26]***
>
> —Andrew Dasburg, July 1973

> ***I looked up universities in the West. One of them was Oregon because [Mark] Tobey was up there. I thought of that and then I happened to see the catalog of the University of New Mexico and it was not Collegiate Gothic. It was adobe style and I said, "That looks like interesting architecture." So I applied. . . . I knew nothing else about the place. . . . I didn't know a thing about Taos. I just wanted to get the hell out of the East.[27]***
>
> —Earl Stroh, January 1985

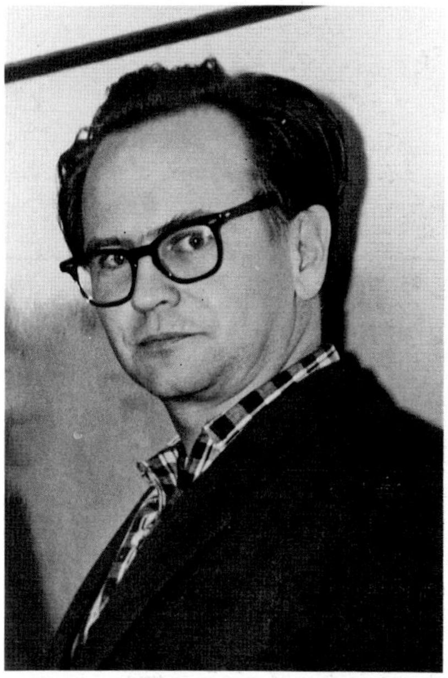

ILL. 18
Earl Stroh. ca. 1959. Photographer: unknown

Earl Stroh began art studies at UNM in Albuquerque, then came to Taos later in 1947 to attend the university's Summer Field School of Art. Students lived and painted at the Harwood Foundation, participating in a program that had begun in 1929. They received art instruction from University of New Mexico teachers and special critiques from established Taos artists, including Andrew Dasburg. Stroh was less interested in getting an art degree than in becoming an accomplished painter. By the following year, he had dropped out of the program in Albuquerque and returned to Taos for private work with Dasburg.

Stroh came to Taos influenced by Cézanne and Marin but, after his work with Dasburg in the 1940s and a 1951 trip to Europe, he began to find his own way as an artist. His work in the early 1950s was "modern in trend," as *El Crepusculo* newspaper termed it, and semi-abstract. By 1953, with *Gray Spring*, he began working with full abstractions, while also continuing figurative work, as in *Dido* (ca. 1956). During an extended stay in Paris between 1957 and 1959, he studied etching, aquatint, and other printmaking methods with Johnnie Friedlander, a highly respected European artist.[28] Stroh developed concepts of internal structure which carried over into his subsequent New Mexico work. In his paintings, there is a seeming paradox: what appears at first glance to be a softness in focus is an effect derived from the soft edges of color bands. But the formal structure within them has been described as being made of steel.

While identifiable subject matter—still life, the figure, landscape, or skyscape—may appear in his work, his intent is not to illustrate nature but to convey a complex elegance through the use of the most limited pictorial means. Nothing is added beyond what is needed. He has maintained the importance of striving for the essential within a particular subject matter, avoiding becoming trapped in its surface. Stroh's art concerns light, its refractions, reflections, and relation to natural forms. Nuances of blended color flow together imperceptibly, giving the work a connected solidarity. Stroh spends an immense amount of painting time to achieve a unity of the surface which will be as complete as the feeling of depth. Strong images—a blue line swallowed by shimmering desert, the sudden curve of a mesa's plummeting descent, a glow within the land—give his work a feeling of limitless space.

AGNES MARTIN (born 1912), first lived in Taos in 1947.

> ***We were misled on some points, but it is not a blank canvas after all—apparently there are color stripes and bars on it.***[29]
>
> —Fergus O'Brien, Lord Mayor of Dublin, Ireland; analysis of Martin's grid paintings, November 1980

> ***When I did the grid paintings, I thought I had finally come up with something no one would possibly want.***[30]
>
> —Agnes Martin, April 1987

Agnes Martin lived in Taos at two different times—the first time as an art student in 1947, the second, in the 1950s, just prior to discovering the balance of line and soft color (or even just the suggestion of color) on which she built a major career. Her paintings display an expansiveness, as of a plain reaching out to the undefined edges of the Canadian prairie (like the area where she grew up), symbolic of the metaphysical reality that inspires her. In Taos she declared her intention to achieve great artistic success and to receive recognition for that success. In this statement of intent, as in her paintings, there is a good deal of the mysterious.

After receiving a master of fine arts degree from Columbia University in 1952, Martin took a teaching job in the Albuquerque Public Schools.[31] She moved to Taos in 1952 to build the basis for the grid which would sustain her. She later said of that time, "I just stayed in my studio and

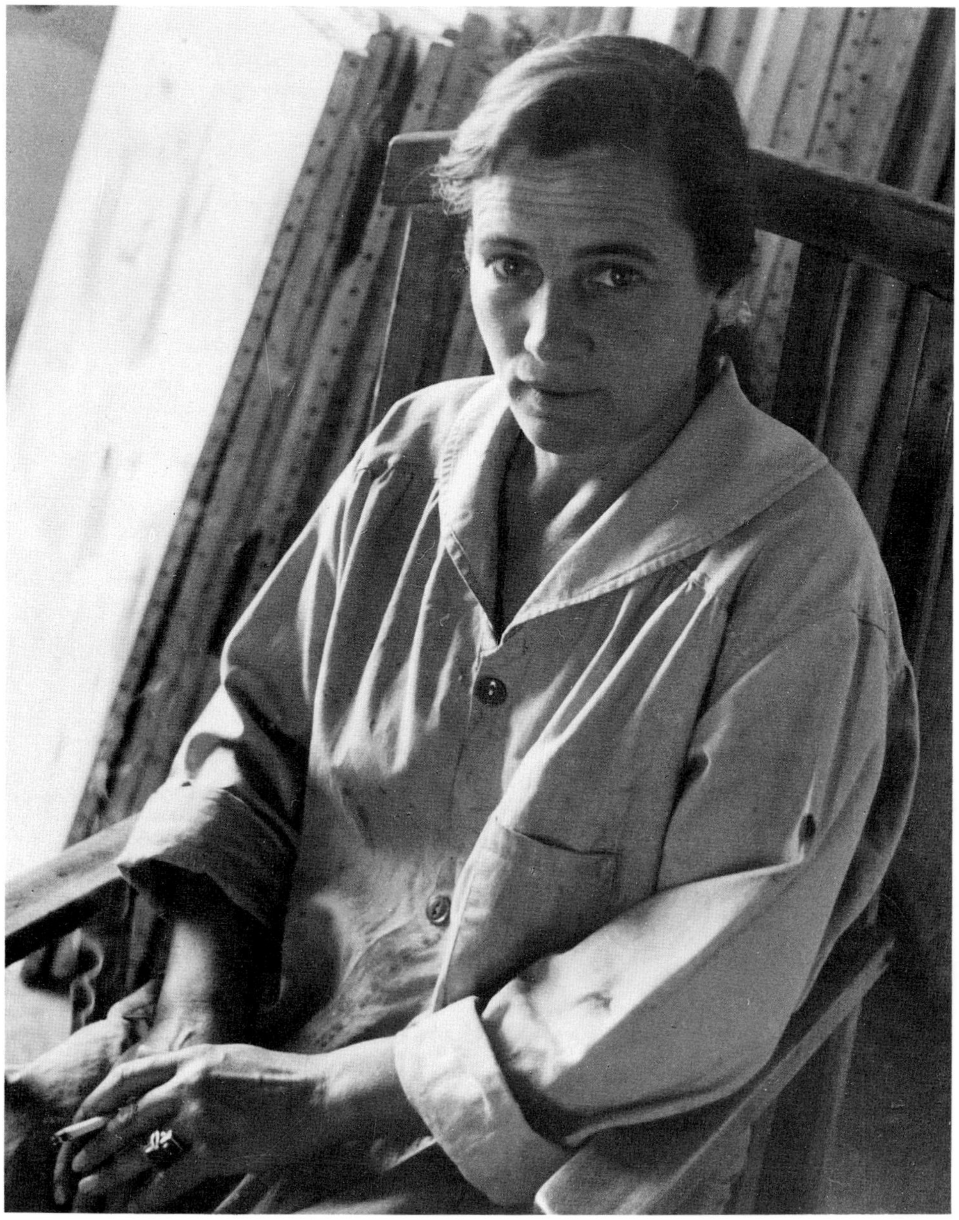

ILL. 19
Agnes Martin in her Taos studio. ca. 1953. Photographer: Mildred Tolbert

fought and struggled with my response to life, and struggled to know it."[32] Martin lived in daytime isolation, seldom leaving her easel, infrequently showing her work except with Ribak and Mandelman at their studio-gallery during the summers. She visited the Ribaks almost every evening; they chose not to talk about art.[33] This simultaneous intimacy of place, and dearth of artistic contact among its residents, continues to be one of the most ironic contradictions of Taos. Martin's experience was typical. The Taos Moderns were more inclined to paint than to talk.[34]

In a town where most of the artists lived at or not far above subsistence level, Martin faced particularly difficult circumstances. She survived the worst of times secure in her determination to get exactly what she wanted. Late in 1954, a grant from the Wurlitzer Foundation enabled her to meet living expenses and to purchase art supplies, but just barely. In her application she listed as references Clay Spohn and Betty Parsons, the New York art dealer with whom she hoped to show her work. The cumulative production of her Taos period impressed Parsons enough that she bought several of Martin's paintings, thus providing the artist with enough income to make the move to New York in 1957. Martin felt that association with Parsons would put her "in the position of one of those contributing to art expression in this country."[35]

She had to wait nearly seven more years before major national recognition finally began to come her way, but this severe focus on achieving critical success—an obsession, according to those who knew her—paid off. Her striving towards artistic fulfillment, her desire to capture "truth and beauty," as Martin terms it, permeated the art community, but few of the others shared her overwhelming drive to become famous. Martin combined artistic integrity with commercial success, never an easy balance nor one often achieved. She clearly stated her artistic intentions in a 1954 letter to the Wurlitzer Foundation:

> *I would like to say that my efforts and interests as an artist are directed toward assisting in the establishment of American Art, distinct and authentic, that I feel we, myself and other artists, will very soon succeed in making not only a successful but an acceptable representation of the expression of the American people. . . . I feel that it is very thrilling to be "in" almost at the beginning as we are.*[36]

Earl Stroh recalled that in 1947 Martin experimented with Rouault-inspired portraits and a few landscapes. By the time she returned to Taos in 1952, she was working to free her painting from reliance on the environment, even its light. Martin developed her emphasis on composition over color even before her 1957 move to New York. The biomorphic or pictographic forms of the Taos paintings such as *Autumn Watch* (ca. 1954) are often separated by areas of subdued, earth-colored flat space. Her reductive approach to painting somewhat resembled minimalist art, but remained warmer due to the influence of abstract expressionism and painters such as Edward Corbett and Ad Reinhardt, a visitor from New York.[37] Martin said, "I think painting is about our most emotional responses to life . . . you could paint anything, really . . . all our feelings."[38]

In 1955 alone, she completed over one hundred canvases, some of which were shown that year in Santa Fe and Albuquerque, and possibly in Taos at the Ruins Gallery. Little of this work survives; except for the few pieces sold, Martin destroyed almost all of her Taos paintings on a return visit from New York in the late 1950s.[39]

OLI SIHVONEN (1921–1991), first lived in Taos in 1949.

> *On a warm blue ground lie five diagonally compressed ellipses of identical size; three cold blue, one brick red, and one alizarin. Their careful spatial and color relationships push and bend the parameters of the canvas, and alter the viewer's balance and sense of personal space.*[40]
>
> —Vivian Milford, 1983

Josef Albers's influence came to Taos with the arrival of one of his students, Oli Sihvonen, who attended Black Mountain College from 1946 to 1948. Albers was for that art school what Clyfford Still had been for the California School of Fine Arts—a dominating presence. For Albers, "Abstraction is the essential function of the Human Spirit."[41] For Sihvonen, this meant that the images created intended no representation of or reference to any other identifiable thing. A painting made in this manner included flat color, no romantic evocations, no gestural expressiveness, but instead a clean, pure, effortless look. In Taos, Sihvonen continued his studies at Ribak's Taos Valley Art School in 1949 and 1950, seven years before he became a full-time Taos resident with the support of a Wurlitzer Foundation grant. By 1950, he worked exclusively with abstract imagery. Before the end of the decade, he was doing work such as *Fenestra #2.*

Not all of it was in paint. He made a group of reliefs for cabinet doors whose linear elements were designed in sheet metal with a hammer and punch. Sihvonen's use of line was nondescriptive. He developed a similar idea in drawing by extending long intricate lines into what appears to be an endless pattern of springy, wiry forms covering the entire surface of the paper.

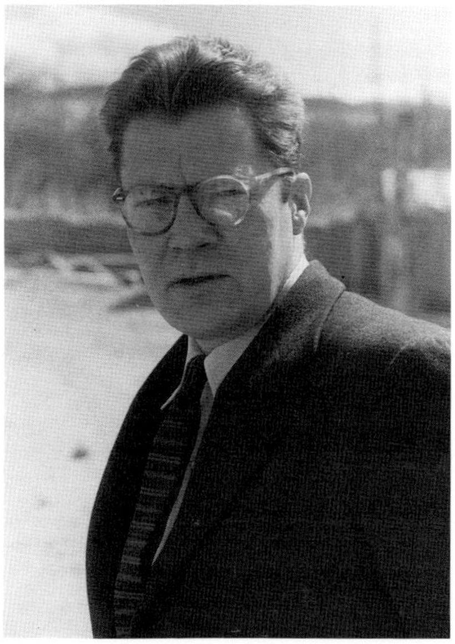

ILL. 20
Oli Sihvonen. ca. 1955. Photographer: Mildred Tolbert

Sihvonen gained recognition outside of New Mexico for a series of ellipses begun in Taos. He described them as "ellipses in a surround. . . . The environment is a surround—one is among, not in it." In the series titled "Dialogue," begun by 1962, he explored the relationship of forms within the composition (often in just two or three colors)—the dynamic integration of forms. This approach was well suited to someone who perceived the "surround." Even here, where the work of a Taos Modern achieved a most extreme reduction, the influence of the natural environment remained. While the shapes in the "Dialogue" series represented no object, the artist speculated that the massive forms of mountains and the giant shadows cast gave at least a suggestion to his artistic course.[42] He painted these elliptical shapes in clear, luminous colors. Many of his paintings were large compared to those of other Taos painters, who seldom attempted to work in sizes much over five by six feet—perhaps because of transportation difficulties. But also, there was little market for paintings on a public-architectural scale then in New Mexico. The broader acceptance of large works in the East, and the inclusion of Sihvonen's work in a major exhibit at the Museum of Modern Art, led him to move to New York in 1967.

TED EGRI (born 1913), moved to Taos in 1950.

> ***His major concern is with that moment of inspiration when the direct visual image is siphoned through his personality. The resulting artistic expression is a synthesis of what was seen and felt. The work, whether abstract or representational, has transformed the experience into a statement about values. Further, for the work to become an aesthetic entity, it must also have structure, principles of balance and design as observed in nature.***[43]
>
> —*Southwest Art,* February 1979

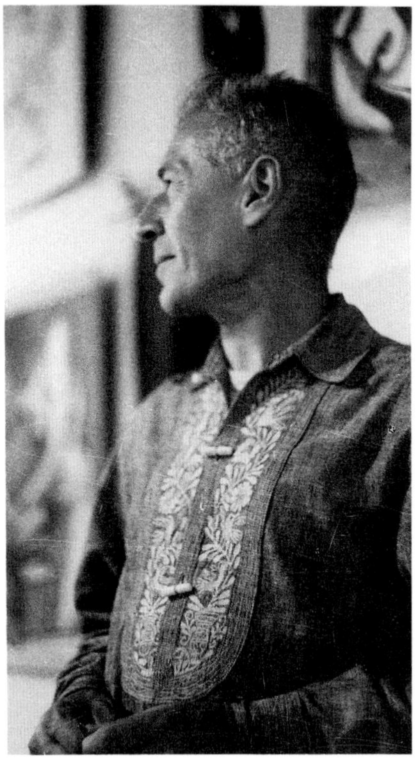

ILL. 21
Ted Egri. ca. 1955. Photographer: Mildred Tolbert

As might be expected from an artist who, while still a child, provided illustrations to the leftist publication *New Masses*, Ted Egri saw art not only as creative expression but also as social responsibility. From the first, his Taos work was highly political, often speaking to issues of oppressed or tormented humankind.[44] But whether his subject is political or religious, his approach representational or abstraction, Egri's work suggests motion. *Struggle*, a 1951 woodcarving, was inspired by a 1949 riot in Peekskill, New York, which ensued when white hecklers prevented African-American singer Paul Robeson from giving an open-air concert. The motion depicted in *Struggle* is unpleasant, reflecting the anger Egri felt over the obscene behavior exhibited by the rock-throwing, jeering Peekskill mob. For him, sculpture was a form of social protest and a means of political activism.

Egri had been a painter before moving to Taos, but while he continued to paint occasionally, the massiveness of the mountains and the dramatic impact possible with three dimensionality made him decide to concentrate on sculpture. This work was meant to express the artist's concern with the relationship of peoples:

> *Many artists have expressed their feelings of man's isolation and the chaos in the world. Even though this indicates their awareness of the world around them, it also indicates that they have not identified themselves with that world. They feel isolated. I believe the artist must identify himself with some vital force, either aesthetic, social, political or philosophical, in his present environment. Man's struggle for human dignity is one of the most dramatic sources for artistic creation today.*[45]

LOUISE GANTHIERS (1907–1982), moved to Taos in 1950.

> *From a study of these paintings it appears obvious that the artist is heading toward a completely non-objective type of painting . . . her work demonstrates how a serious painter holds the mental conception within the bounds of plastic color.*[46]
>
> —Alfred Morang, 1952

Louise Ganthiers came to Taos with the hope of becoming an artist. An administrator in a textile business, she had a longstanding interest in art and studied with the figurative-fantasy artist Rufino Tamayo in New York. In Taos, she became familiar with the artistic concepts of Hofmann, and applied the results of all her training to her work.[47] In a statement about her relationship to art for the catalog of a one-person show, she said:

> *I don't paint with ease. I wish I were capable of the smashing directness of some of my contemporaries. Some of these sketches have that quality. In carrying them further will I move toward the lyric, the muted understatement of the beautiful and gentle? I have been struggling to reach further into the abstract to break up forms in new ways*

to fix a space dimension on the canvas that has not been my approach. Yet if I find that I am saying something that infers crassness or harshness I won't be happy. I have tried to speak in different ways against tragedy, injustice and waste but my way is not that of harshness.[48]

Ganthiers waged a struggle on both artistic and economic fronts. In the 1950s, she sold frozen custard to tourists during the summer; she also went to San Francisco to find work and to show her paintings. There her paintings caught the attention of prominent art critic Alfred Frankenstein, who wrote several reviews of her work over the years. He may have seen the encaustic painting *Buffalo Dancer* (1954). There is an undeniable wildness to the figure which seems to be of another world. The dancer clearly has merged with the animal spirit he portrays. Frankenstein wrote:

Miss Ganthiers, who is exhibiting at Studio 44, is a painter who likes a rich, complex impasto, lays on her color most often with the palette knife, and brings off whatever she does with great skill and finely imaginative design. Her abstractions are excellent, but most striking of all are her pictures derived from the Indian dances she has seen in Taos, where she lives. Her big single figures are magnificently drawn, and her studies of group choreography handle the rhythms, the color, and the mysterious character of their subjects equally well. With the possible exception of Niagara Falls, nothing in the United States has led to more dull, literal minded painting than the Indian dances and dancers of the Southwest, and it is therefore doubly refreshing to see this theme handled by a creative artist who brings it genuine imagination, selectivity and power over the expressive values of paint.[49]

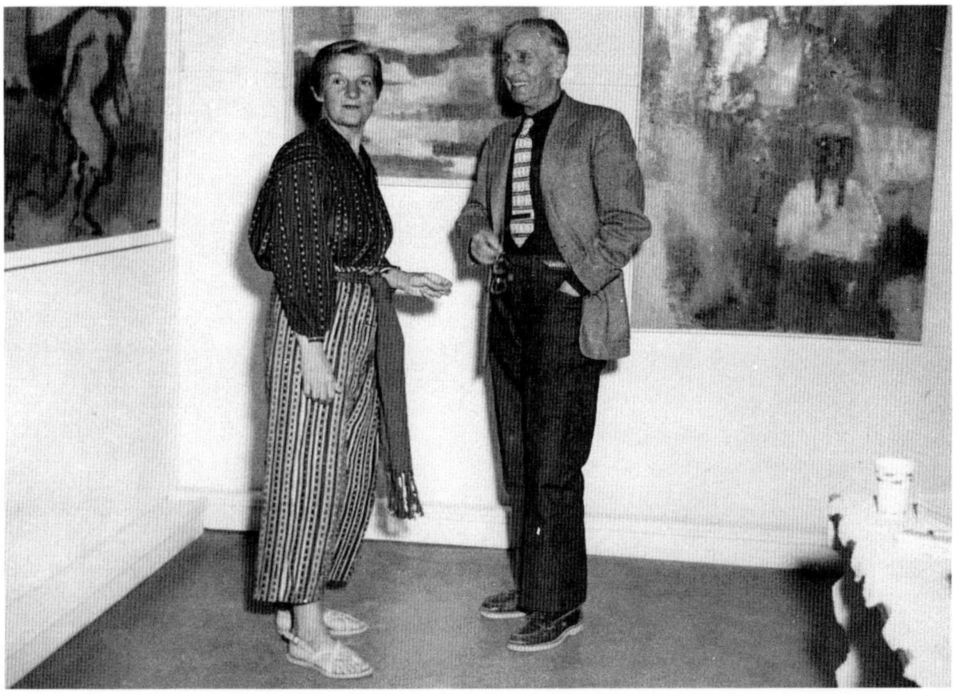

ILL. 22
Louise Ganthiers and Thomas Benrimo in Taos at an opening reception for a show of Alfred Rogoway's paintings. ca. 1955. Photographer: Martin Shaffer

CLAY SPOHN (1898–1977), moved to Taos in 1951.

> ***I do not believe in anything which restrains, limits or suppresses the spirit of man, or the spirit of his works, nor which binds his art to any conventionality of idea, theory, or method, or to conscientious and self-conscious description, or to that which would otherwise jeopardize the discovery of new experiences and awarenesses.***[50]
>
> —Clay Spohn, 1953

A native of San Francisco, Clay Spohn attended art schools in the Bay Area, New York City, and Paris, exhibiting regularly on the West Coast from the late 1920s. Highly regarded locally, he was a natural choice as a teacher at the progressive California School of Fine Arts. He promoted no particular "brand" of art but stressed the use of imagination. For instance, Spohn claimed that he suggested the idea of the twisted wire mobile to sculptor Alexander Calder. He was an early proponent of the concept of temporary art, art meant to exist only in a particular moment, and instituted what may have been the first "art happenings" on the West Coast. The best known of these was the 1949 "Museum of Unknown and Little Known Objects" at the school, in which mundane substances such as rotting rice or bedroom lint were crazily rearranged or reinterpreted, forcing viewers to see things in a new way. For all their zaniness, he intended the happenings as serious exercises in the imaginative process and as challenges to the prevailing ideas of what constituted art. Although these happenings were statements of the moment, he meant his paintings to have lasting value.

Spohn painted abstractly even before the Second World War, but it was afterwards, while teaching in San Francisco, that his modern ideas about painting became best known. By the time he moved to Taos in the spring of 1951, his work clearly could be seen as a part of that broad category of abstract expressionism, although he repudiated the label and, in an antiestablishment gesture not uncommon to artists, claimed that his work fit neither here nor there, and could not be labeled.[51] Unfortunately, he was taken at his word, and having rejected being included with the artists of the New York School, his career came to a standstill. He continued to desperately want a major art show in New York while taking swipes at precisely those mechanisms through which he might have achieved that recognition. In 1959, he wrote to two of his closest Taos friends, Wolcott and Georgette Ely:

> ***Ran into Ad Rinehardt [sic] on the street about an hour ago on my way to work. He lives just up the street from the N.Y.U. Library. I see him occasionally. Today he spoke of the publicity received by Clyfford Still, Kline, De Kooning and Rothko (in this week's issue of Life Mag.)—and he was amazed that they should go along with Life mag's identifying their work with the visual shapes and forms or qualities of nature—with fire, steel girders, grass and sunsets. All of it catering to and talking down to the baser comprehensions of the public—just the sort of thing their principles have been opposed to—the sort of thing they have, for years, talked against.***

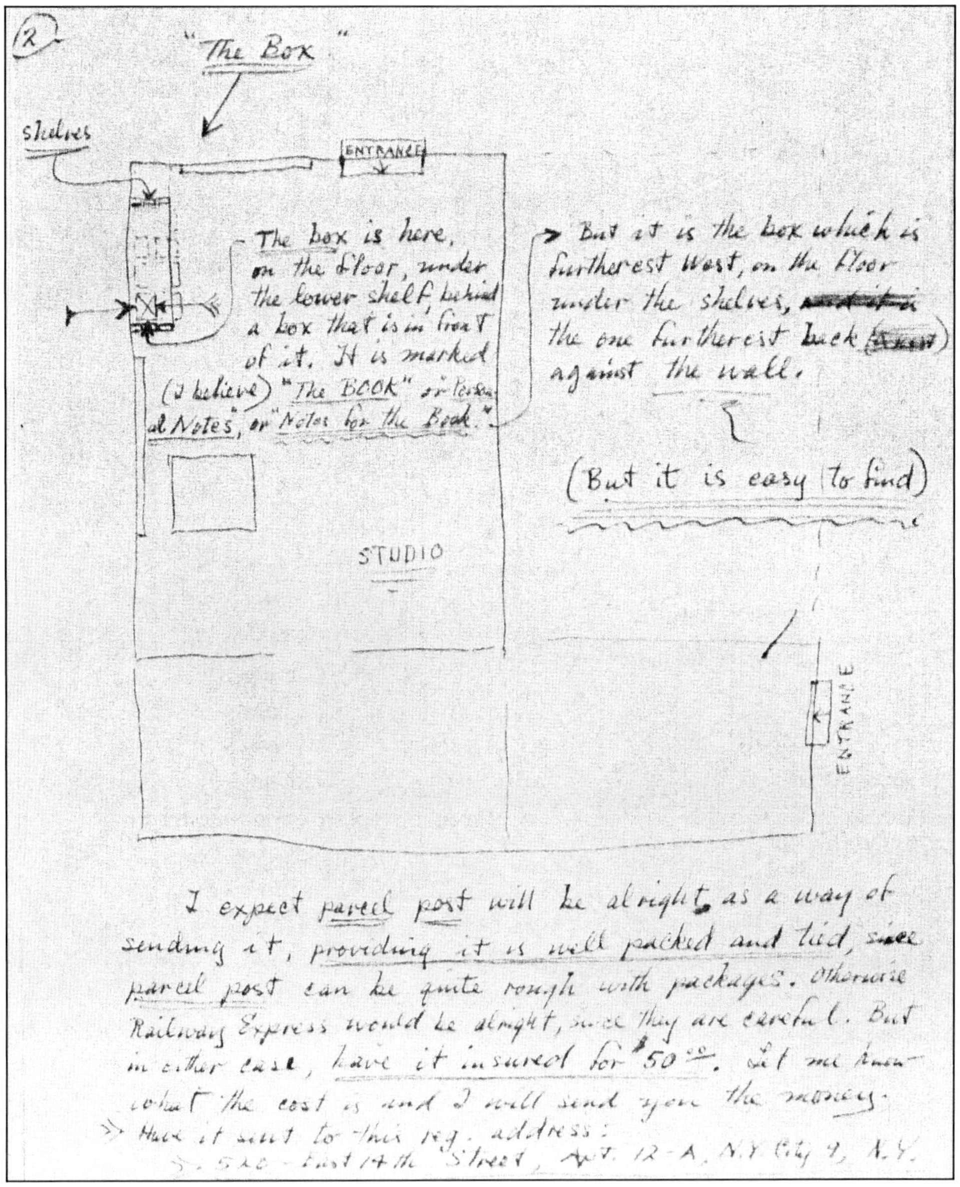

ILL. 23
Clay Spohn had an encyclopedic memory. He wrote from New York to friends in Taos asking them to retrieve a box for him. He was able to describe the precise location of any one particular box from among the hundreds stored in his house.

> ***Ad couldn't help referring to this as another Charles Van Doren incident or condition in which they have allowed their standards to be compromised in the face of opportunity—for the sake of expediency. But perhaps they didn't know how Life was to present it. I doubt if they did know. So it is Life that I blame for keeping the public in ignorance. I expect there will be many letters written to Life about this. Perhaps we should do so too!***[52]

If Spohn accurately reported Reinhardt's belief, this is rather mysterious since, as we have seen, the abstract expressionists, and the Taos Moderns, including Spohn, created nature-based imagery. And it is all the more strange since Spohn rejected the hegemony which the New York School hoped to impose on the art world. Spohn had confirmed his position toward artistic freedom when he resigned his teaching post at the California School of Fine Arts rather than give in to the conservative tone that began there in 1950.

Afterwards, sojourning for a time in New York City (he moved back and forth between Taos and New York, maintaining a house in Taos), Spohn decided against joining with the abstract expressionists in their campaign to establish the validity of their stylistic intentions. By then his friend Still was in New York and was included in the East Coast group. Being part of the group would have meant accepting their label and as Spohn later explained, he found the group's intentions too bent on domination of the art world.[53] Clyfford Still, in particular, proved to be a master manipulator of museums, a propensity based, curiously enough, on his supposed antiestablishment attitudes. The exclusion of all artistic criteria, other than what the New York School abstract expressionists deemed acceptable, made it impossible for Spohn to go along, even though his painting fit their category—or might have expanded it. By isolating himself he became, unlike Still, truly antiestablishment, and paid a severe price as a result. It was not surprising that he might leave the New York group who talked anarchy to join the Taos group who practiced it.

Spohn rejected the notion that the avant-garde painting of the New York School was radical enough to be absolutely unique and unrelated to preceding styles—a view held by some in Taos as well as in New York. He was a serious dissenter but also erratic; no doubt part of his charm derived from a certain contrariness—doing the unexpected, defying convention, sometimes merely to amuse his friends. There was also an encyclopedist-like aspect to his personality. He developed a vast personal archive which occupied as much space as a modest studio with its many shoebox filing cabinets and indexed Kress's five-and-dime paper bags. He carried the complete index in his head and could instantly recall subjects and their file locations.

Spohn was also clear about his work on canvas. He explained his intentions in a statement sent to Stables Gallery director Leone Kahl:

> ***The whole statement lies purely in the physical aspect of the painting itself. The only subject matter intended is made up of the color involvements and interrelationships, together with paint texture and manner of brush strokes and other qualities, so arranged—it is hoped—to create a dramatic situation of these elements as an honest response to the artist's experience of living. No literal meaning is intended or implied, but rather only feeling—meaning as a subjective and objective response. Any literal meaning the observer might interject or read into it is of the observer's own invention and choosing and not consciously or deliberately intended by the artist.***[54]

Spohn always spoke of his painting in the present tense, as if it were underway at that very moment (which it seldom was in his final years). The question of when he had last worked was not an issue. He often worked on his paintings for extended periods; he may have had trouble completing them to his satisfaction. As late as 1971 he expressed his desire to rework a small group of his 1926 Paris abstractions.[55]

His continuing concern was to create deep spacial relationships, as in *Gray Tones* (1958), which is painted in soft light-dark patterns of great intensity. He avoids single focal points and creates fields of activity with open boundaries. In his paintings, no area is trapped or prevented from interacting with others. Vortices of forms pull the eye into places which seem far off.

Spohn lived for the excitement of the artistic chase, as if for the sensation of constant movement. For him, there was not enough time to form lingering relationships with fixed styles.

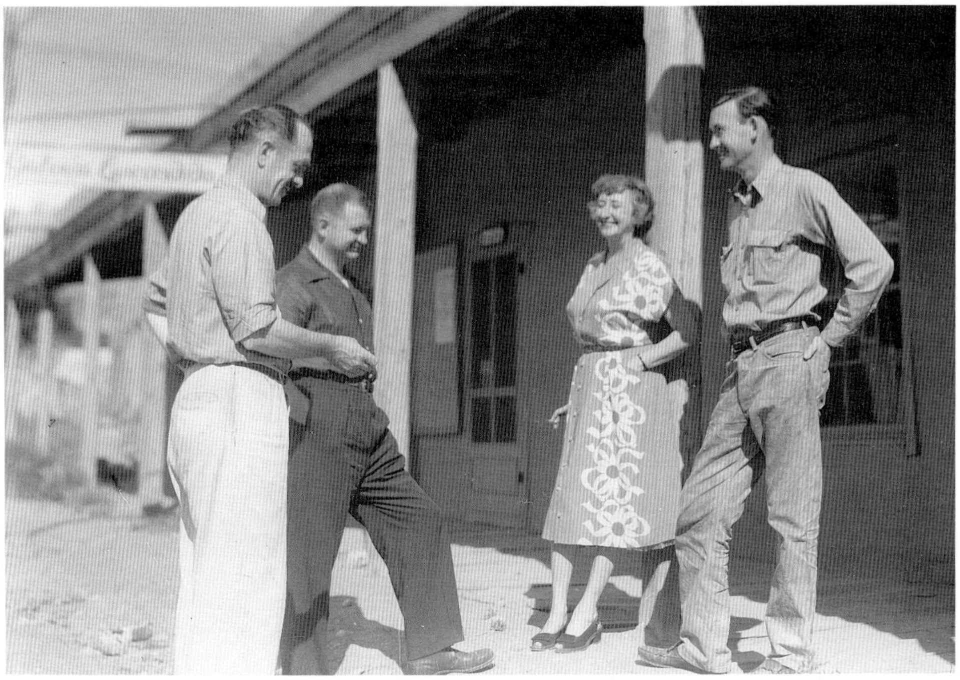

ILL. 24
From left to right, Clay Spohn, Ad Reinhardt, Eulalia Emetaz, and Edward Corbett in front of La Galeria Escondida. Unlike now, they did not then have to worry about dodging traffic. ca. 1952. Photographer: Mildred Tolbert

EDWARD CORBETT (1919–1971), moved to Taos in 1951.

> ***I intend my work as poetry.***[56]
>
> —Edward Corbett, 1952

Edward Corbett, twenty years younger than Spohn, came from the same artistic milieu of San Francisco. He believed, with the rest of the abstract expressionists, that the value of art was intrinsic. Speaking of the postwar period in the Bay Area, Corbett reflected on his own intentions as a painter and intellectual at grips with ideas that dominated his world at the time:

> ***I knew that I had to find a way of painting that I could do as well as [the Europeans] did their Surrealism and Cubism . . . and I had to literally work towards a discovery. I didn't know what I was working towards. It was a mystery. The end was there but it was imagined. The end, I could imagine without knowing what it looked like in the painting. . . .***[57]

By the time he was included in the Museum of Modern Art's 1952 "15 Americans" exhibit, Corbett had found the imaginative track he would continue to follow. The process had begun with his childhood in the Southwest and continued through his time as a student at the California School of Fine Arts, and, after the war and on the recommendation of

Spohn, as a teacher there.[58] He made his first visit to Taos as early as 1947. By the time he moved there in January 1951, he had already made several summer visits.[59]

Corbett completed only four or five paintings during his time in Taos; the balance of his works were drawings in charcoal, chalk, pastel, pencil, and occasionally, casein. The paintings, measuring about five by six feet, suggested the influence of the wintry expanse of snowy mesas nearly engulfing the narrow, black chasm of the Rio Grande gorge. He started painting by placing colors on the canvas and then gradually eliminating or lessening them by covering them with white.[60] The canvases were not blank, but filled with almost imperceptible detail. These paintings were of major significance to Corbett for they provided the structural and thematic basis for much or perhaps most of his later work. In an untitled charcoal and pastel (ca. 1953), he achieved similar effects of elusive color beneath what appears at first glance to be a black-and-white drawing.

Much of Corbett's work concerns edges. Concentration on those borders or the ways they rub up against each other was an important concern, a matter of achieving balance. For much of his work, he held little concern for which side might be designated as "up," believing that if a composition were truly in balance, any side could equally serve as the top.

According to Corbett, "Abstract appearances are seen, the matter is felt, the experience is emotionalized, and through continual experience the symbol is formed."[61] Abstract appearances—suggested by the land and by the native architectural forms which grow out of nature—led to a symbology of the land, not landscape pictures. Corbett, however, was equivocal about the natural environment as a catalyst for art. He wrote to art historian Gerald Nordland, "I admit to being influenced by not only nature out-of-doors, but nature within," and concluded a few sentences later, "If sources of nature exist, I trust they do not influence the painting."[62] Perhaps this denial of the influence of natural forms served as a defense measure: Fully abstract work could have lost some of its magic if described with words such as "this is a flame," or, "this is a cliff."

It is also likely that Corbett wished to convey that he had not been seduced by the saccharine aspect of the Southwest, but neither did his creations come out of a void. Since we are of nature, there can be no form on any canvas which is not rooted somewhere in nature between the level of the atomic and the level of the universal, be that image of the spiritual or of the profane.

Whatever they were based on, Corbett's images suggest the fullness of night, heavy snow, deep canyons, stark light; subtle hues fill paper and canvas with considerable life force, the understated vigor of immensely rugged land overflowing with delicacies of color and movement and light flashes. In his Taos drawings, the interplay of negative and positive create depth; their soft-edged forms interlock in a lyric poetry of form. His work, often in grays and browns, shows that the successful use of hue is a matter of making combinations and relationships rather than the degree of pigment saturation. In the use of color, it is the effect of hues on one another which makes a work come alive. Corbett's exacting drawings create the tension of anticipation, "not the experience of possessing an event, but a mystery . . . about what might happen."[63]

As is true with the work of Agnes Martin and other masters of nuance, it is impossible to experience the full impact of Corbett's work through photographs, and even difficult to sense fully through glass. A suddenness of line emerges from a color field—or does it actually disperse, not into fragments, but into soft focus? Constant, immense variations of form suggest depthless atmosphere or the ground floor of the atmosphere seen from an undetermined height, giving at one moment what appears to be a clear picture of detail while, in the next, drifting past the edge of clear perception, forcing the viewer to wonder which perception or which detail is the correct one. This description merely illustrates the complexity of Corbett's dilemma in talking about his work, for an image such as the untitled brown drawing (ca. 1952) can be a "landscape" only in metaphor since it is instead a picture, an idea. The art which makes claim to being "new" is that which outruns language's ability to adequately encompass it with words.

JOHN DEPUY (born 1927), moved to Taos in 1952.

> *He paints an [sic] hallucinated, magical, and sometimes fearsome world—not the one we think we see but the one, he claims, that is really there. A world of terror as well as beauty—the terrible beauty that lies beyond the ordinary limits of human experience, that forms the basis of experience, the ground of being.*[64]
>
> —Edward Abbey, 1981

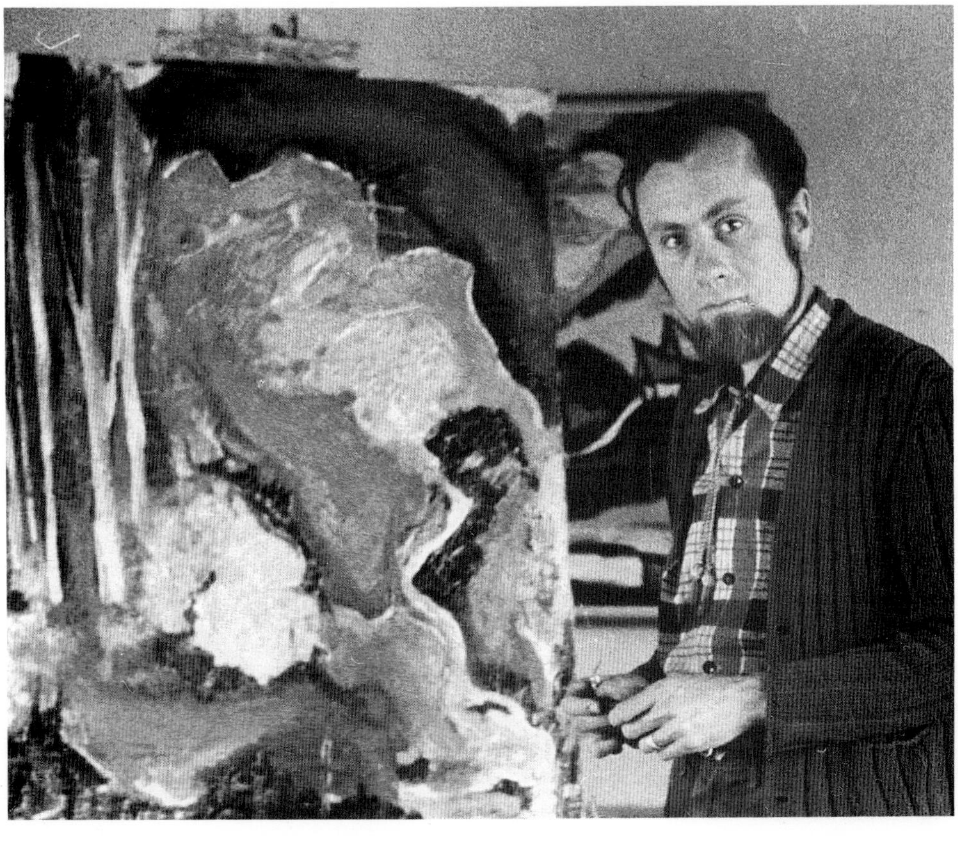

ILL. 25
John DePuy. ca. 1959. Photographer: Regina Cooke

John DePuy has said that in Taos, with the exception of Ted Egri's work, "The painting was not political, the lifestyles may have been, but not the painting."[65] Nonpoliticized art was not unique to Taos. Catalogs from the University of Illinois "Contemporary American Painting and Sculpture" series show an interest in war and political themes just after World War II, changing to less political and increasingly abstract imagery as the exhibitions continued into the 1960s. The Taos Moderns were more often preoccupied with the "new" than with politics in their art. In 1835, Alexis de Tocqueville described this American fascination with the new, a preoccupation that resides in the core of the American character. DePuy noted that by the early 1950s the Taos Moderns thought they had found "the ultimate philosophy of art." How could they not have been excited about the great wave of modernist expression in which they found themselves? DePuy explained:

> ***I think we all felt in those days that we were the primitives of a new art. And we were sadly disillusioned. I think that all abstract expressionists expected that their work would develop into a new art. There was no nihilism, no cynicism [in Taos], there was the sense of the beginning of something new. I think this is why Rothko committed suicide. . . . Rothko, who was in many ways the master of that period, felt that his work would be the beginning. . . . I think he felt that he was establishing a tradition that would last a hundred years, and then he realized that was impossible.*** [66]

When DePuy first moved to Taos, still under the influence of his teacher, Hans Hofmann, he painted nonobjectively. Over time, Hofmann's influence receded, but his advice to paint from nature remained. For DePuy, the influence on art in New Mexico was "mainly the land" and (as with Ribak) the inspiration Pueblo Indians provided in their connection with the land. In DePuy's work, the purely surface qualities of the land are often eclipsed by the land's sheer power. Subtle gradations of color on walls or in the sky or on limitless plains form a shifting, lively backdrop for suns which shimmer and rivers which slide away and mesas which stand darkly. DePuy wrote, "This land speaks of another time sense than our Western-European lineal time." By this he refers to the Western concept whereby time proceeds from one definable moment directly to a later, equally definable moment. The land DePuy began painting by the mid-1950s exists within spatial time, where moments do not proceed to any destination but repeat endlessly in the regular cycle of days, years, millennia, always returning, circular rather than linear.[67] As such, nature may contradict our expectations. In an untitled oil painting (ca. 1955), the artist presents a world which seems to have flipped upside down.

ROBERT D. RAY (born 1924), moved to Taos in 1954.

> ***There is in his work the magic of a court jeweler working with the materials of our time.***[68]
>
> —Robert A. Ewing, 1968

By the time Robert D. Ray decided to leave his native Denver and move to Taos, he had served in the navy in the South Pacific during World War II, earned art degrees in California and Mexico, and lived in Europe for a year. His decision to move came after being invited by Eulalia Emetaz to exhibit at La Galeria Escondida. In Taos, Earl Stroh introduced him to Helene Wurlitzer, who, to encourage him to remain, provided him with a studio-residence. He thus became one of the first beneficiaries of Mrs. Wurlitzer's generosity. When she commissioned several Taos artists to paint portraits of her for family members, she included Ray: "It was her way of keeping all of us alive."[69] He showed his work in regional and national exhibitions and sold some, but during the quiet winters of the 1950s when Taos nearly shut down economically, he was forced to return to Denver for a few months of employment.

The most frequent subjects of his early Taos oil paintings and woodcut prints were still lifes and semi-abstract landscapes. He was fascinated by the light of the Taos Valley—not just the light itself, but the way in which the quality of light defines the place.

In his work, intense concentrations of light contrast abruptly with darkness and fragmented forms. *Snow and the River* (1958) shows how light may define place. In this painting, the viewer looks straight down on a dark water path winding through an otherwise white, frozen river; the scene achieves depth through the suggestion of red willow clumps at the top.

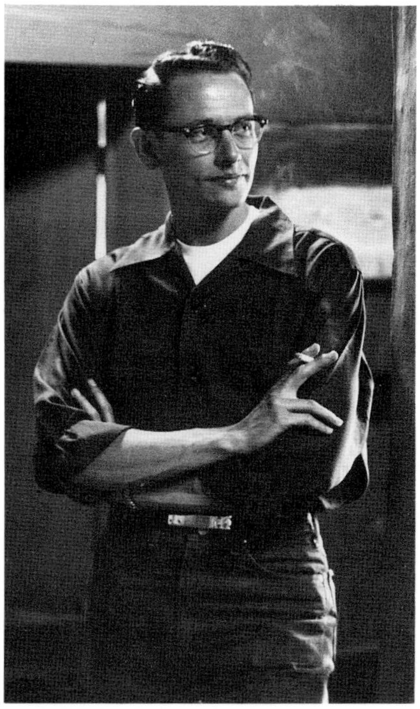

ILL. 26
Robert D. Ray. ca. 1955. Photographer: Mildred Tolbert

■ ■ ■

In this book, I have concentrated on the dynamic milieu and events of the immediate postwar era in Taos. Of course, numerous artists discussed here continued their work through subsequent decades—the subject for another book. Moreover, many of the Taos Moderns continue to live and work in Taos, producing some of the most advanced art being made in the region. Almost fifty years have passed since the period of the Taos Moderns began. They can look back on their participation in the revolutionary period of postwar modernism that transformed both American and world art. The scores of resident and visiting modernist artists made Taos in the 1950s, along with San Francisco and New York, one of the important centers of modernism.

The Taos Moderns avoided imitation while consciously or unconsciously interpreting the power of the land and the light in their art. The journey has not been easy. Edward Corbett once said, "Unfortunately, the only way to be paid for art is to enjoy being an artist. Enjoy being an artist as you might enjoy life-for-its-own-sake after a narrow escape from death."[70]

New Mexico is not the idyllic land of the romantic myth portrayed by the Taos Society of Artists, but a harsher place whose heart is enigma. Agnes Martin has captured precisely this aspect of New Mexico. At the end of her driveway (or the beginning of it, depending upon your perspective) a sign of faded black letters on peeling white paint exists as a beacon or as a warning: "At your own risk."

PLATES

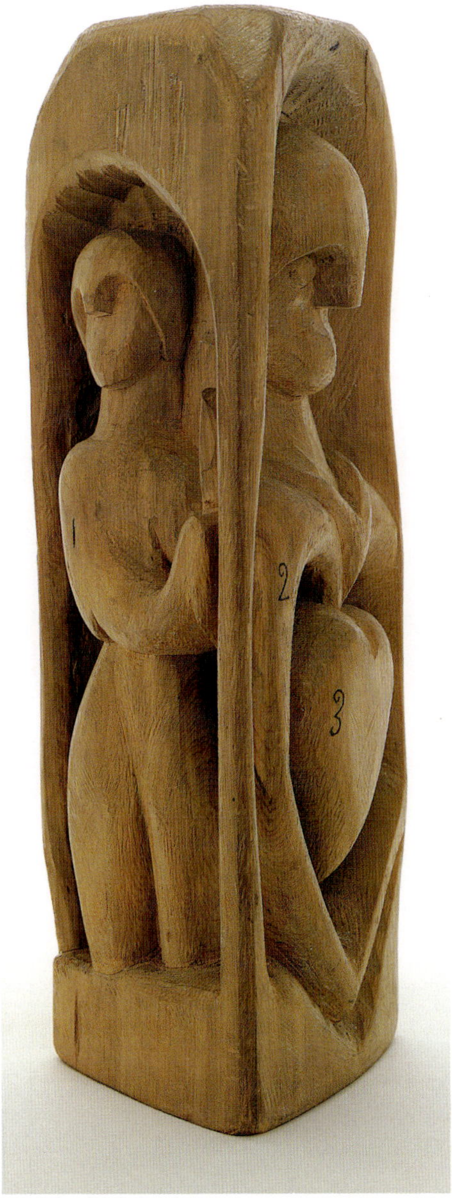

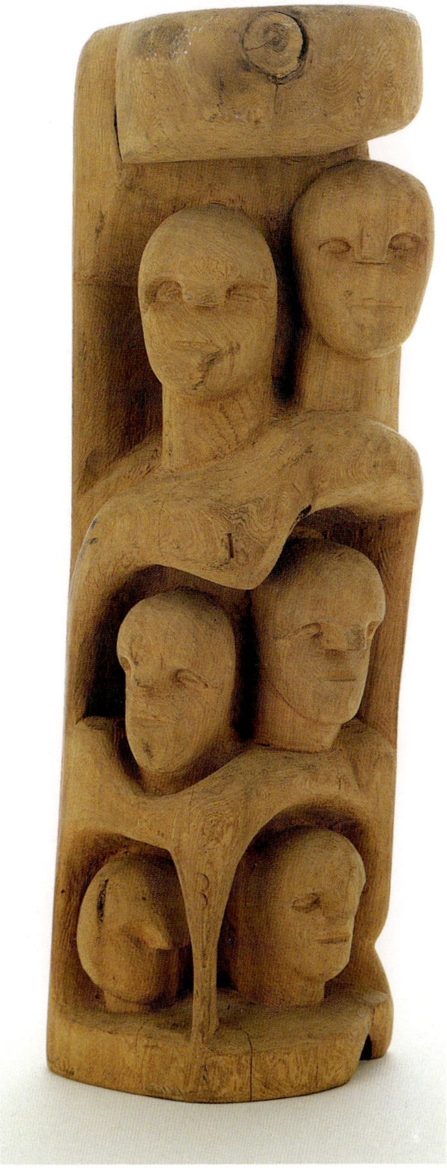

1. (LEFT)
PATROCINIO BARELA
El Fiel, 1941
38.6 x 13.6 cm
juniper wood
Harwood Foundation

2. (RIGHT)
PATROCINIO BARELA
Untitled
48 x 14.7 cm
Harwood Foundation

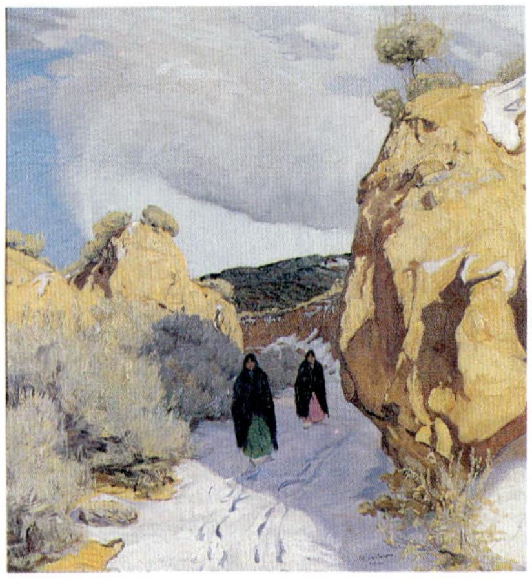

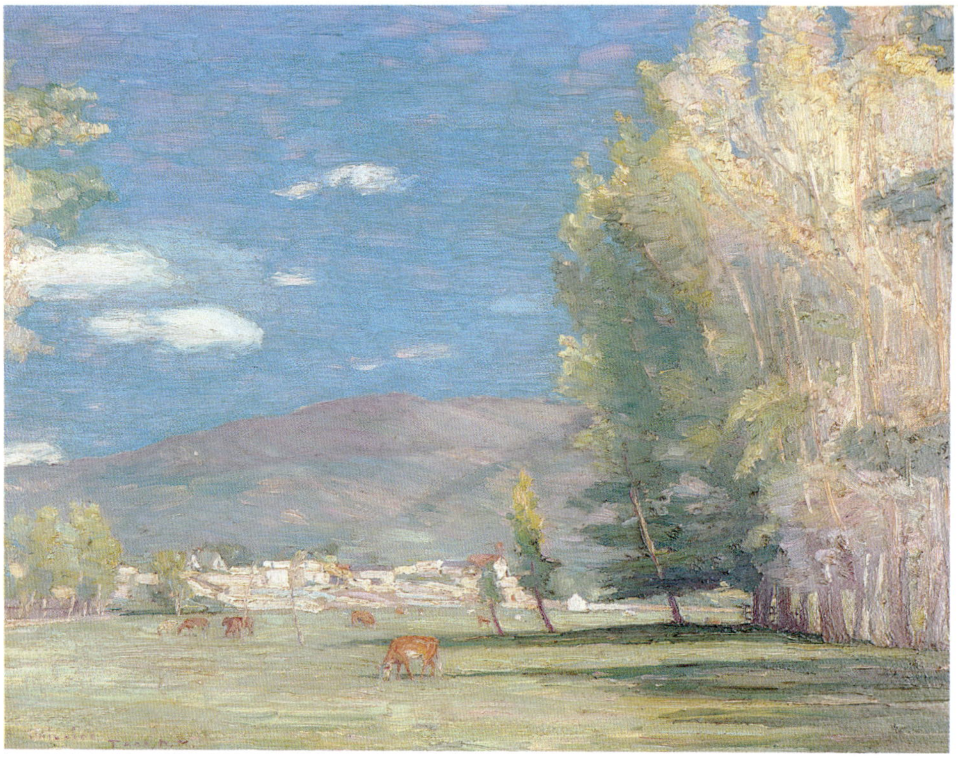

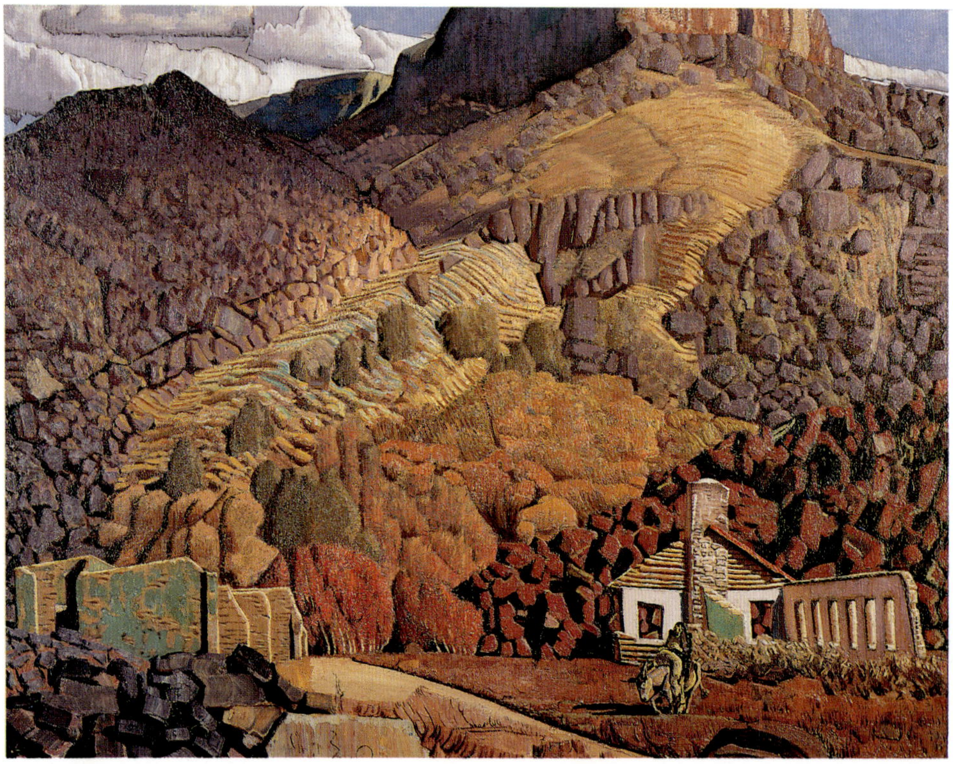

3. (TOP LEFT)
WALTER UFER
Winter in New Mexico, ca. 1930
56.5 x 51.4 cm
oil on canvas
Harwood Foundation

4. (TOP RIGHT)
BERT PHILLIPS
Taos Valley, N.M., before 1940
38.5 x 49 cm (sight dimension)
oil on board
Harwood Foundation

5. (BOTTOM RIGHT)
ERNEST BLUMENSCHEIN
Deserted Mining Camp, 1936–1940
68.6 x 84 cm
oil on linen
Harwood Foundation

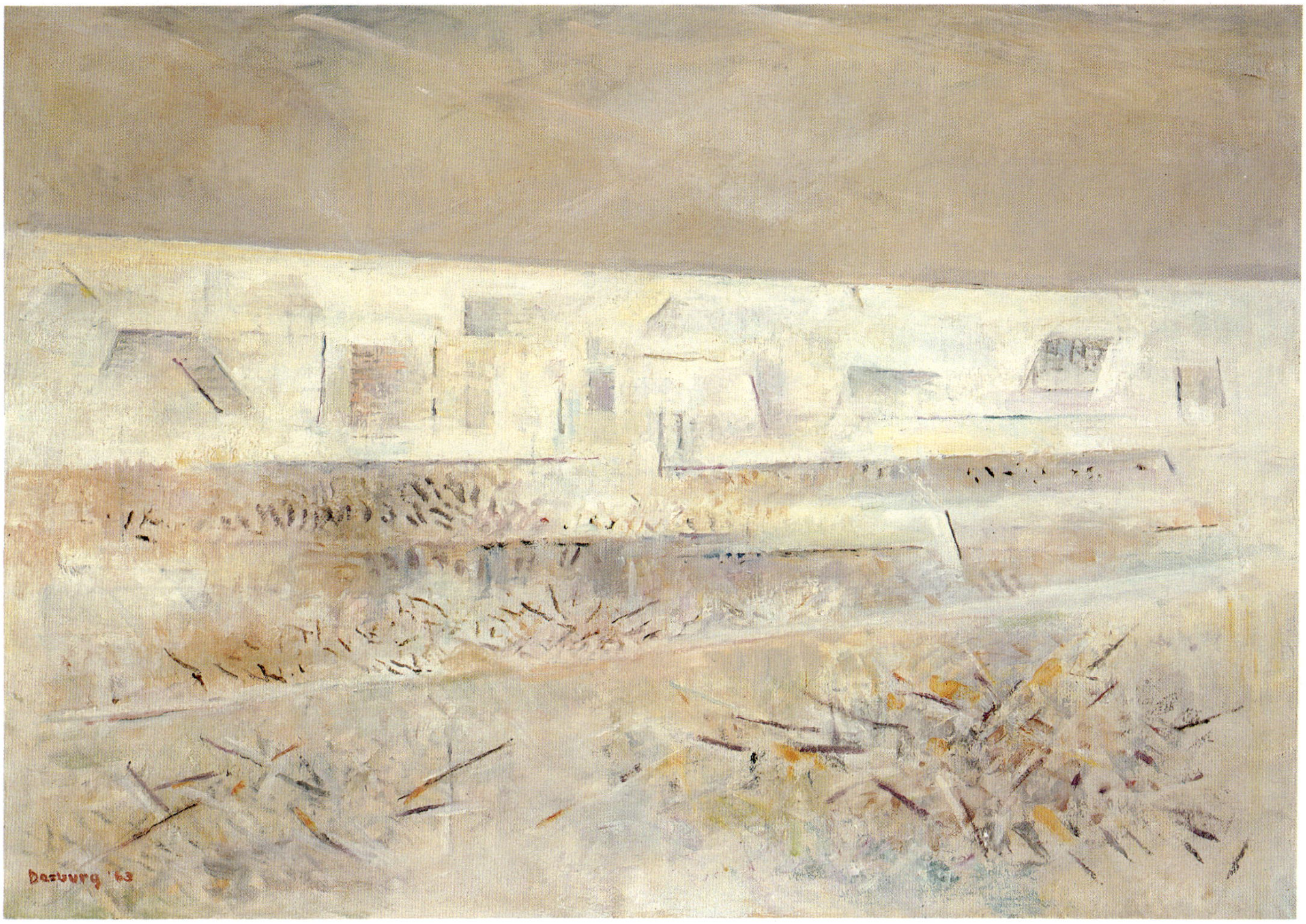

6.
ANDREW DASBURG
White Morning, 1963
63.5 x 81.3 cm
oil on canvas
Private Collection

died 1979

landscapes
balance of
originality + tradition

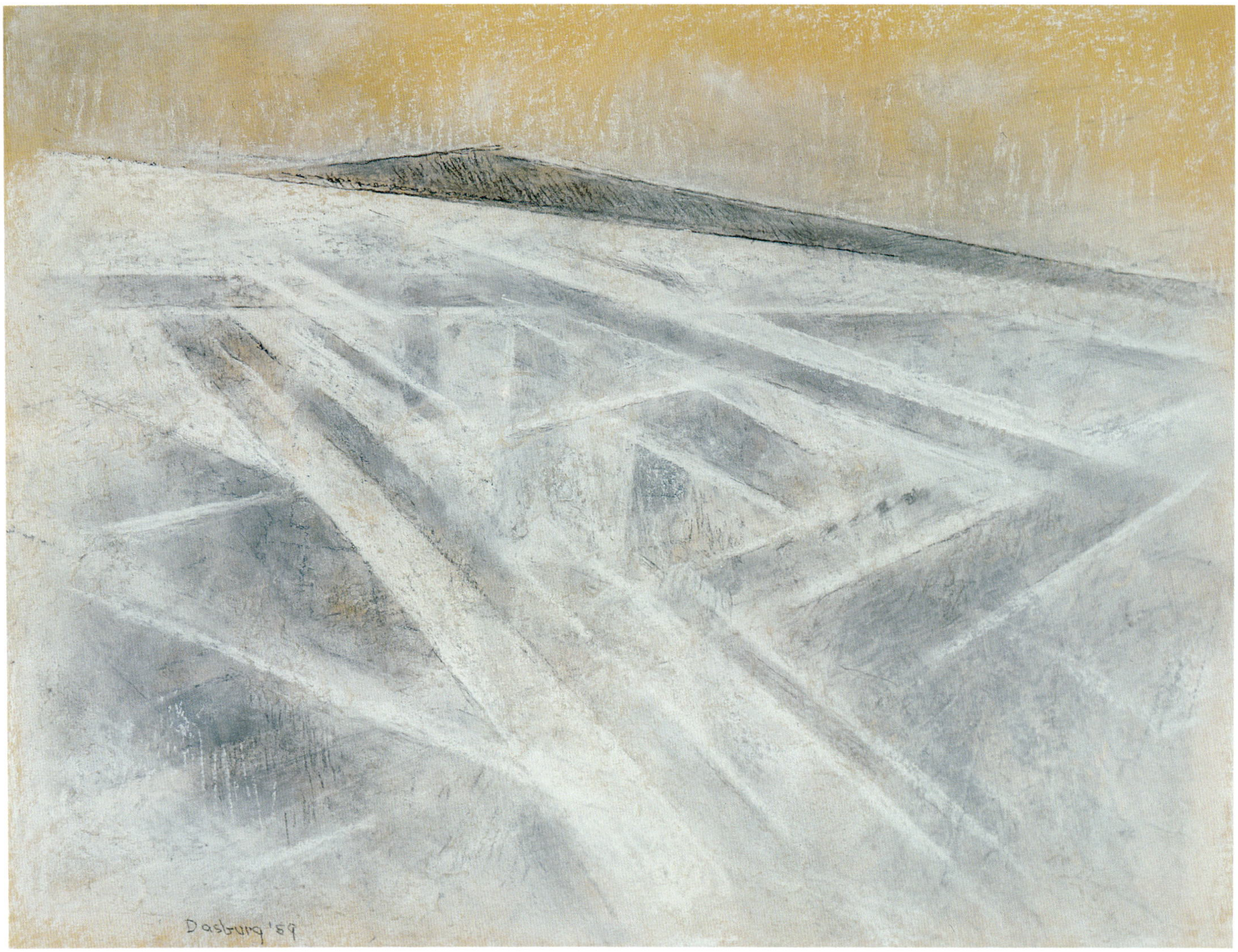

7.
ANDREW DASBURG
Winter Planes, 1959
43 x 55.9 cm
pastel
Private Collection

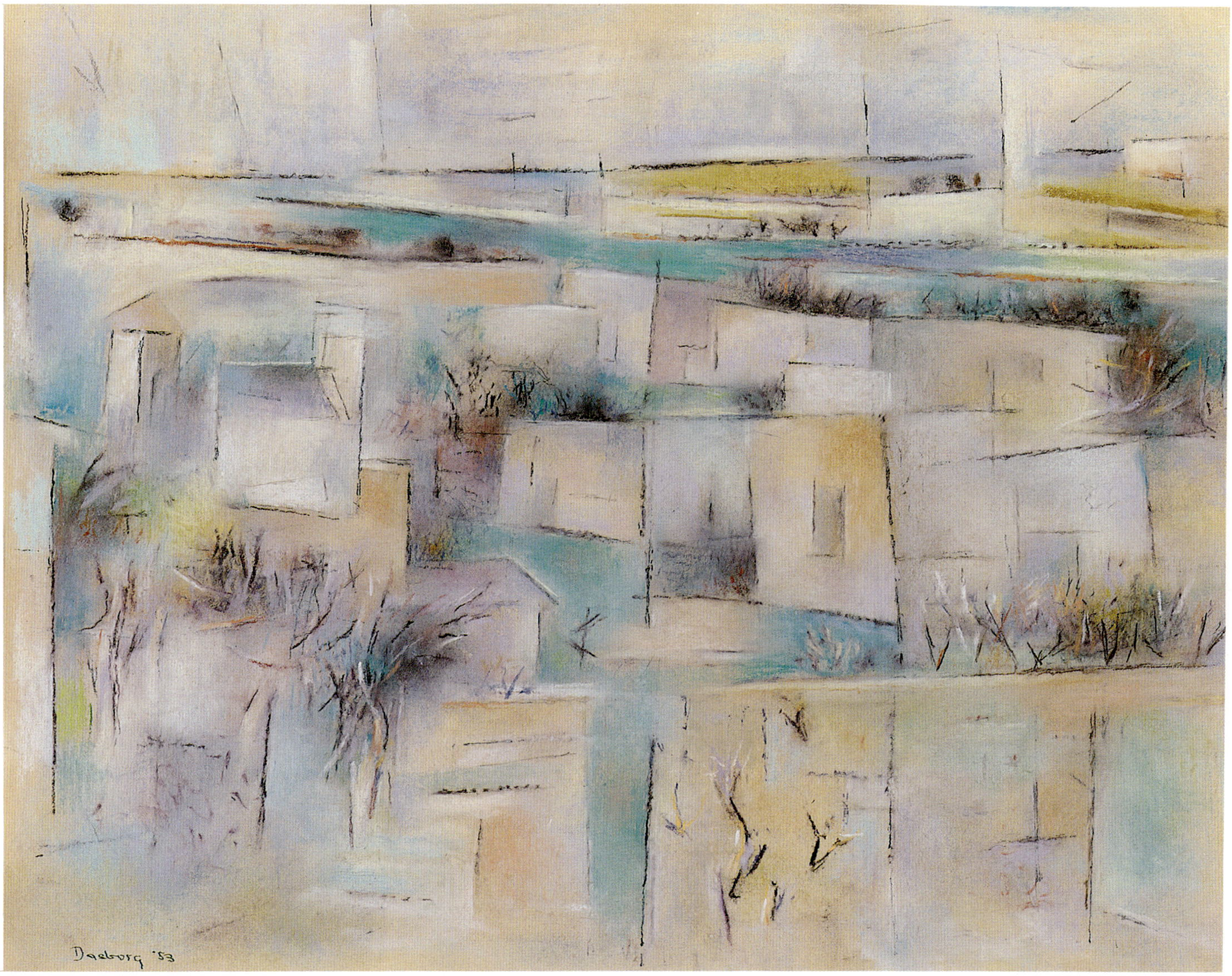

8.
ANDREW DASBURG
Llano Spring, 1953
41.8 x 53.4 cm (sight dimension)
pastel
Private Collection

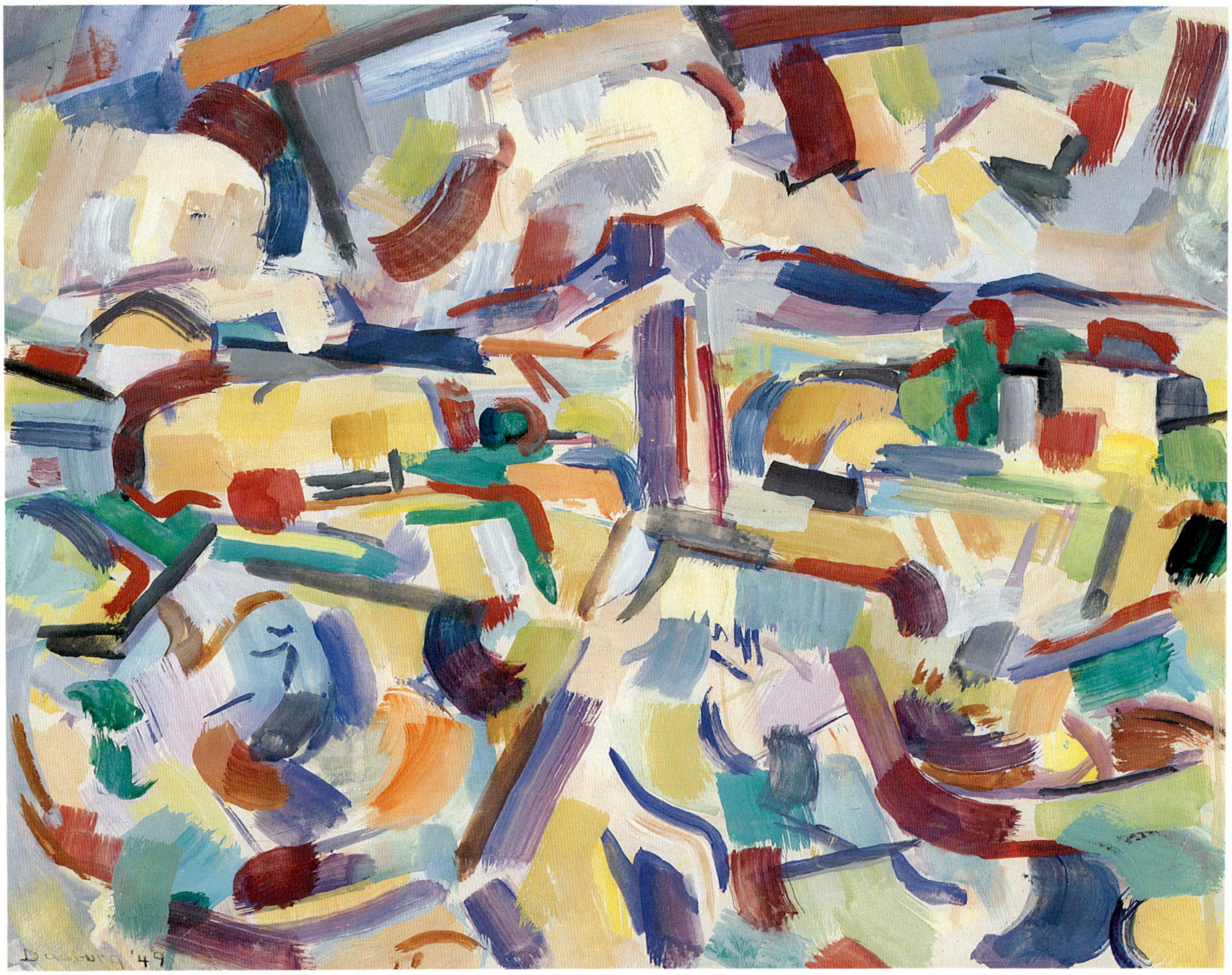

9.
ANDREW DASBURG
Road to Ranchos, 1949
40 x 49.5 cm (sight dimension)
casein on paper
Private Collection

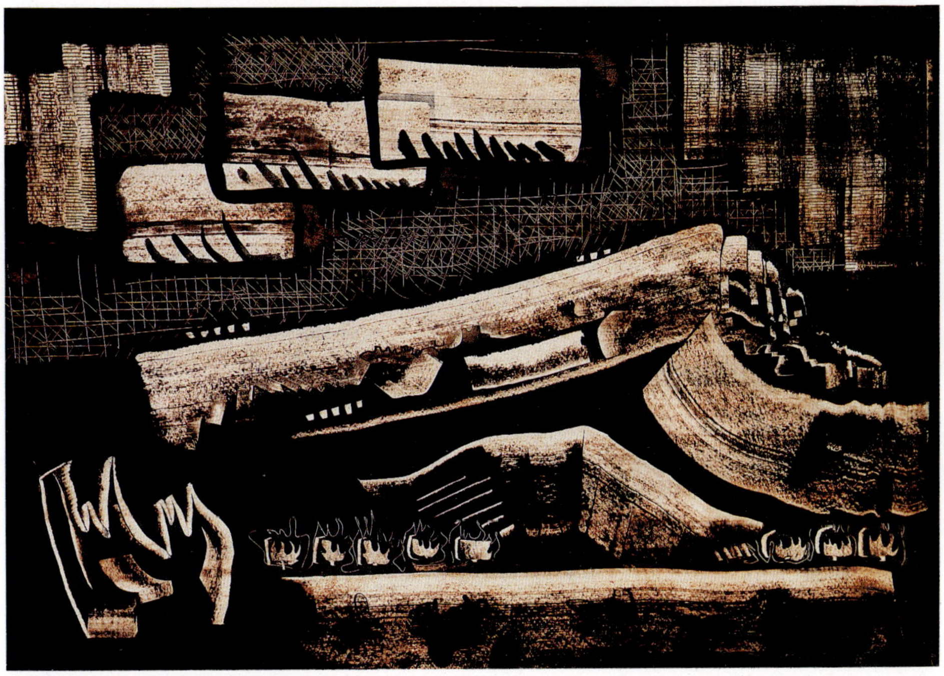

influence of Marsden Hartley

energy

10.
CADY WELLS
Brown Barranca 54, ca. 1952
37.2 x 52.4 cm
watercolor w/gesso
University Art Museum,
The University of New Mexico

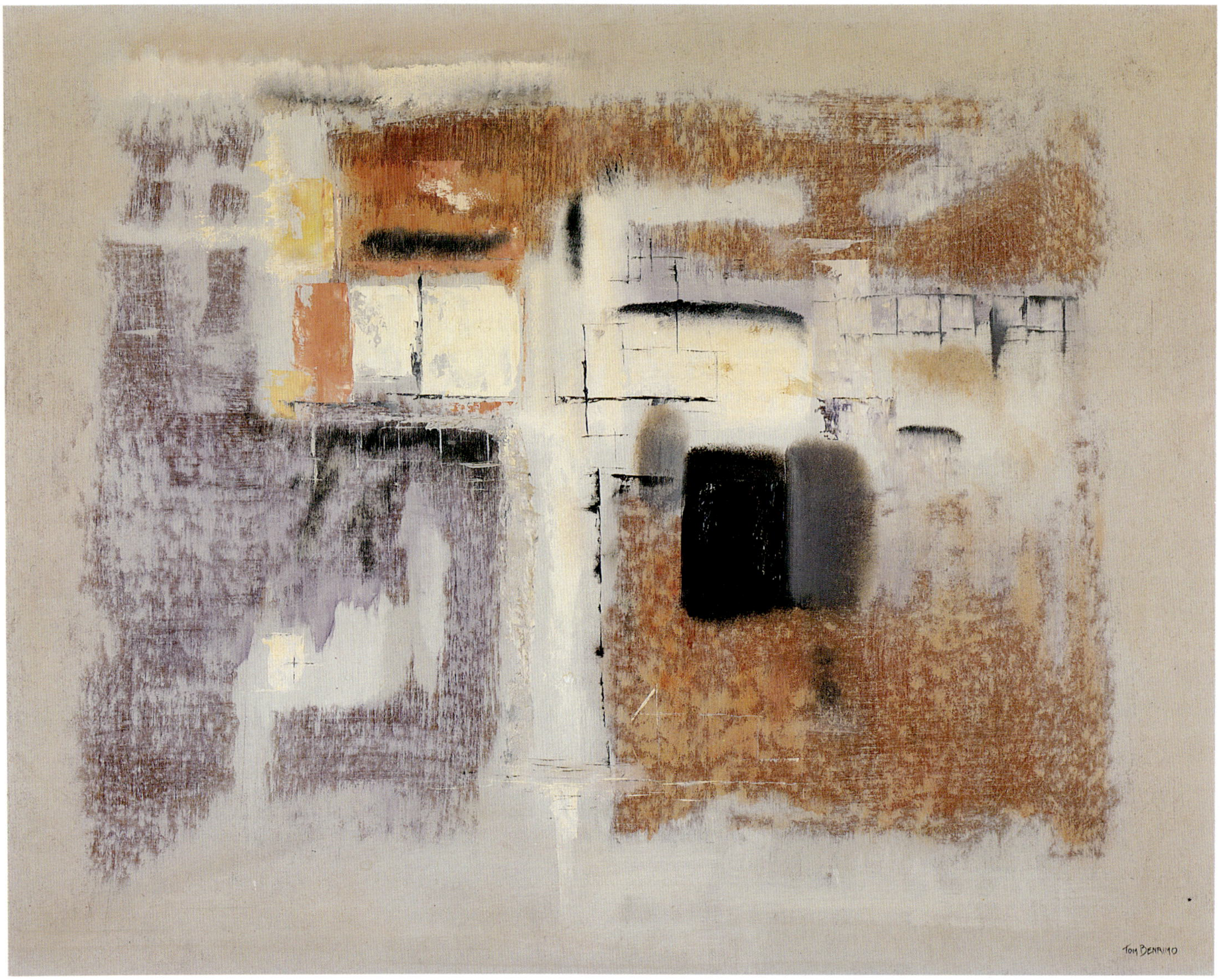

11.
THOMAS BENRIMO
Facade #2, 1950s
61 x 76 cm
oil on masonite
Private Collection

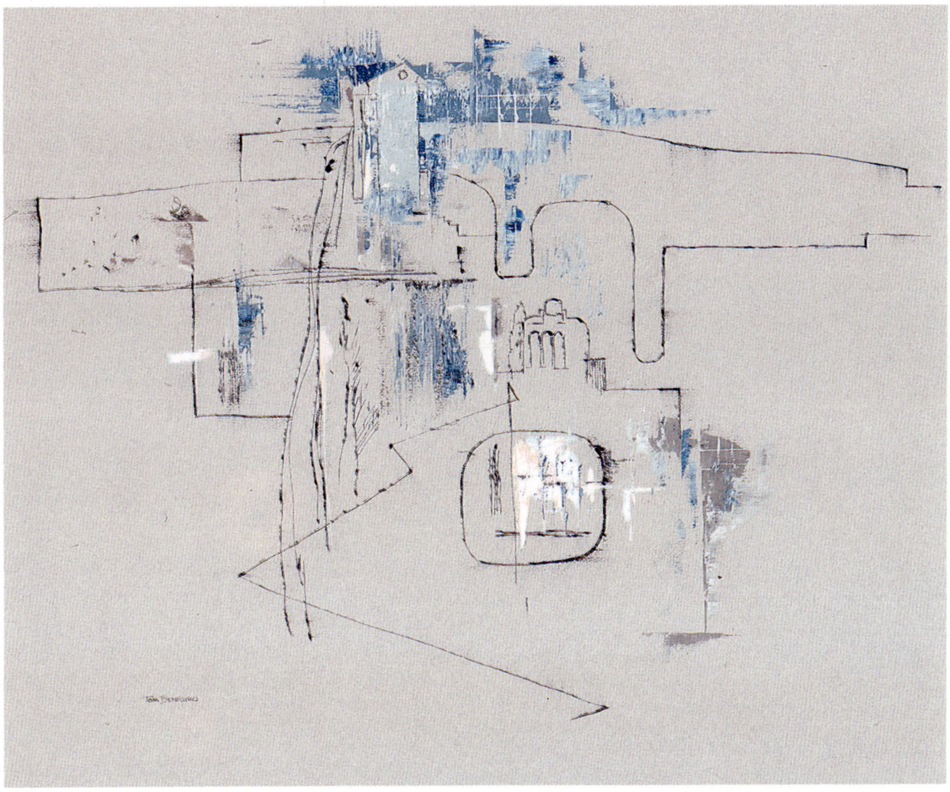

12.
THOMAS BENRIMO
Untitled, ca. 1957
45 x 55 cm
casein and ink on paper
Harwood Foundation

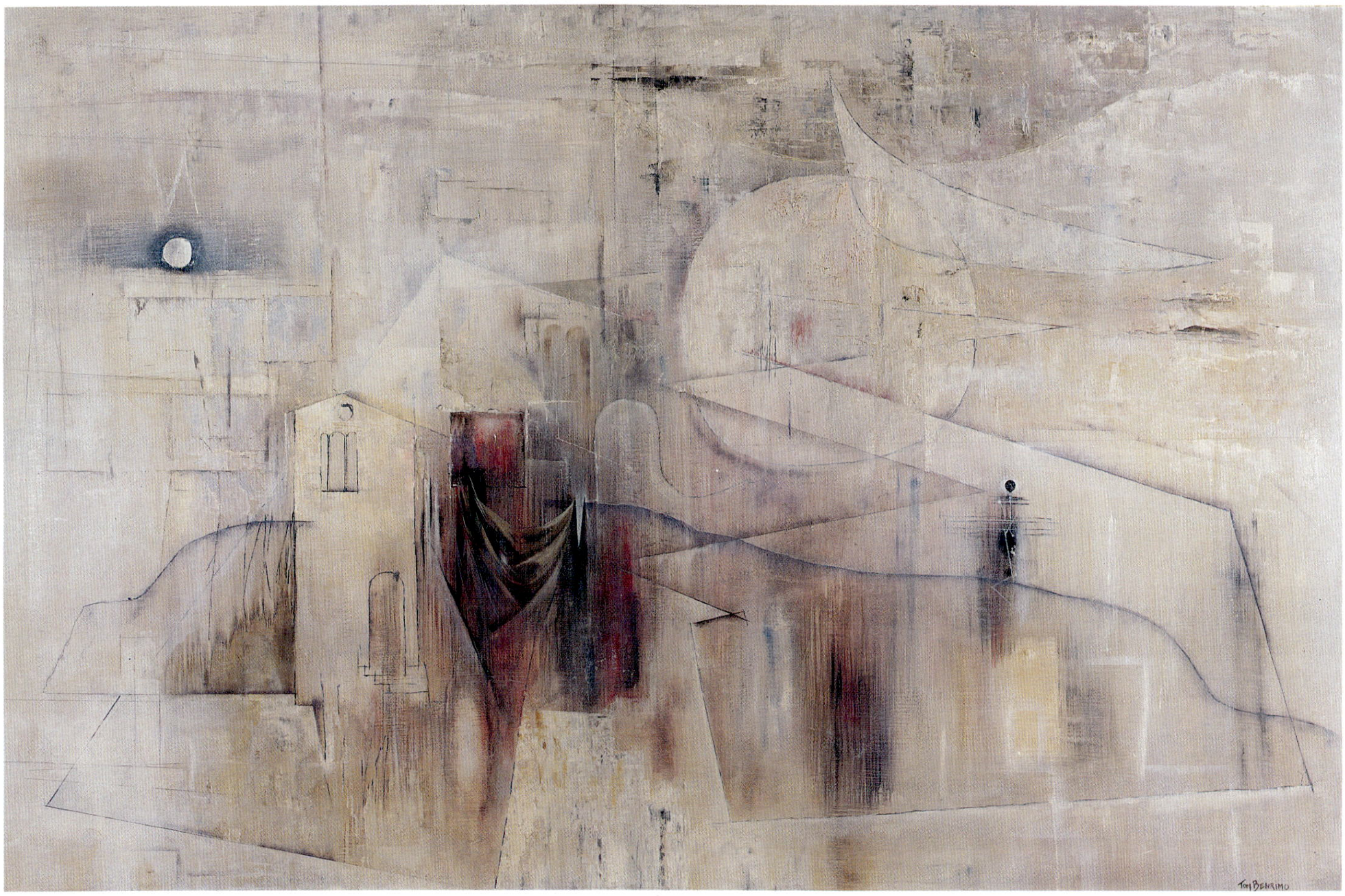

13.
THOMAS BENRIMO
White Moon Number Two, ca. 1954
81.3 x 122 cm
oil on masonite
Harwood Foundation

flat patterned
post cubist
color composition

feeling + form

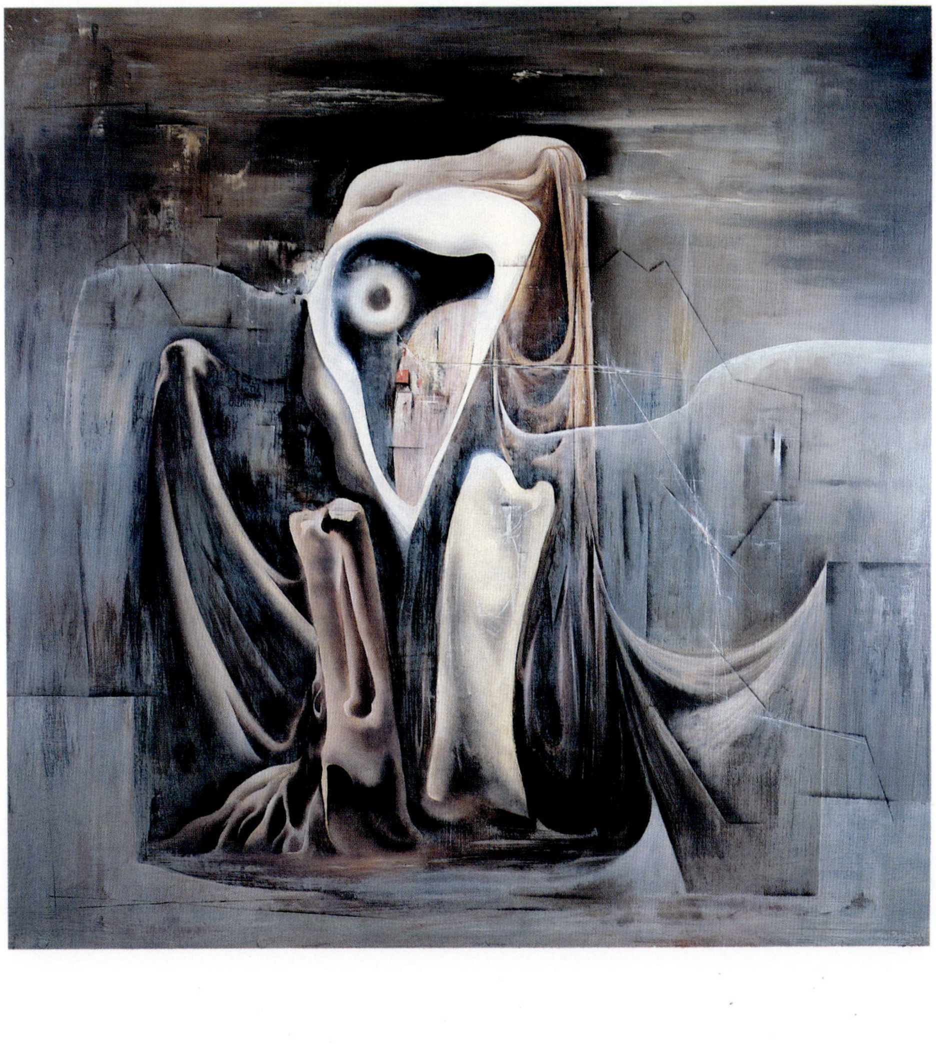

refined brushwork

surrealist

14.
THOMAS BENRIMO
The Hollow Men, 1946
116 x 116.3 cm
oil on masonite
Private Collection

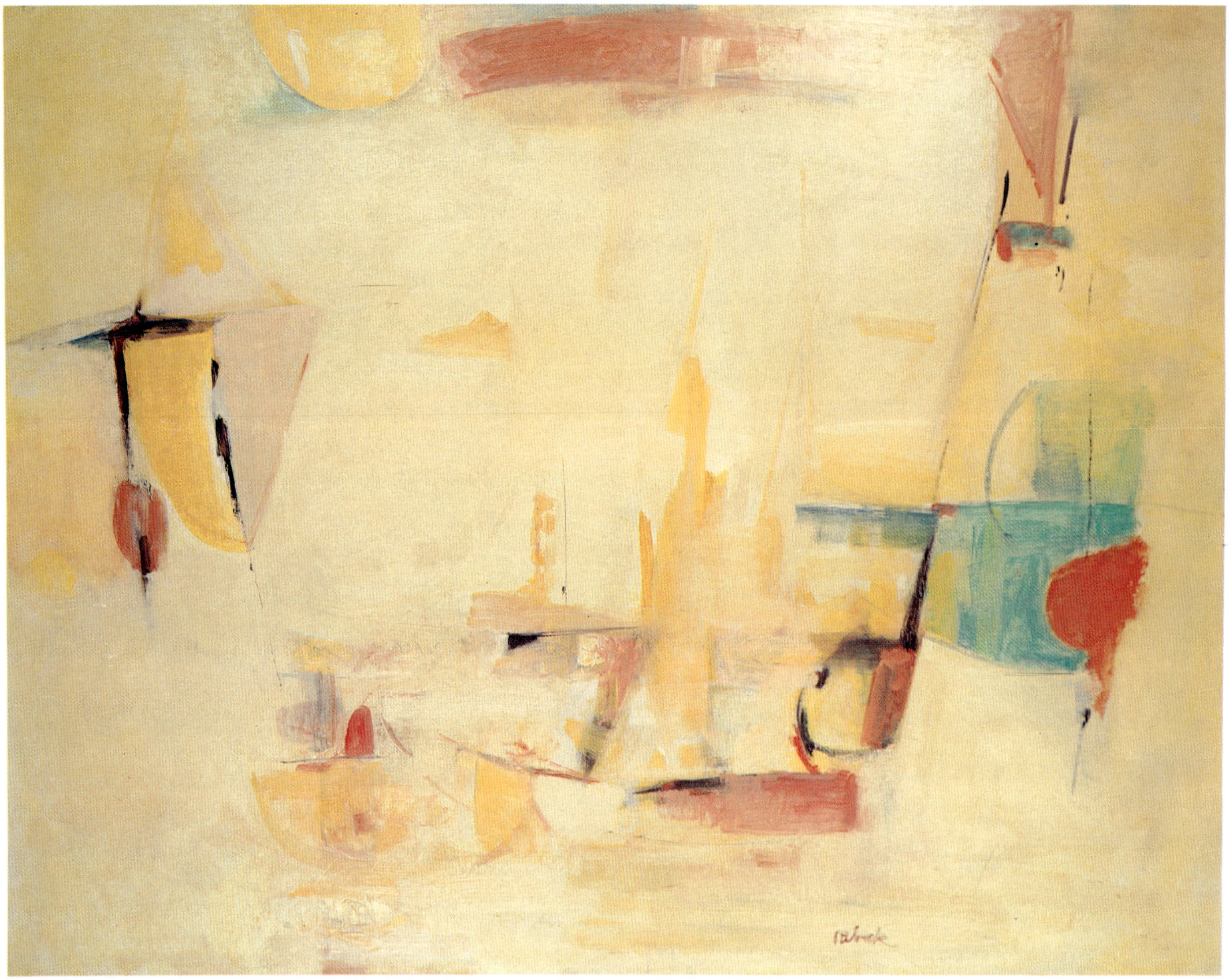

15.
LOUIS RIBAK
Canyon Series, 1950s
122 x 152.5 cm
oil on masonite
Courtesy of
Beatrice Mandelman Ribak

married
to Beatrice Mandelman

Taos Valley Art School 1947

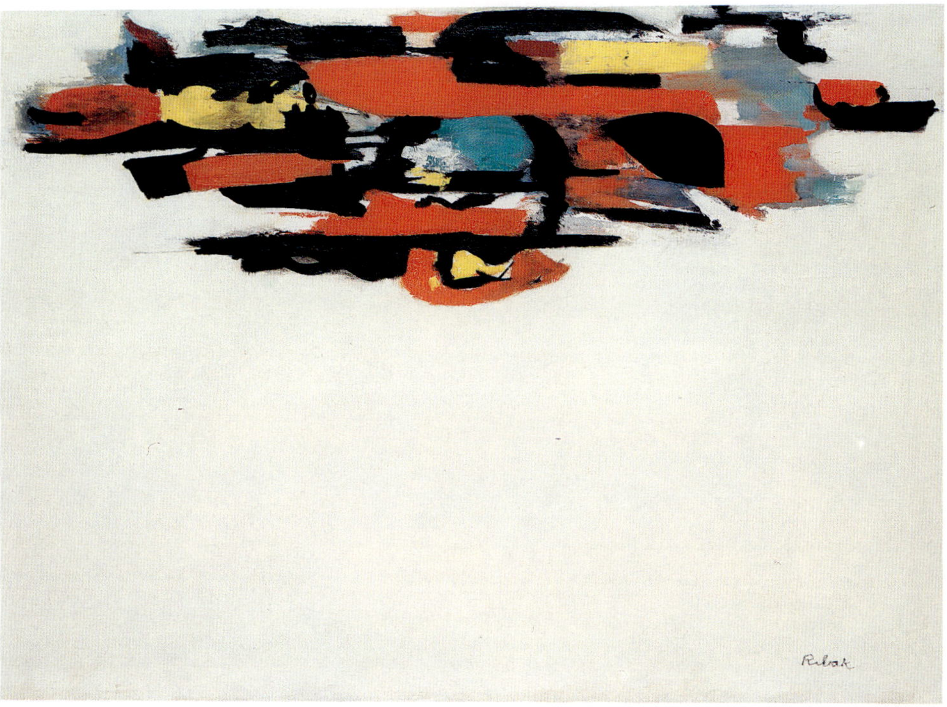

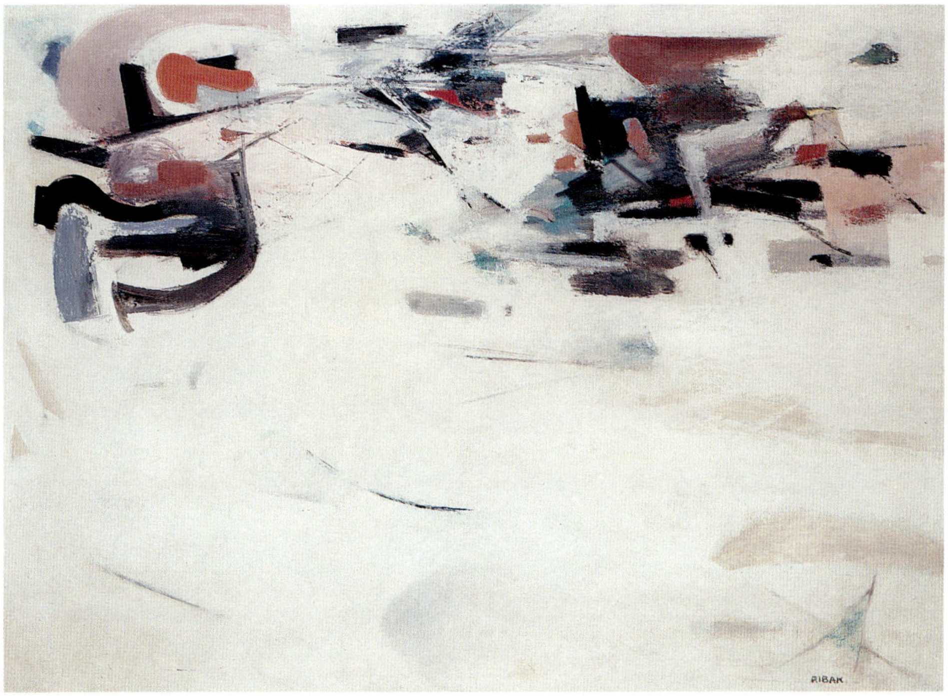

painterly

16. (TOP)
LOUIS RIBAK
Movement No. I, 1950s
91.5 x 122 cm
oil on masonite
Courtesy of
Beatrice Mandelman Ribak

17. (BOTTOM)
LOUIS RIBAK
Movement No. II, 1950s
91.5 x 122 cm
oil on masonite
Courtesy of
Beatrice Mandelman Ribak

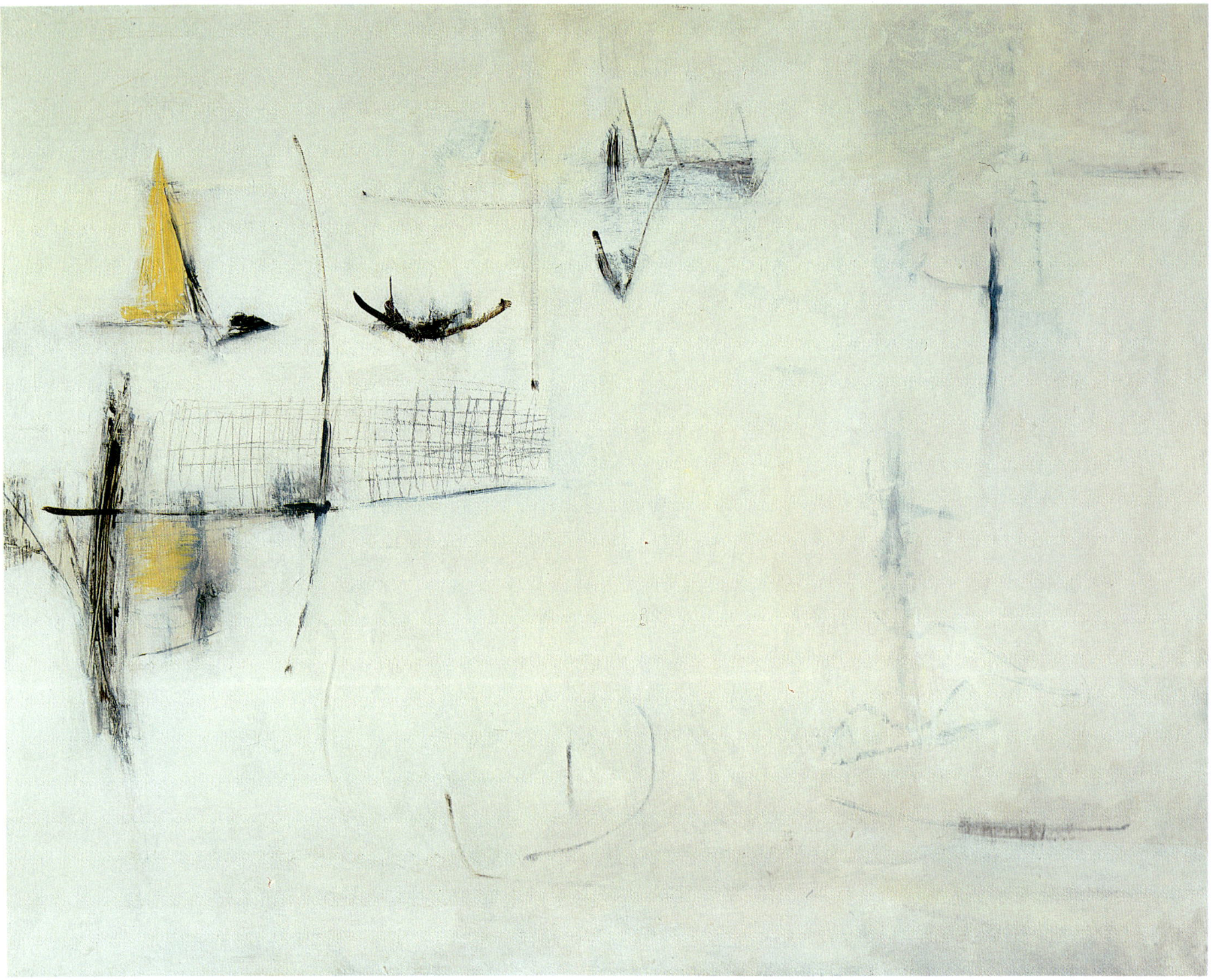

18.
LOUIS RIBAK
Untitled, 1950s
61 x 75.6 cm
oil on masonite
Courtesy of
Beatrice Mandelman Ribak

19. (FAR RIGHT)
BEATRICE MANDELMAN
Experimental Reflections, 1954
122 x 91.5 cm
oil on masonite
Courtesy of
Beatrice Mandelman Ribak

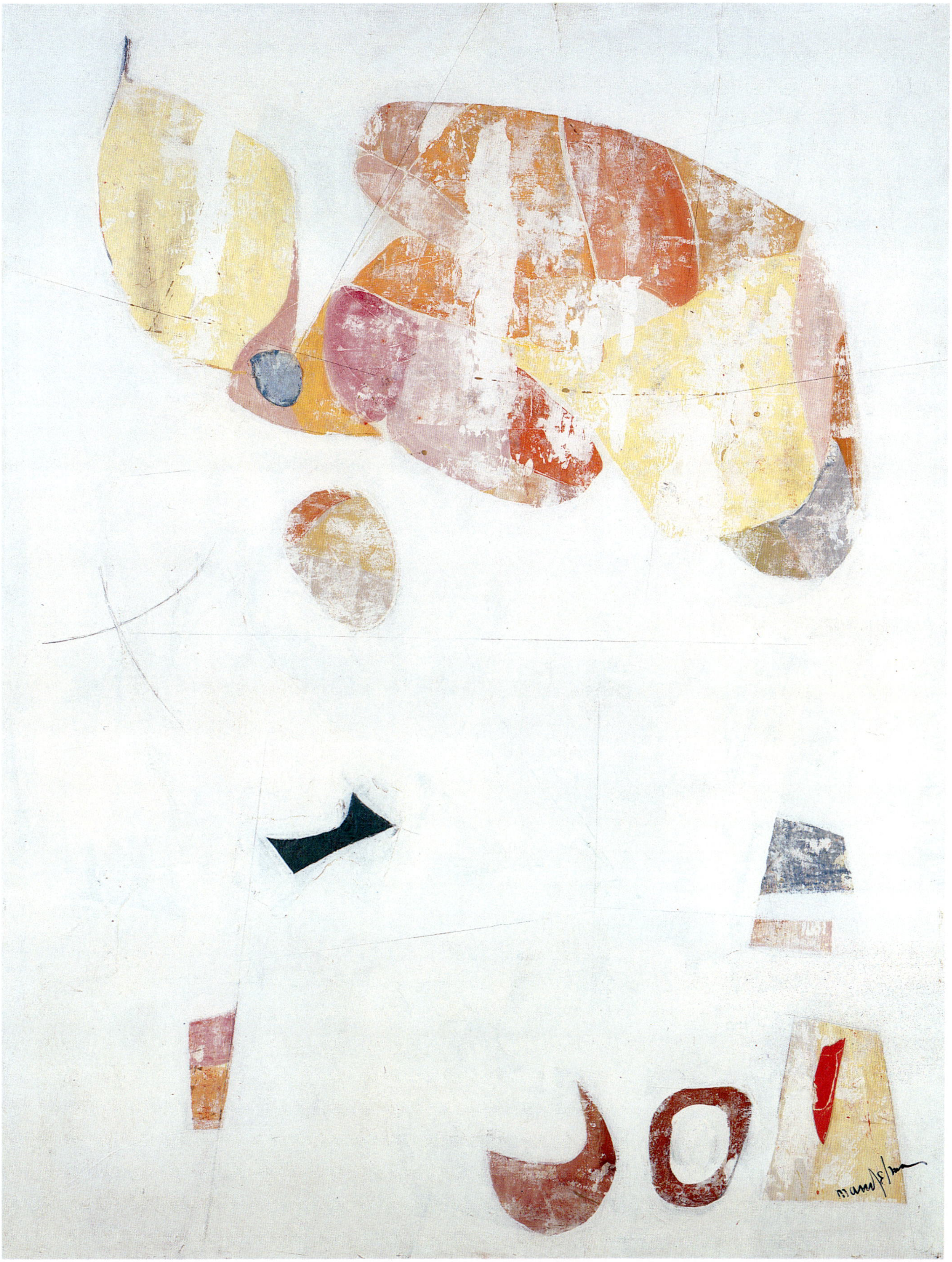

20.
BEATRICE MANDELMAN
Winter, 1954
122 x 91.5 cm
oil on masonite
Courtesy of
Beatrice Mandelman Ribak

21. (FAR RIGHT)
BEATRICE MANDELMAN
Noon, 1953
58 x 44.5 cm
oil on masonite
Courtesy of
Beatrice Mandelman Ribak

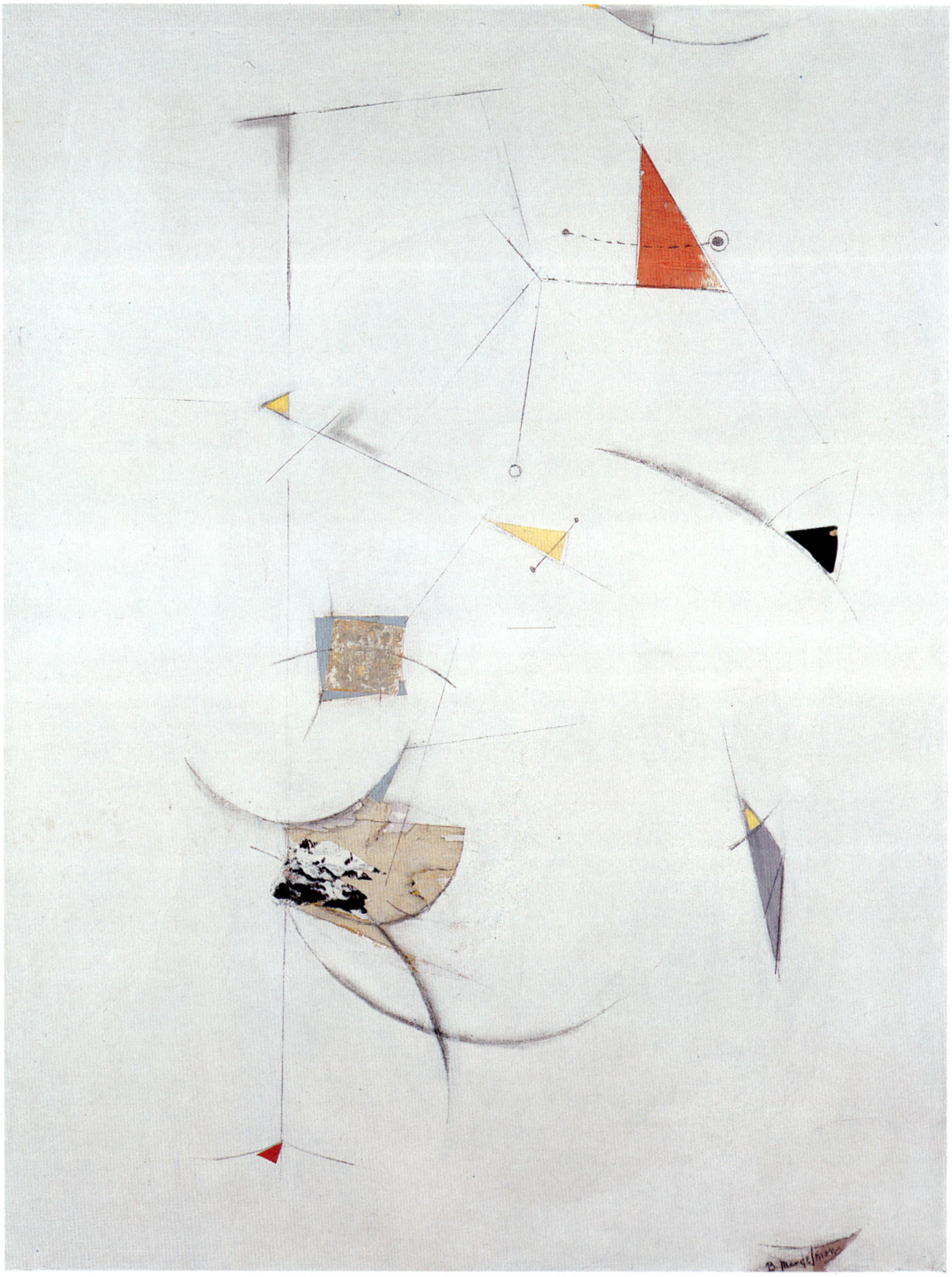

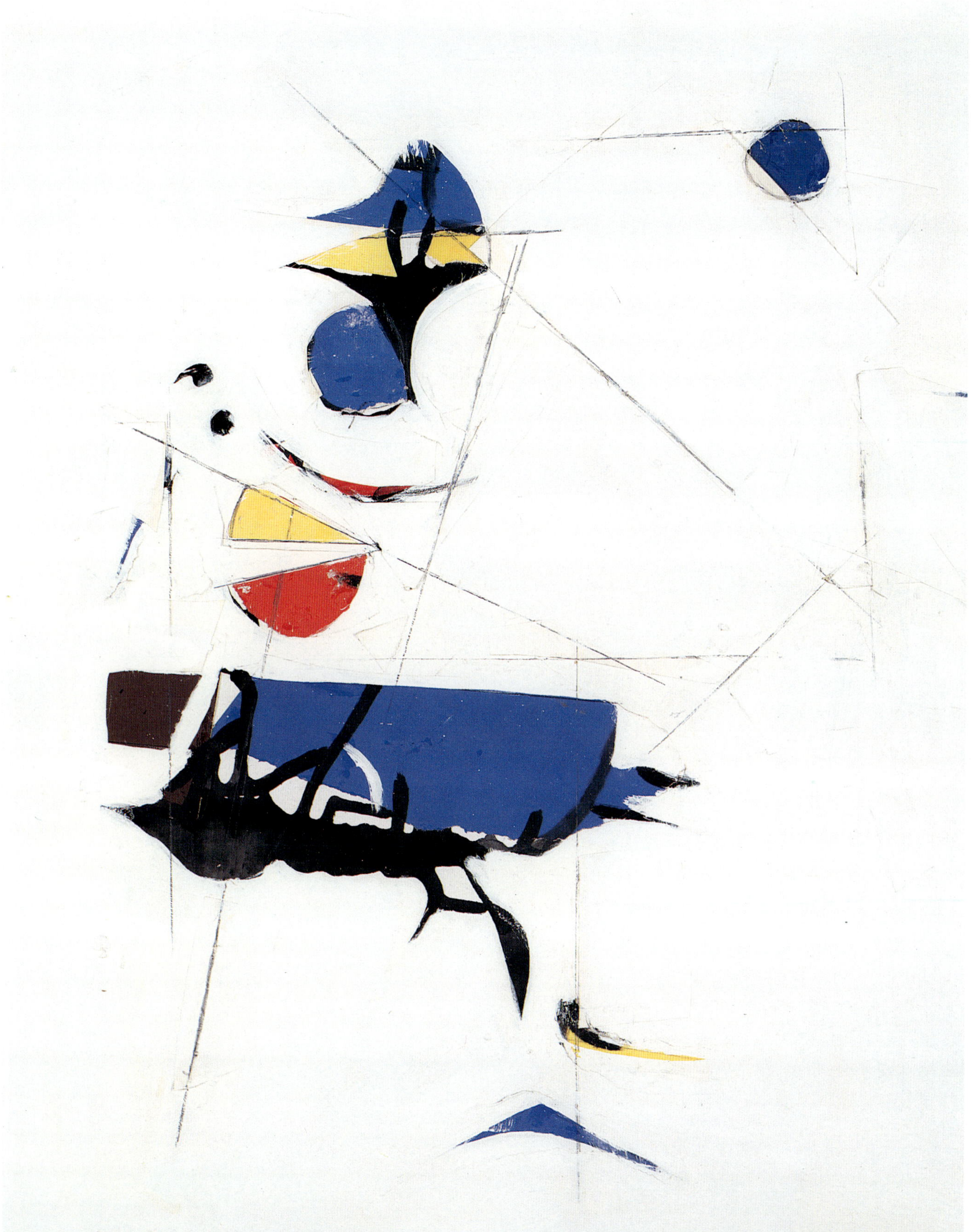

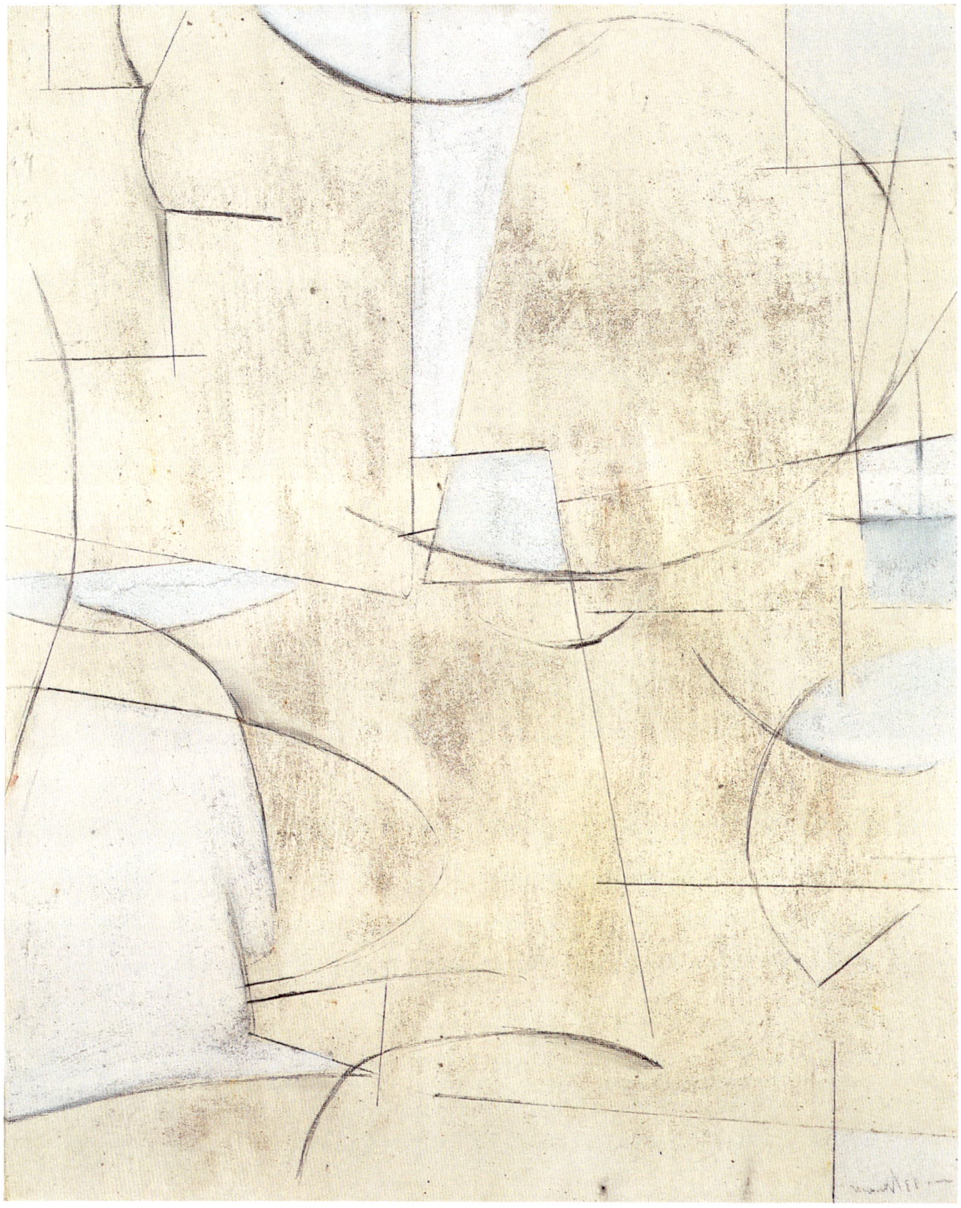

22.
BEATRICE MANDELMAN
Untitled, ca. 1951
71 x 55.3 cm
oil on artist's board
Courtesy of
Beatrice Mandelman Ribak

23. (FAR RIGHT)
EARL STROH
Dido, ca. 1956
91.5 x 71.1 cm
oil on canvas
Private Collection

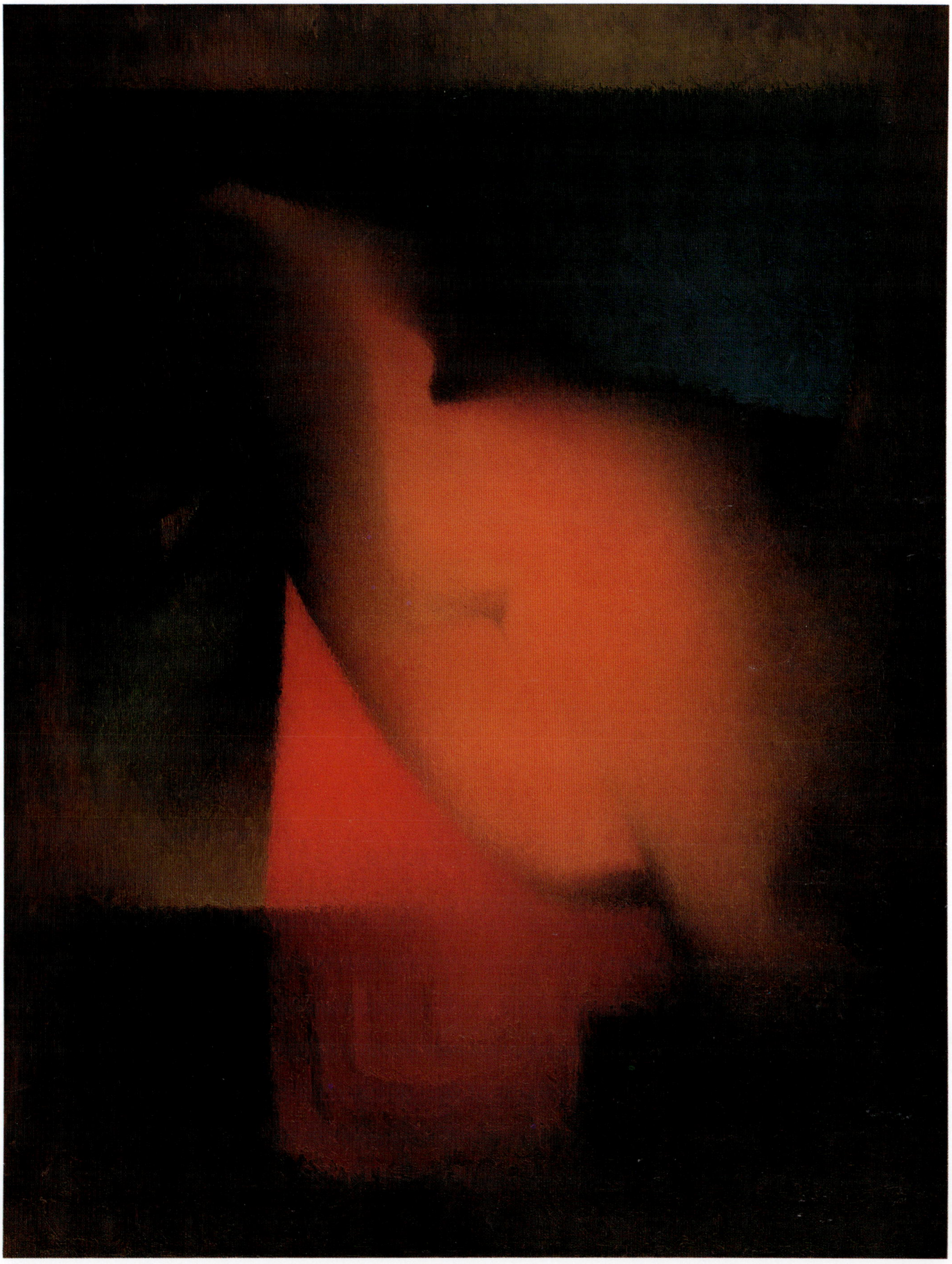

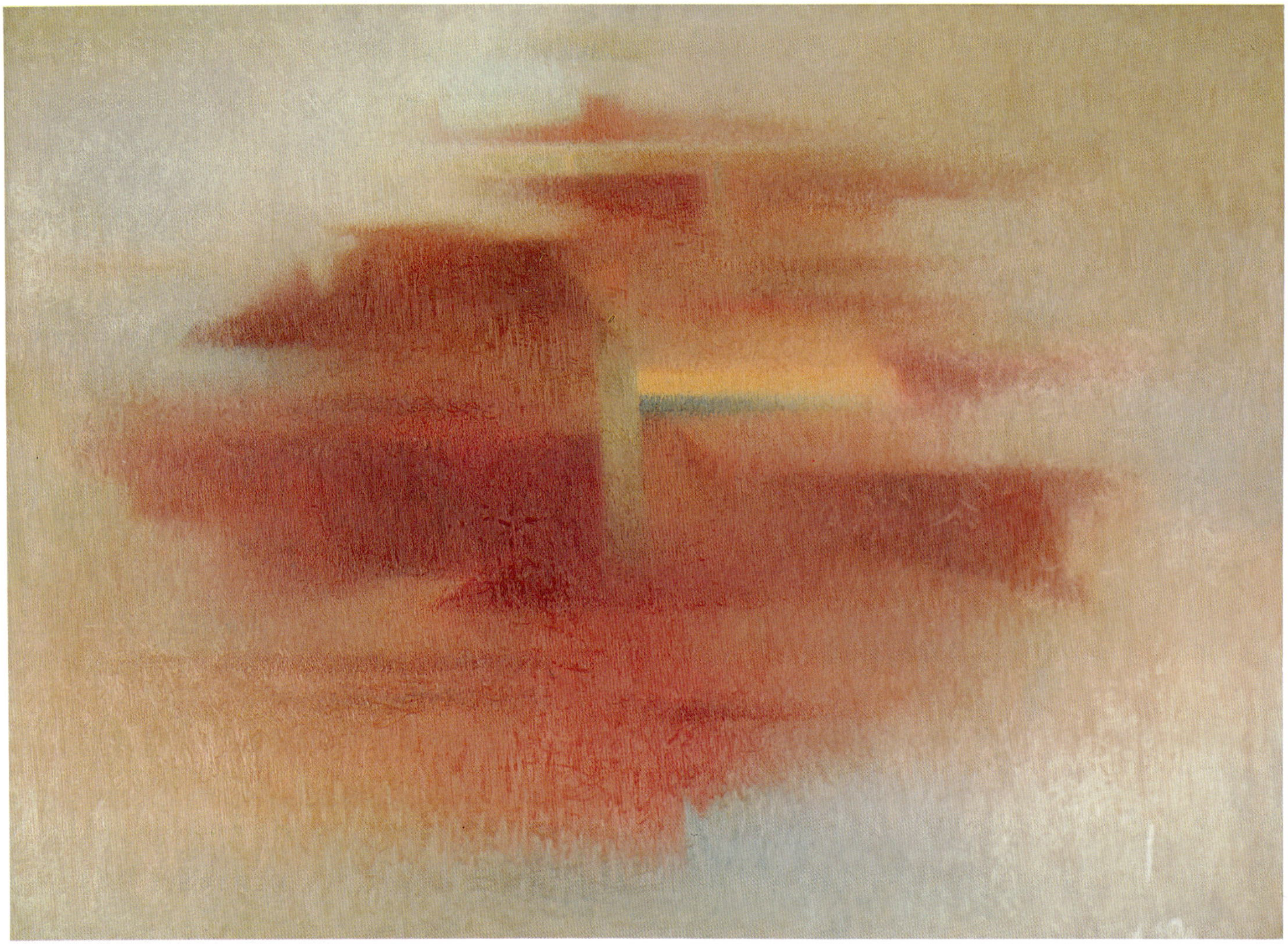

24.
EARL STROH
Red Mirage, 1958
96.5 x 129.5 cm
oil on canvas
Harwood Foundation

abstract
landscape poetry

only essentials
nothing extranious

soft edges of color bands
but toughness within

light reflections
refractions

glow
limitless
space

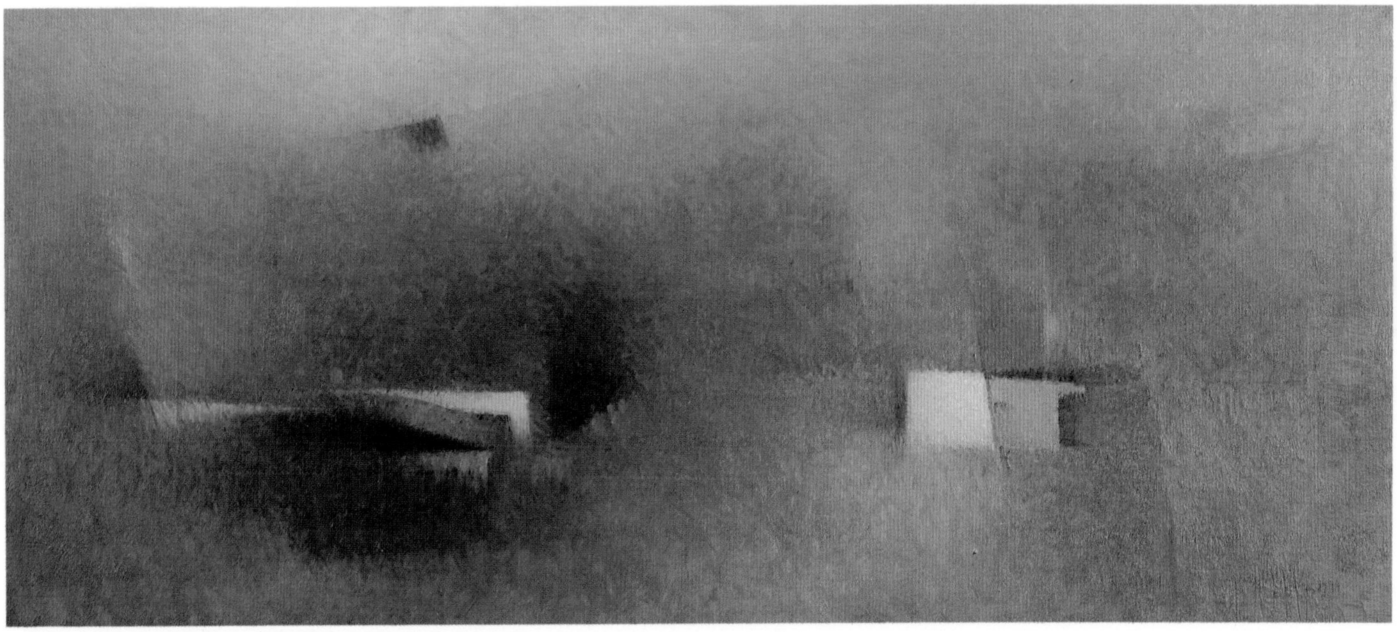

25.
EARL STROH
Gray Spring, 1953
56.2 x 122 cm
oil on masonite
Courtesy of Helen M. Derbyshire

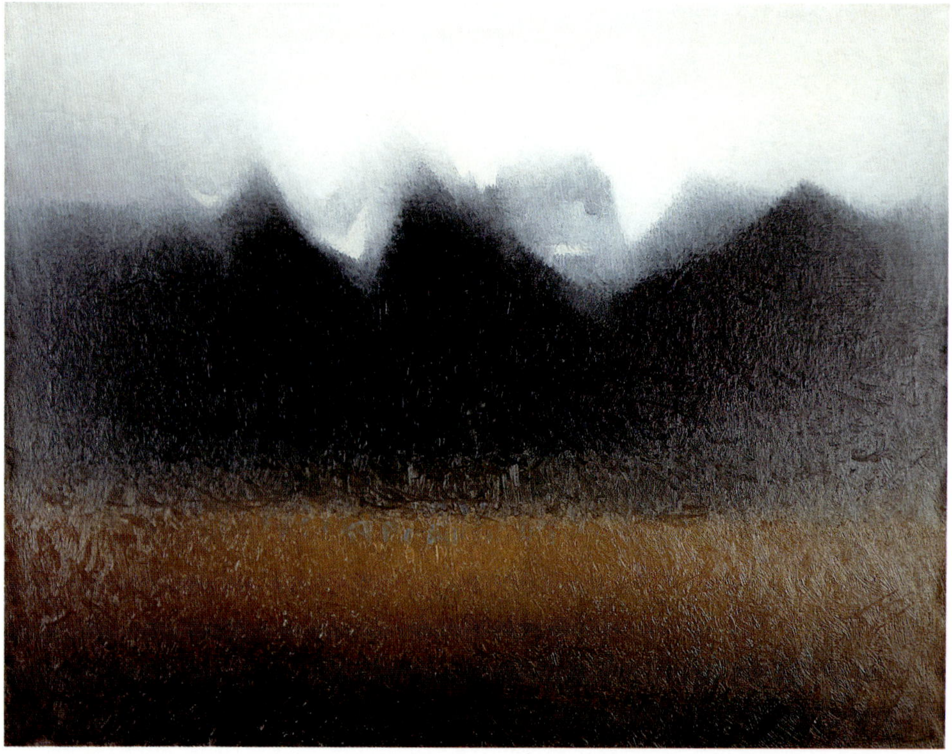

26.
EARL STROH
Dark Mountain, 1960
61.2 x 76.4 cm
oil on canvas
Courtesy of Robert Sonora

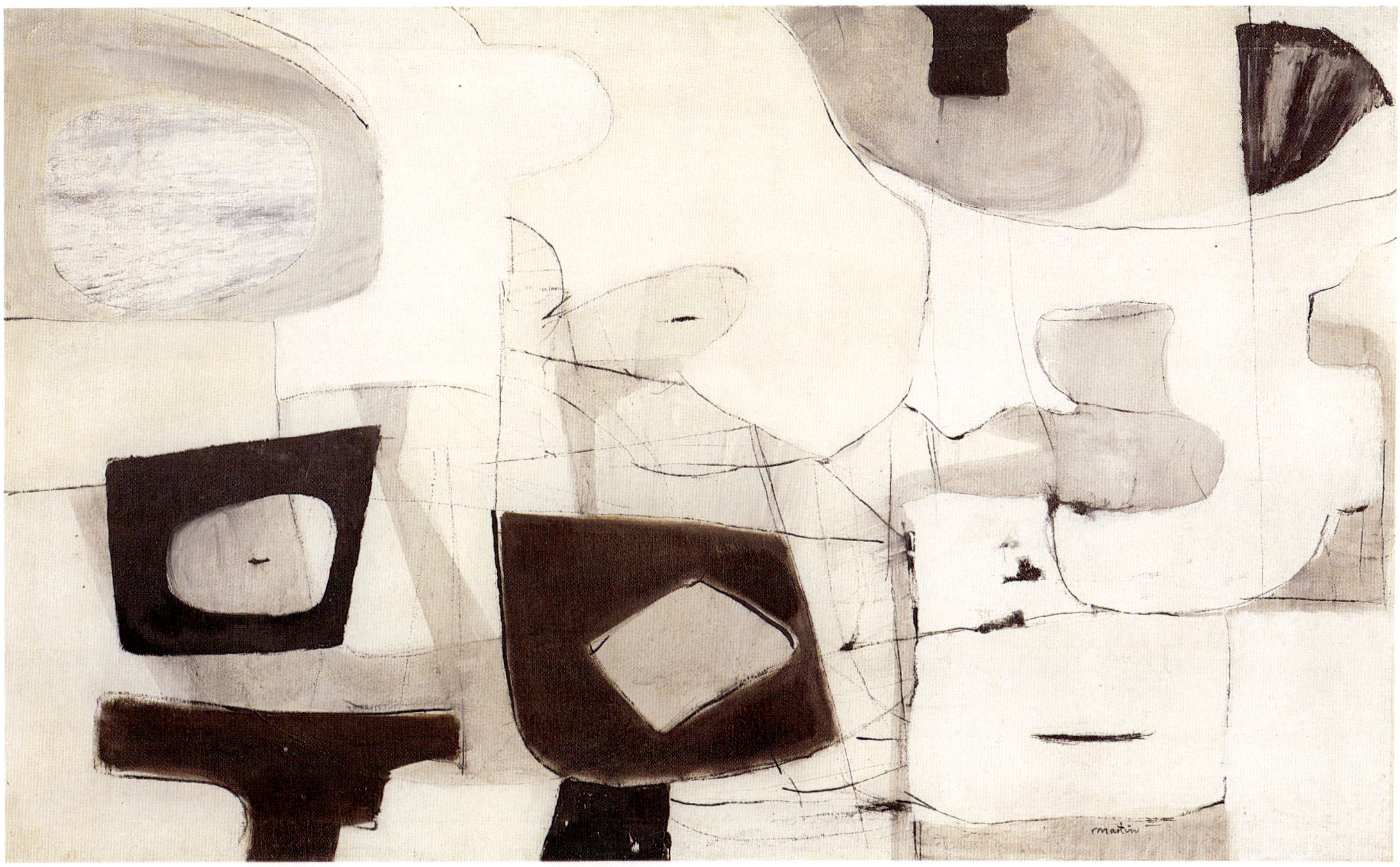

abstract compositions
with shapes, color + space

27.
AGNES MARTIN
Autumn Watch, ca. 1954
83.5 x 134.4 cm
oil on canvas
Private Collection

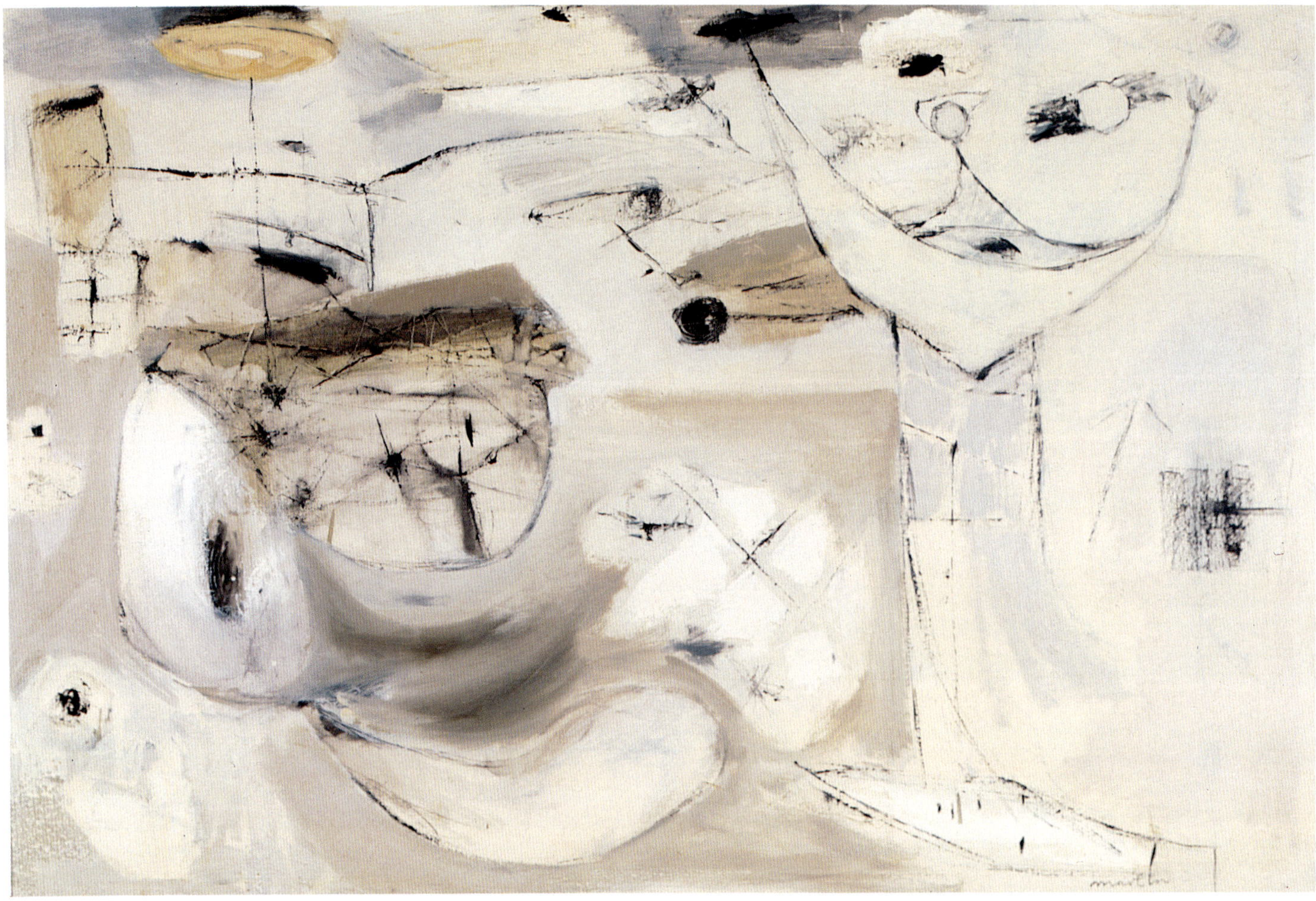

28.
AGNES MARTIN
Two People in Moonlight, 1954
71.5 x 101.7 cm
oil on canvas
Private Collection

minimalist?

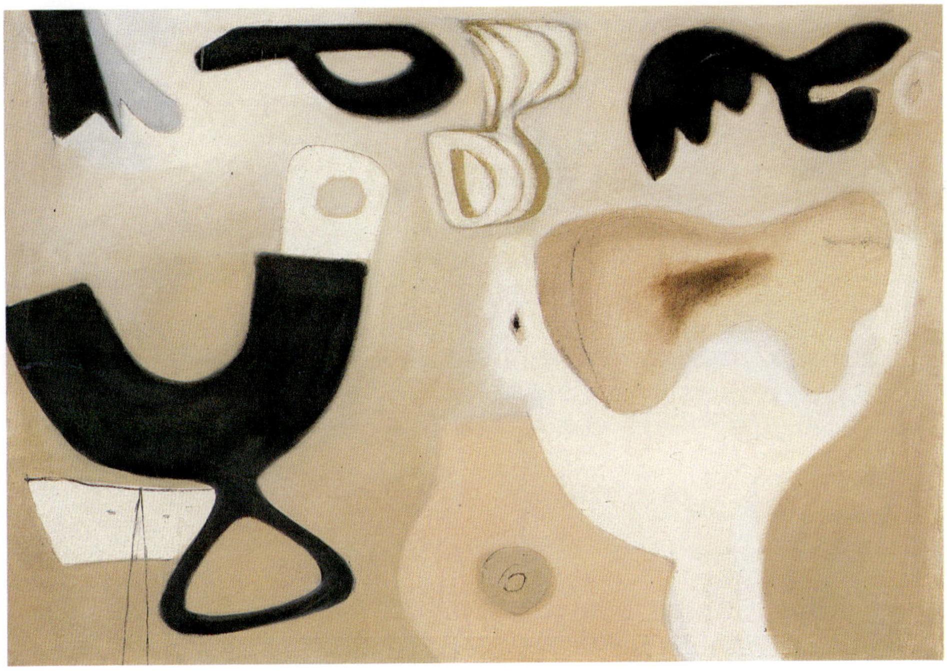

29.
AGNES MARTIN
Untitled, 1953
85.5 x 121 cm
oil on canvas
Courtesy of Mildred Tolbert

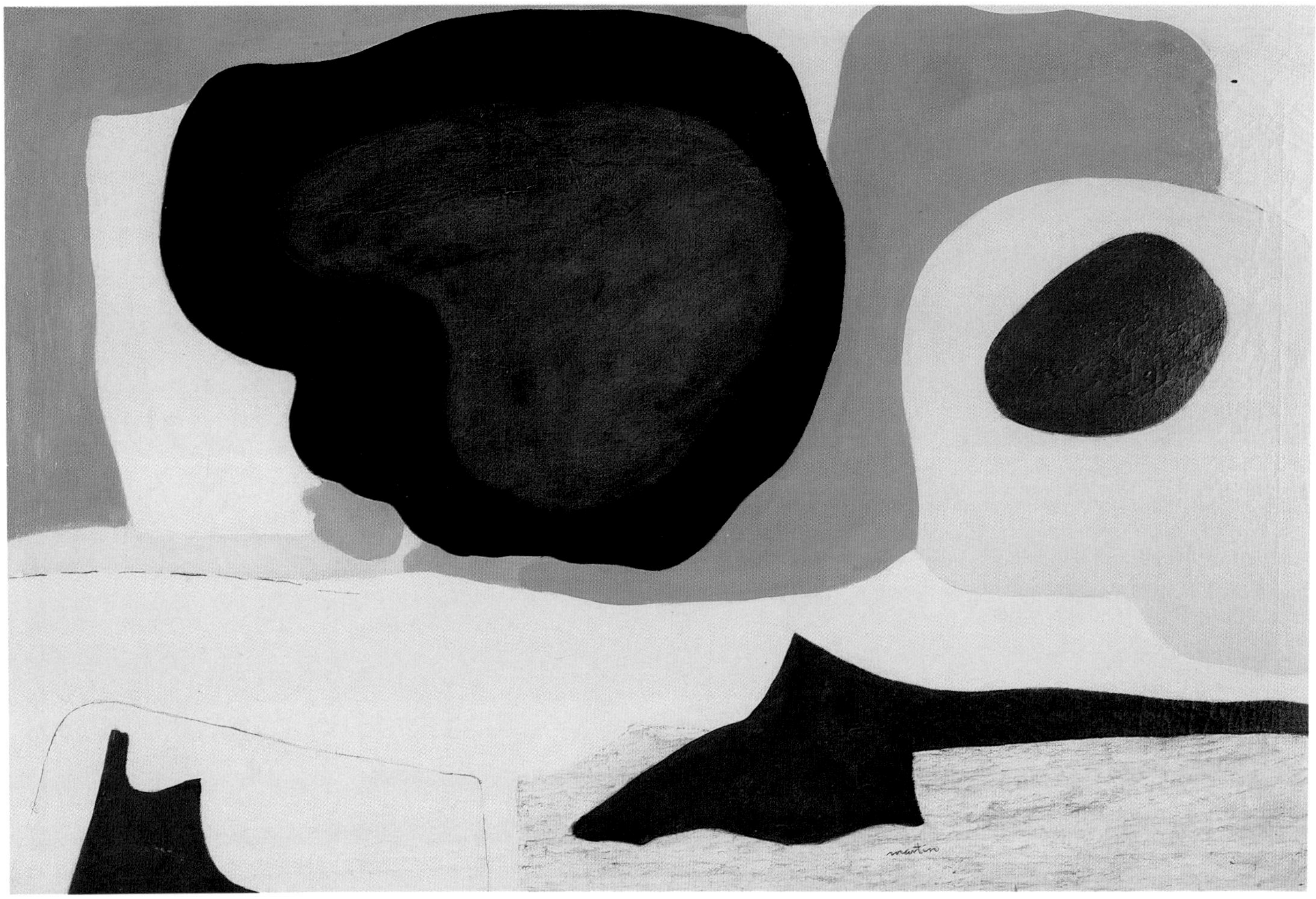

30.
AGNES MARTIN
Midwinter, ca. 1954
84.3 x 122 cm
oil on canvas
Taos Municipal Schools

31. (FAR RIGHT)
OLI SIHVONEN
Fenestra #2, 1950s
76.3 x 44.5 cm
oil on masonite
Private Collection

Black Mt w. Albers
color field

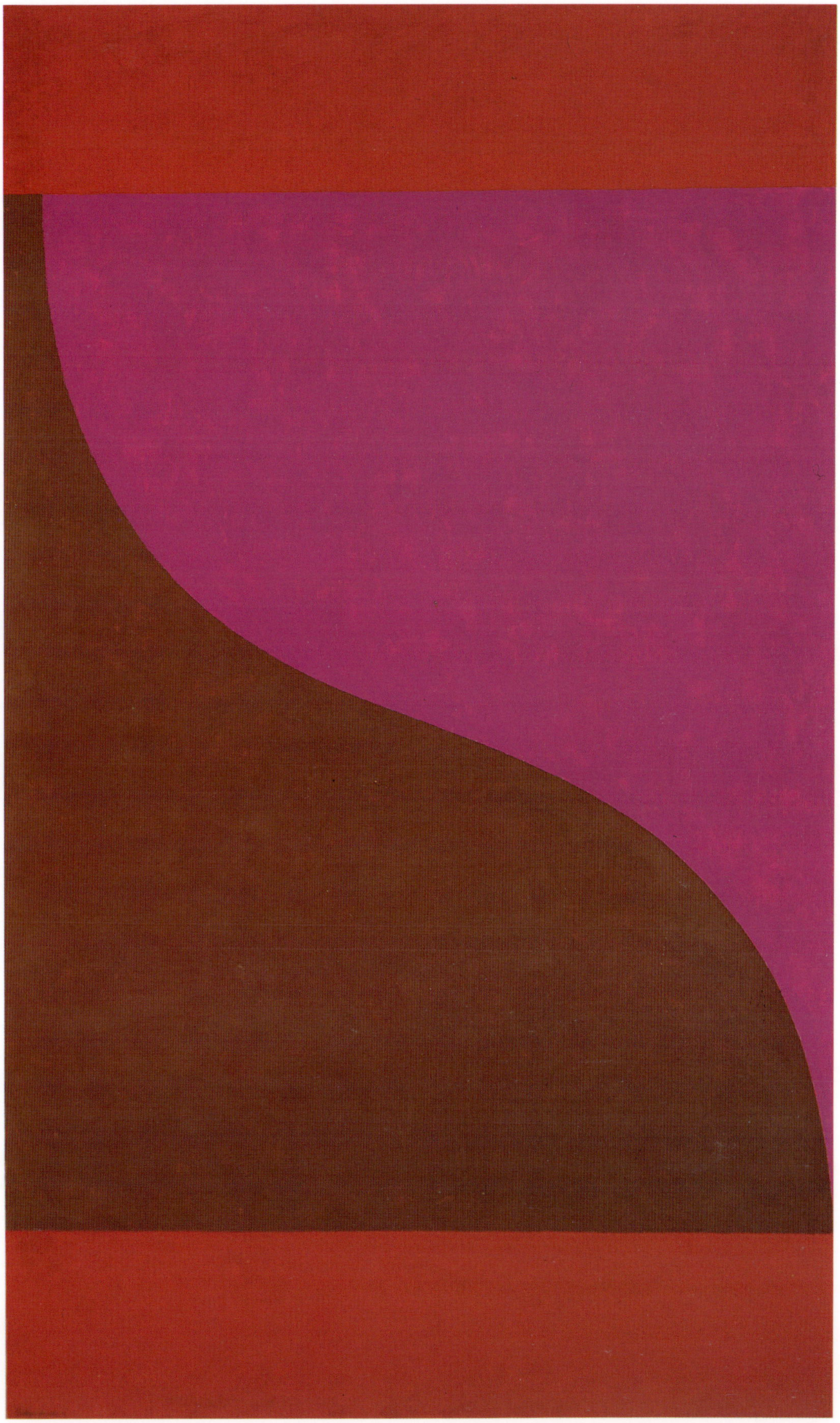

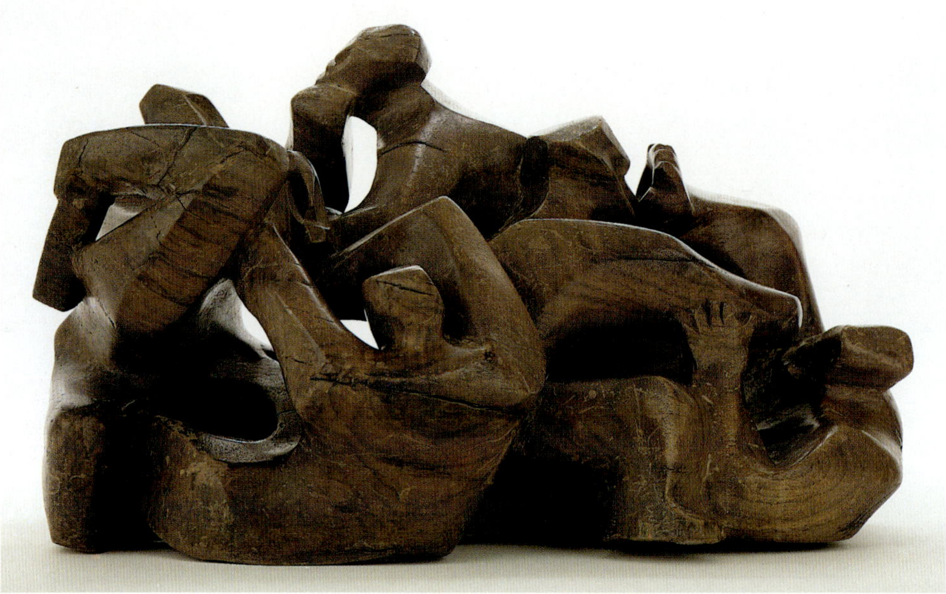

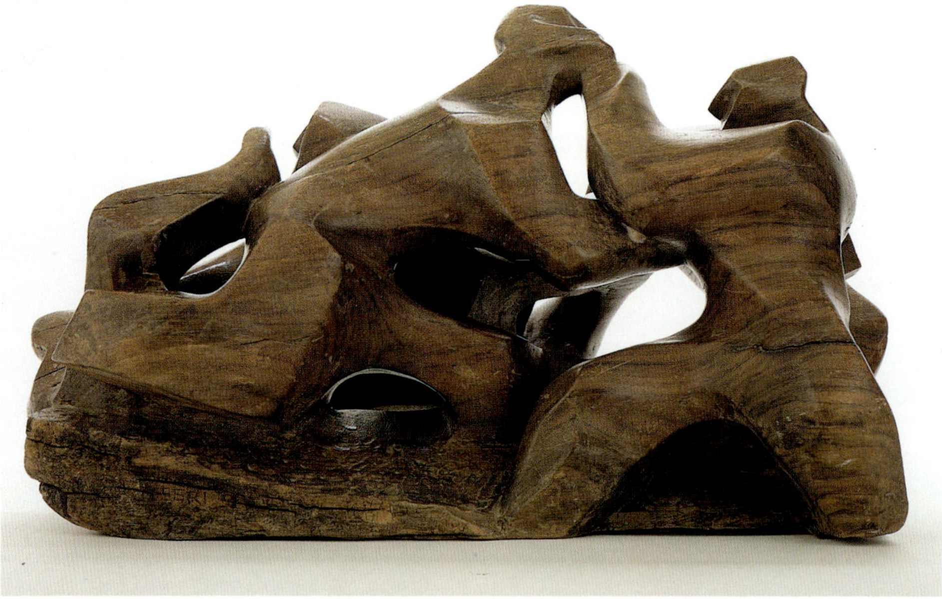

32., 33.
TED EGRI
Struggle, 1951
34.3 x 56 cm
wood
Courtesy of Ted Egri

34. (FAR RIGHT)
LOUISE GANTHIERS
Buffalo Dancer, 1954
81 x 61 cm
encaustic on masonite
Courtesy of Mildred Tolbert

>John Young-Hunter came to Taos in 1917, around the same time as the subject of his portrait, Mabel Dodge Luhan. Both of them purchased large estates and would remain friends for nearly forty years of living in Taos. Mabel was important in making Taos known to the rest of the world both through her writing and through inviting many important artists and writers to visit here.

>The other co-founder of the "art colony", Burt Phillips, made Taos his home in 1898, and lived here for fifty-eight years. This painting is darker than a typical Phillips, but it does demonstrate the romanticism for which he and many of his Taos contemporaries were well known.

>Patrocino Barela was an important figure in the art history of the Southwest. He work drew upon both the old tradition of Spanish religious art and a sensitivity which is clearly "modernist." By this, I refer to his sophisticated shaping of space in his wood carving.

>Thomas Benrimo was among the early American modernists. He came to Taos in 1939, and while here developed a distinctly personal vision in art. Notice the masterful refinement of his brush work. You may be able to better see this painting by taking a "tour" of it - this method can be used with any painting.

Stand ten feet away, close one eye, put your hand in front of the other, bringing fingers and thumb together so that you can look in the same manner as you would look through a telescope. Tour through the painting, noticing intersections of line, patches of color, to focus in on one element of the composition at a time. Then again look at the complete work and see if your perception of it has changed.

>Doel Reed was fascinated by entry ways and the structures which form them. Take a close look at this painting to see how many different paths you can find between and behind the elements in the composition.

>Unlike many of his contemporaries, Herbert Dunton concentrated on the Anglo culture in New Mexico, depicting its old time cowboys and hunters. In this one, Ginger looks back nostalgically at a mule drawn wagon which has become just a memory from the past.

>This abstraction by Andrew Dasburg was painted in New York subsequent to his first Taos visit in 1918. He was one of the first modernist painters in America, and an important teacher in New York before permanently moving to New Mexico in 1930.

>Another artist who arrived here in 1918 was Leon Gaspard, a Russian painter whose life was as colorful as his palette. Before finally settling in Taos in 1924, his exploits included a two year honeymoon trip through Siberia with his wife Evelyn, and a later solo horseback trip through China and Tibet. He has achieved much popularity for his sketch-like painting style.

>In this final section we see represented an earlier group of Taos painters, the santeros' interpretation of the icons of Catholicism. Working with rather primitive materials, they created a unique American art which is both pius and fresh at the same time. This collection was gathered by Mabel Dodge Luhan who was among the first Anglo outsiders to recognize the inherent beauty and importance of this work.

THE ART OF TAOS

DAVID L. WITT, CURATOR, THE HARWOOD FOUNDATION

Welcome to our exhibition - our hope is that you will find it an informative introduction to the Taos art community.

>Just ahead as you enter the gallery is the best known painting in our collection, *Winter Funeral*, by Victor Higgins. Created during the winter of 1931-1932, it shows the relationship of humanity to the immensity of nature. But it is not a gloomy scene. Look for the blue sky where the clouds are beginning to break.

>Ernest Blumenschein probably painted this scene south of Taos at the confluence where Taos Creek joins the Rio Grande. Rugged fields of basalt boulders frame the high mesa behind which looms 800 feet above the rivers. The geometry of the rocks gives this painting a sculptural feel. "Blumey" became one of the co-founders of the Taos "art colony" in 1898, and of the Taos Society of Artists (TSA) in 1915.

>A later addition to the TSA was Kenneth Adams who resided in Taos between 1924 and 1938 and maintained a lifelong connection to the community. For much of his career after leaving Taos he taught art at the University of New Mexico in Albuquerque. He worked with a wide range of subject matter, including portraits.

>This Walter Ufer painting shows how the light of the Taos Valley has so fascinated the artists who come here. Many artists came here accustomed to using more somber colors. The brilliant stark light of New Mexico has led many artists to do brighter work in which the quality of light has become a sort of subject in and of itself. Ufer was also a member of the TSA.

>On the wall opposite (starting from the door) is a work by TSA member Oscar Berninghaus who first visited Taos just after the turn of the century to begin a fifty year association with the community. This scene, set in the corrals on the south side of Taos Pueblo, features a finely painted portrait of Santiago, a Taos Indian who worked as a model for many of the painters.

>The crisp clear air of fall makes that season the favorite of many of us who live here. TSA member E. Martin Hennings used elements both of landscape and still life in this September view. The chamisa (rabbitbrush) nicely sets off the stalks of sunflowers just behind and the yellow aspen groves on the mountains east of Taos.

>Blanche Grant painted this work on the porch of one of the oldest houses in Taos. Located about a block west of here, it subsequently became the studio of artists Beatrice Mandelman and Louis Ribak. During the twenties, this artist became a writer. She edited the Taos newspaper and wrote the first history of Taos, <u>When Old Trails Were New</u>.

>Ward Lockwood may have painted this portrait of his wife when he lived next door to the Harwood. The bold abstract pattern of the Navajo blanket with its brightness and stark clean lines has much in common with the similar sharpness of the Southwestern landscape. Hard economic times in the thirties launched Lockwood away from Taos into a university art teaching career.

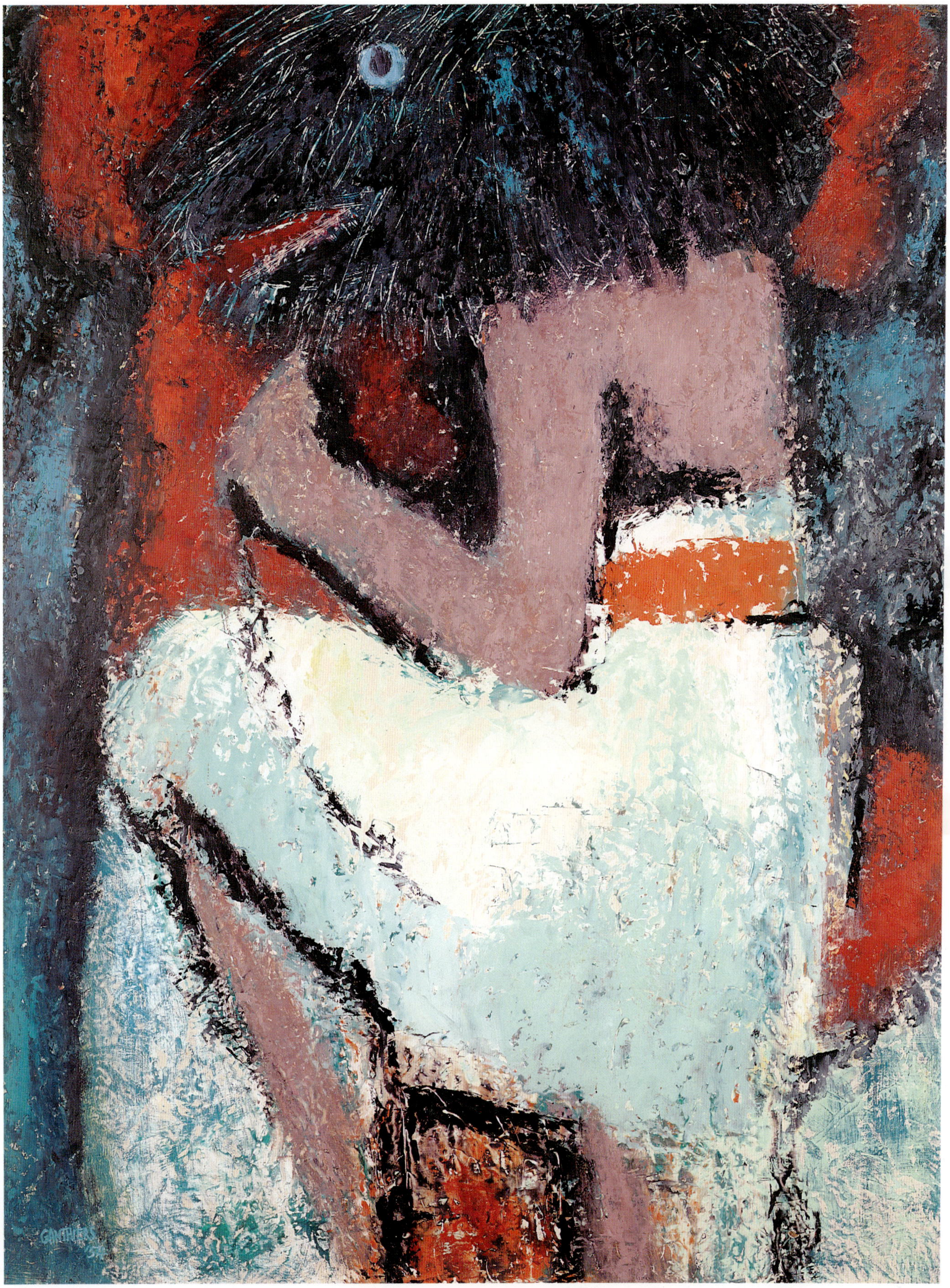

heavily impasto

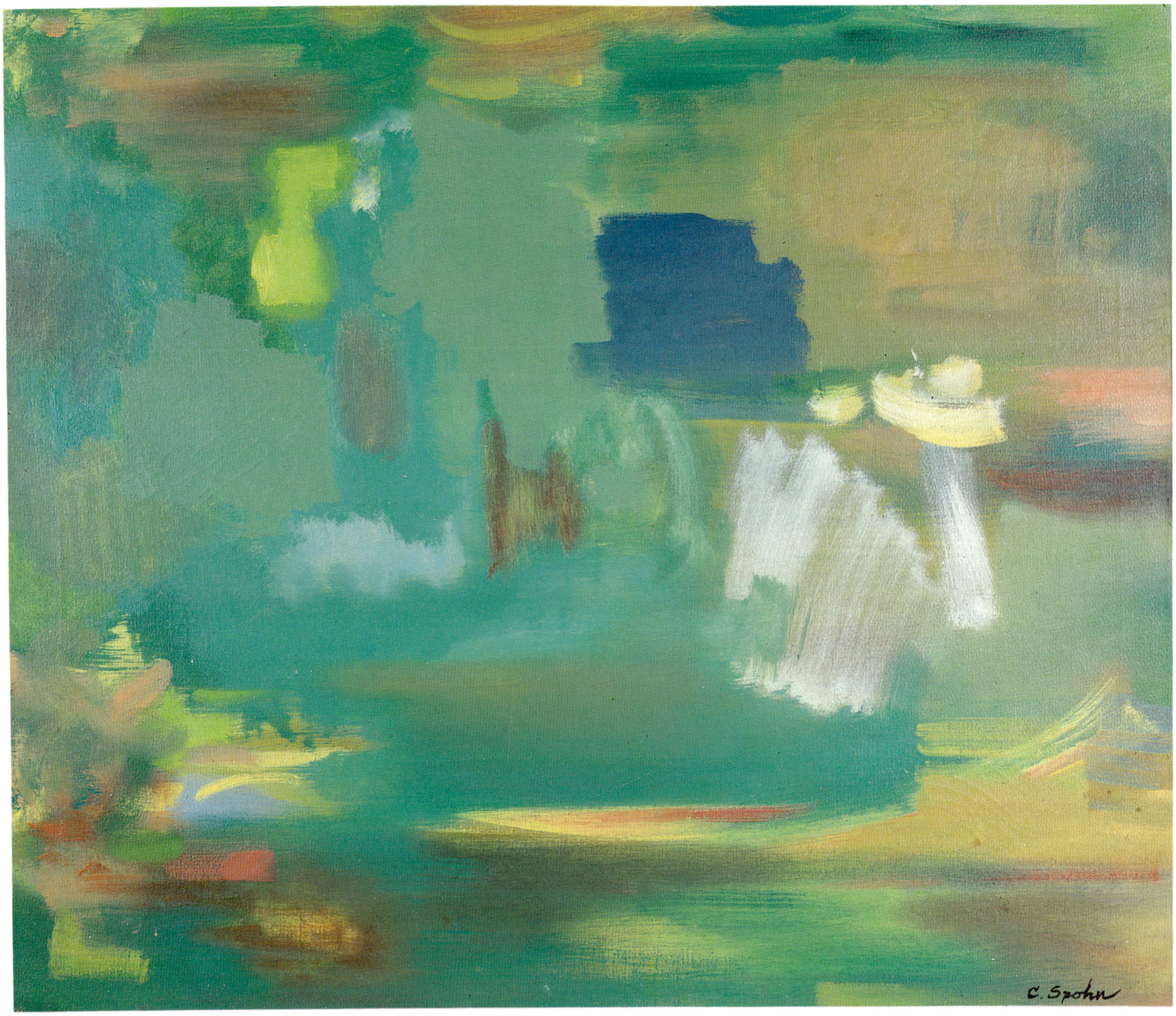

35.
CLAY SPOHN
Elements of Spring: The Rains, 1952
71.3 x 81.7 cm
oil on canvas
Harwood Foundation

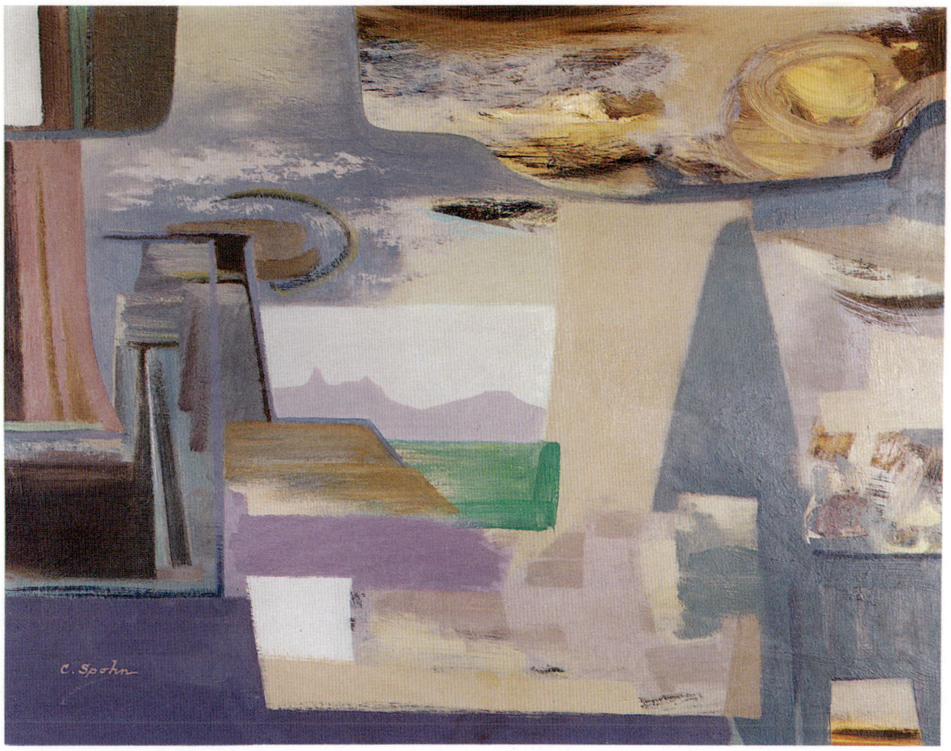

36.
CLAY SPOHN
Impressions of a Landscape, ca.
1952
55.2 x 70.5 cm
oil on masonite
Harwood Foundation

Diebenkorn?

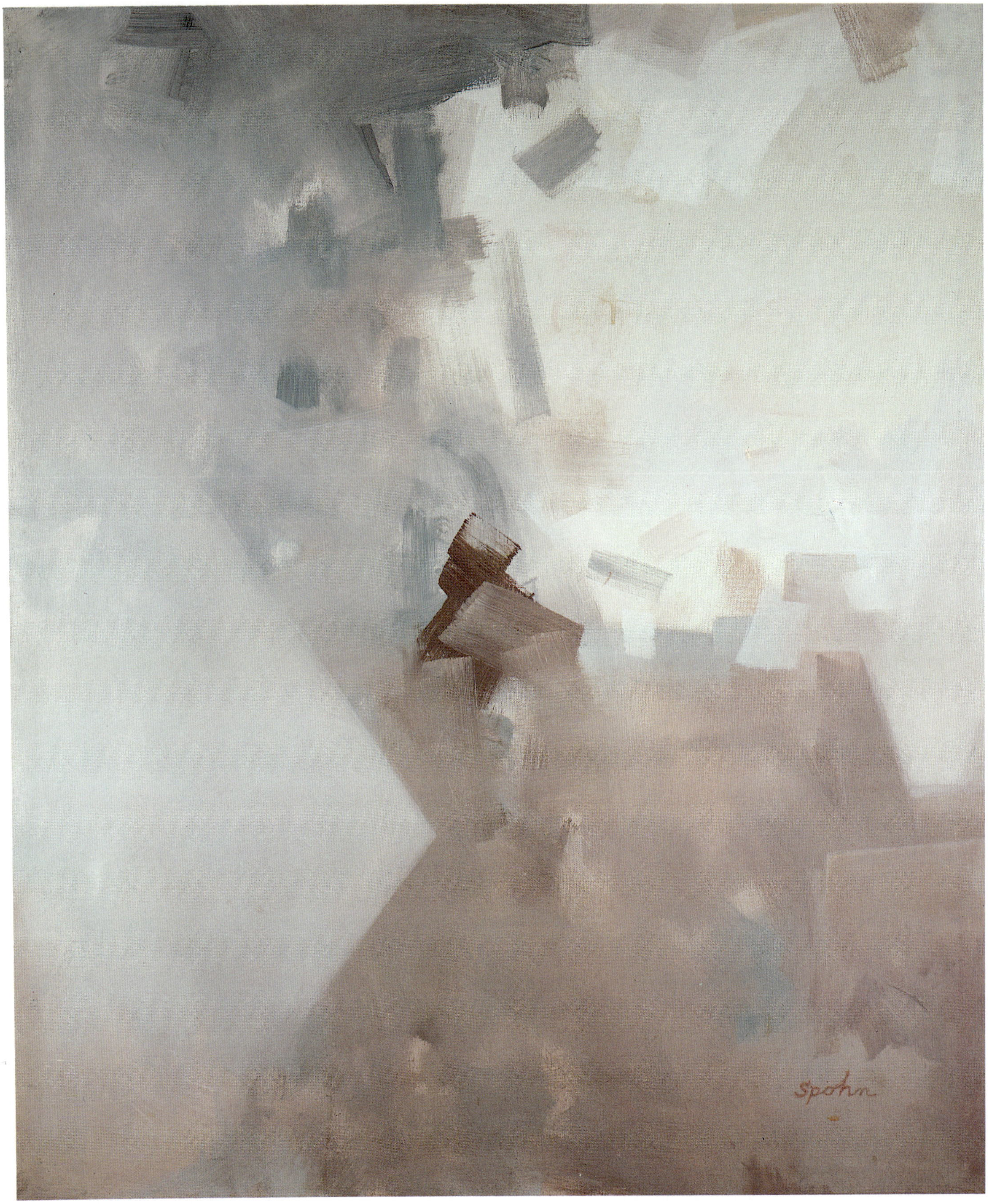
Spohn

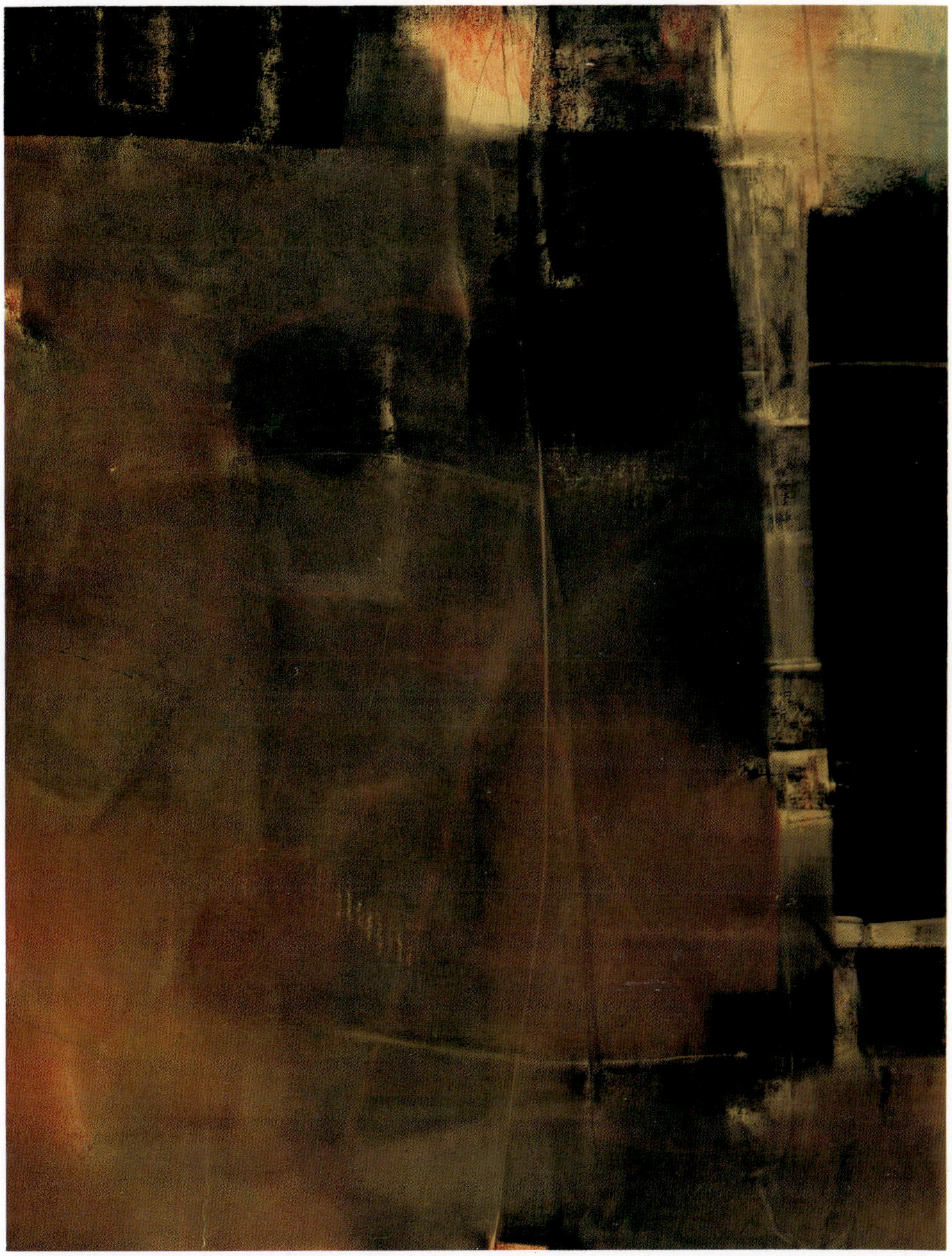

37. (FAR LEFT)
CLAY SPOHN
Gray Tones, 1958
106.3 x 86.3 cm
oil on linen
Albuquerque Museum

38.
EDWARD CORBETT
Untitled, ca. 1952
86.3 x 68.6 cm
charcoal and pastel on paper
Courtesy of Mildred Tolbert

39.
EDWARD CORBETT
Untitled, ca. 1953
40 x 26.4 cm
gouache and charcoal on paper
Private Collection

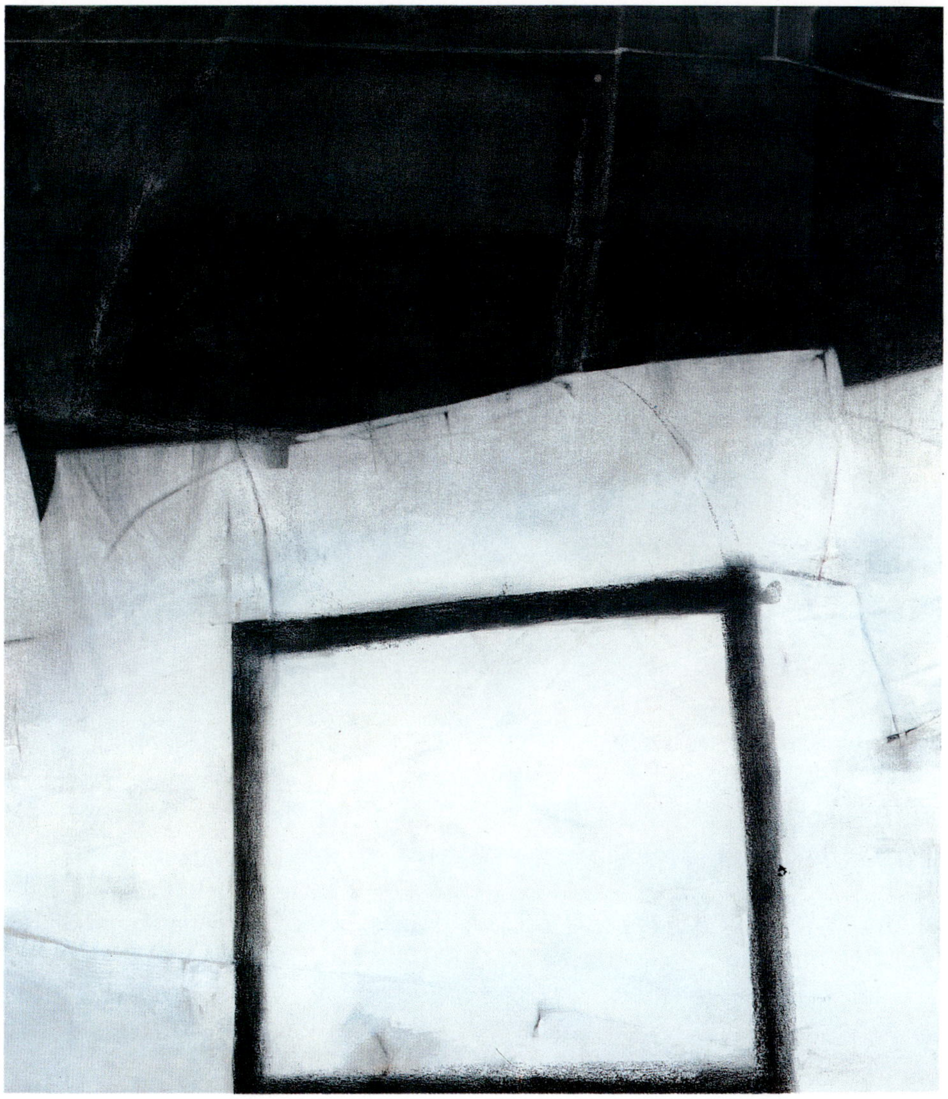

40.
EDWARD CORBETT
Untitled, ca. 1953
73.4 x 64.3 cm
charcoal and pastel on paper
Courtesy of Mildred Tolbert

reflection of light & nature of Northern desert

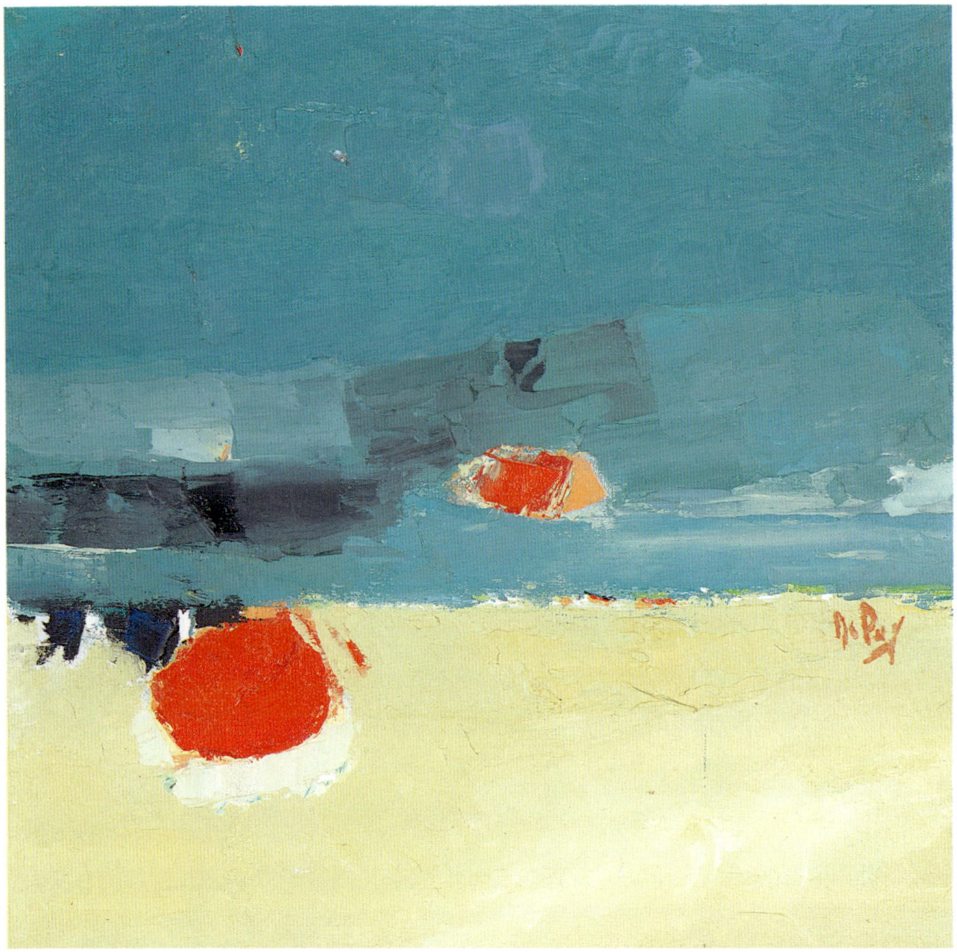

Hans Hoffman
sensitivity of a
naturalist

41.
JOHN DePUY
Untitled, ca. 1955
50.7 x 50.7 cm
oil on canvas
Courtesy of Mildred Tolbert

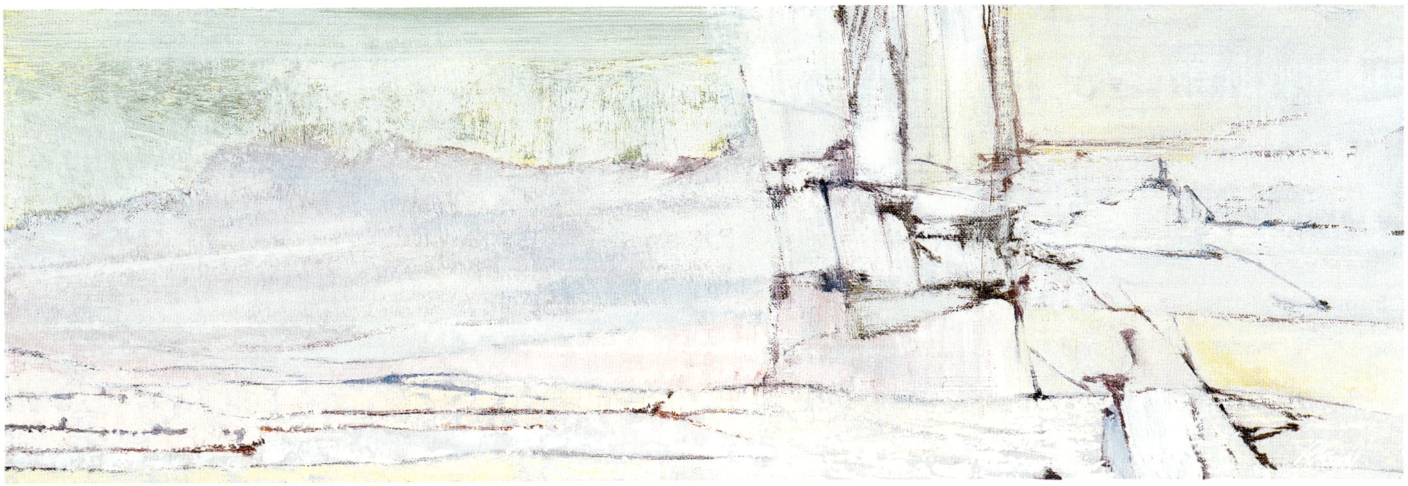

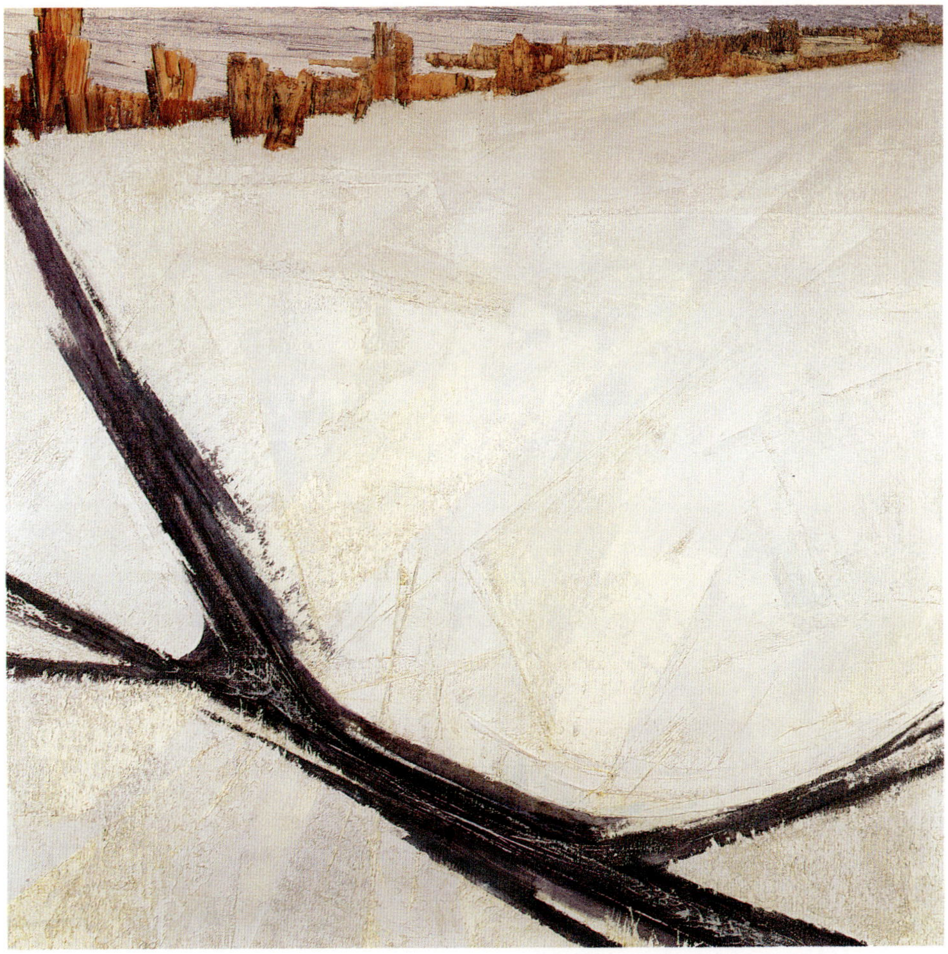

expresses delicacy + harshness of landscape e.g. light

*42. (TOP)
ROBERT D. RAY
Moods and Mornings, 1962
20.3 x 59.4 cm
oil on masonite
Harwood Foundation

43. (BOTTOM)
ROBERT D. RAY
Snow and the River, ca. 1958
106.7 x 106.7 cm
oil on linen
Private Collection

serene colors

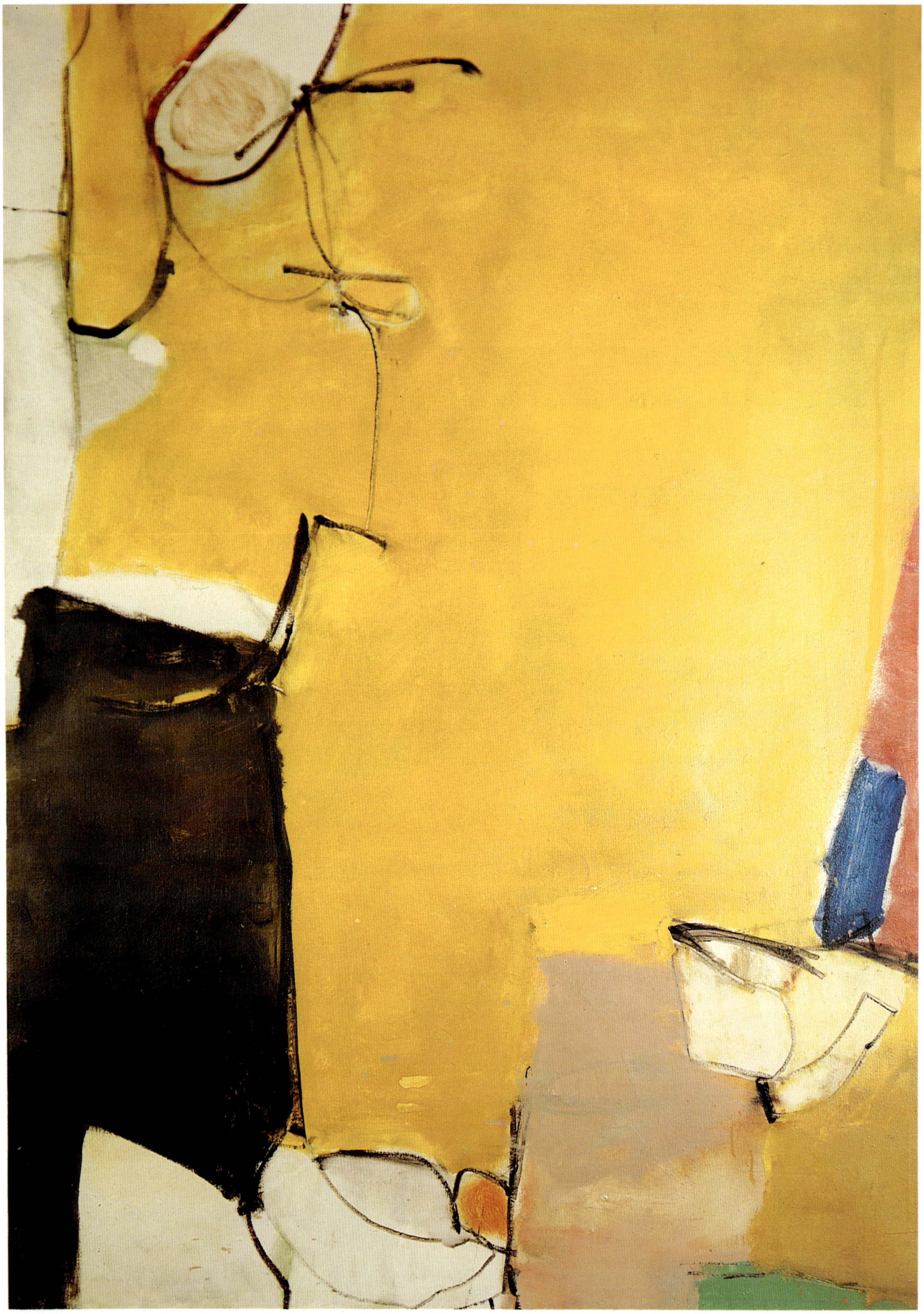

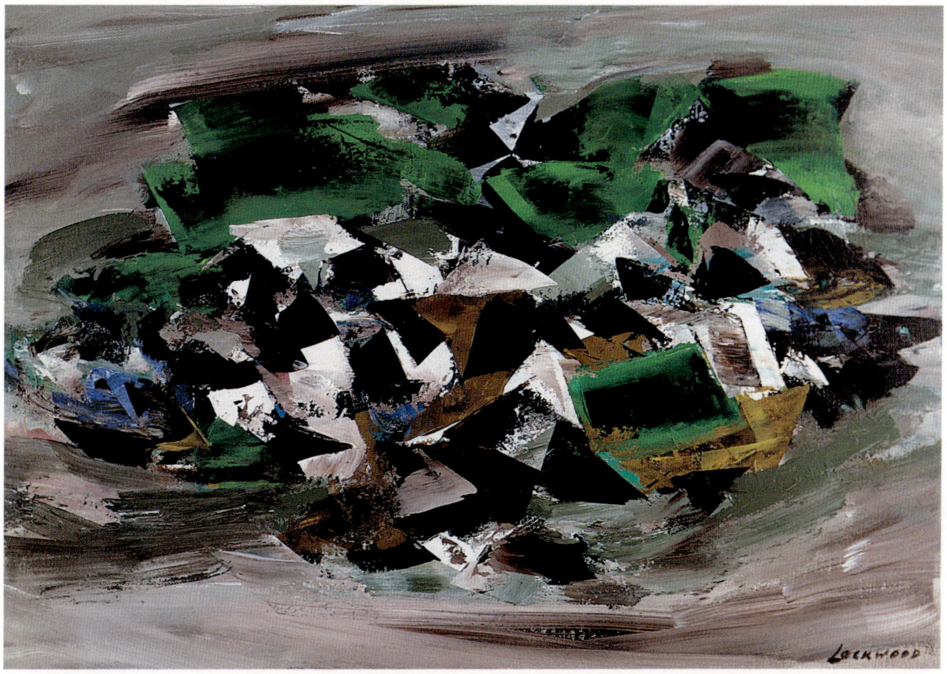

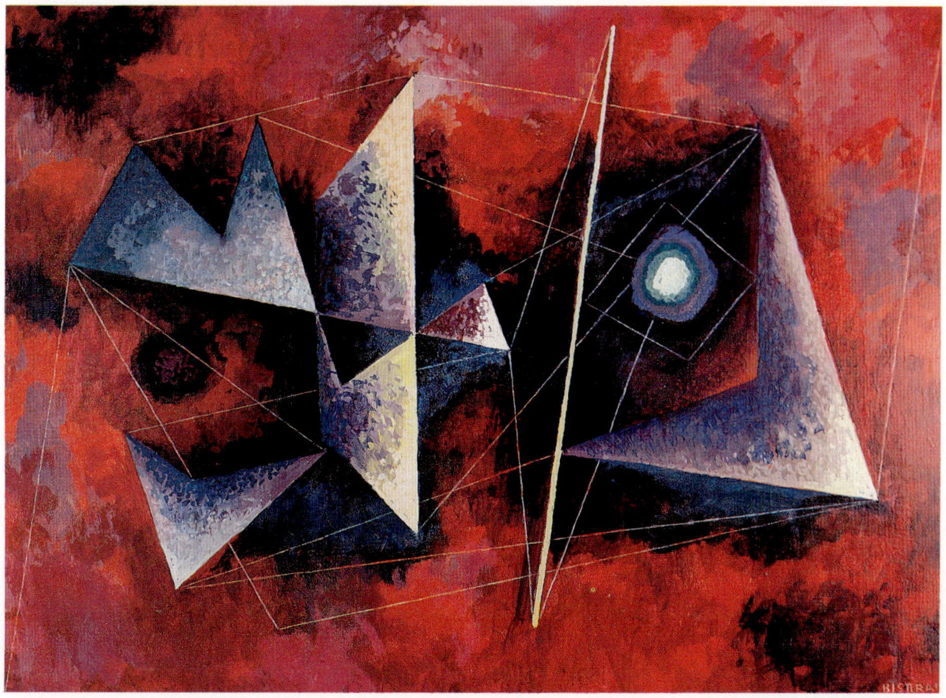

44. (FAR LEFT)
RICHARD DIEBENKORN
Untitled, 1951
139 x 96 cm
oil on canvas
University Art Museum,
The University of New Mexico

45. (TOP)
WARD LOCKWOOD
Episode, ca. 1958
82.5 x 114.5 cm
oil on canvas
Harwood Foundation

46. (BOTTOM)
EMIL BISTTRAM
Out of Space, 1954
68.8 x 91.5 cm
casein on board
Harwood Foundation

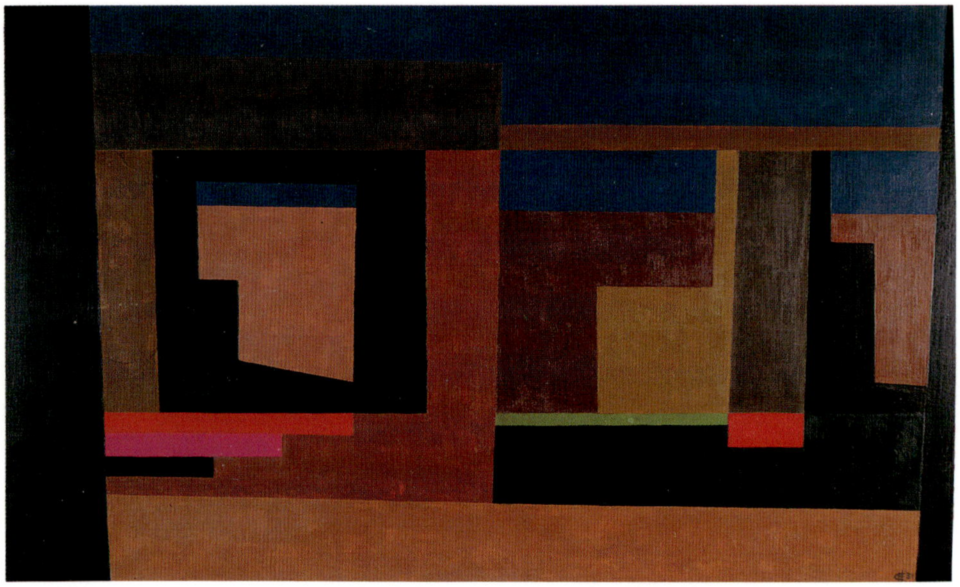

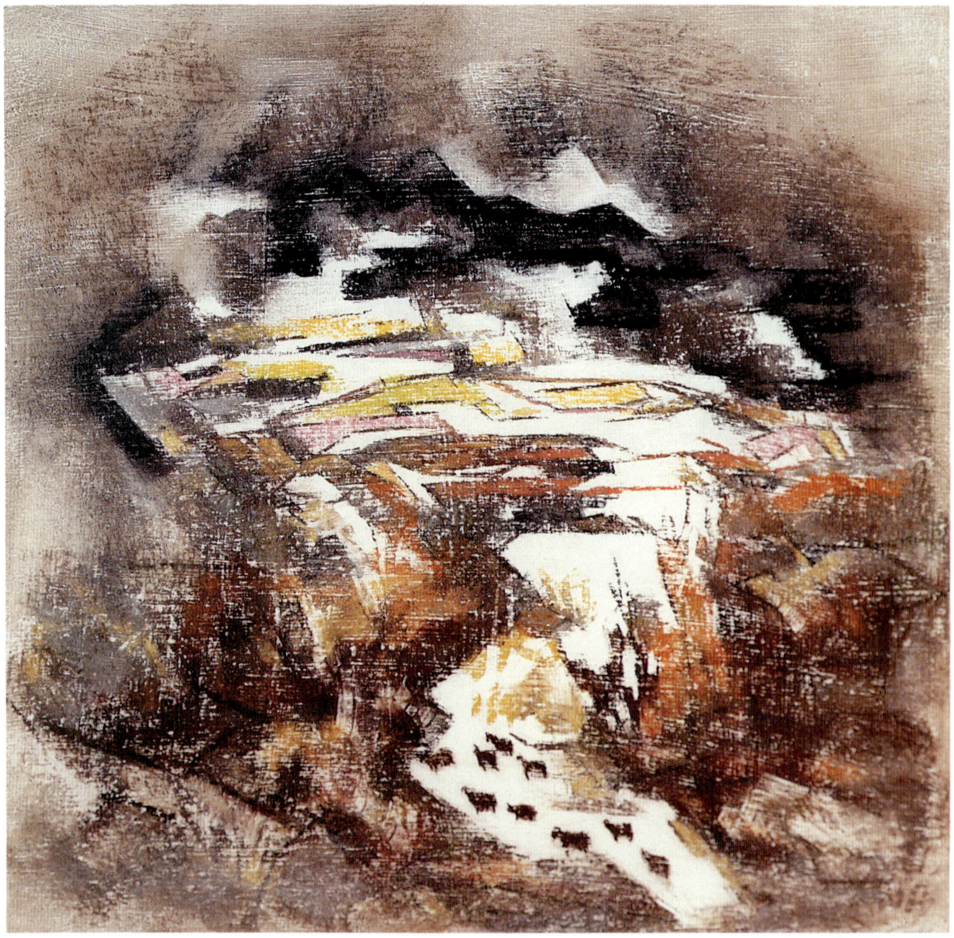

47. (TOP)
CLIFF HARMON
Construction 51-1, 1951
35.6 x 55.9 cm
oil on masonite
Harwood Foundation

48. (BOTTOM)
HOWARD COOK
Ranchos Valley Winter, possibly 1950s
43 x 43.3 cm
oil on board
Harwood Foundation

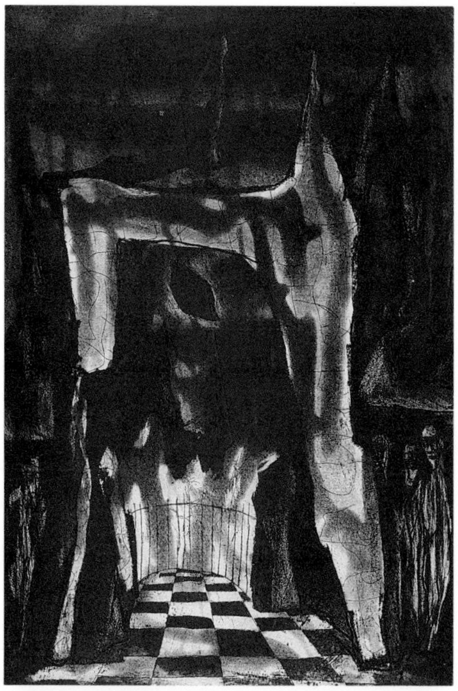

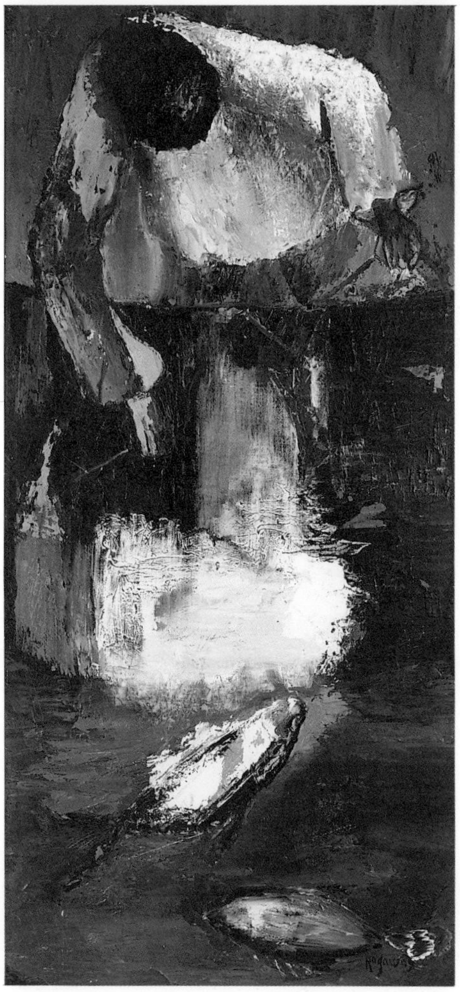

49. (TOP)
ARTHUR JACOBSON
The Long Wait, 1950
33 x 23 cm
aquatint
Harwood Foundation

50. (BOTTOM)
ALFRED ROGOWAY
Untitled, 1950s
130.3 x 61.3 cm
oil on masonite
Harwood Foundation

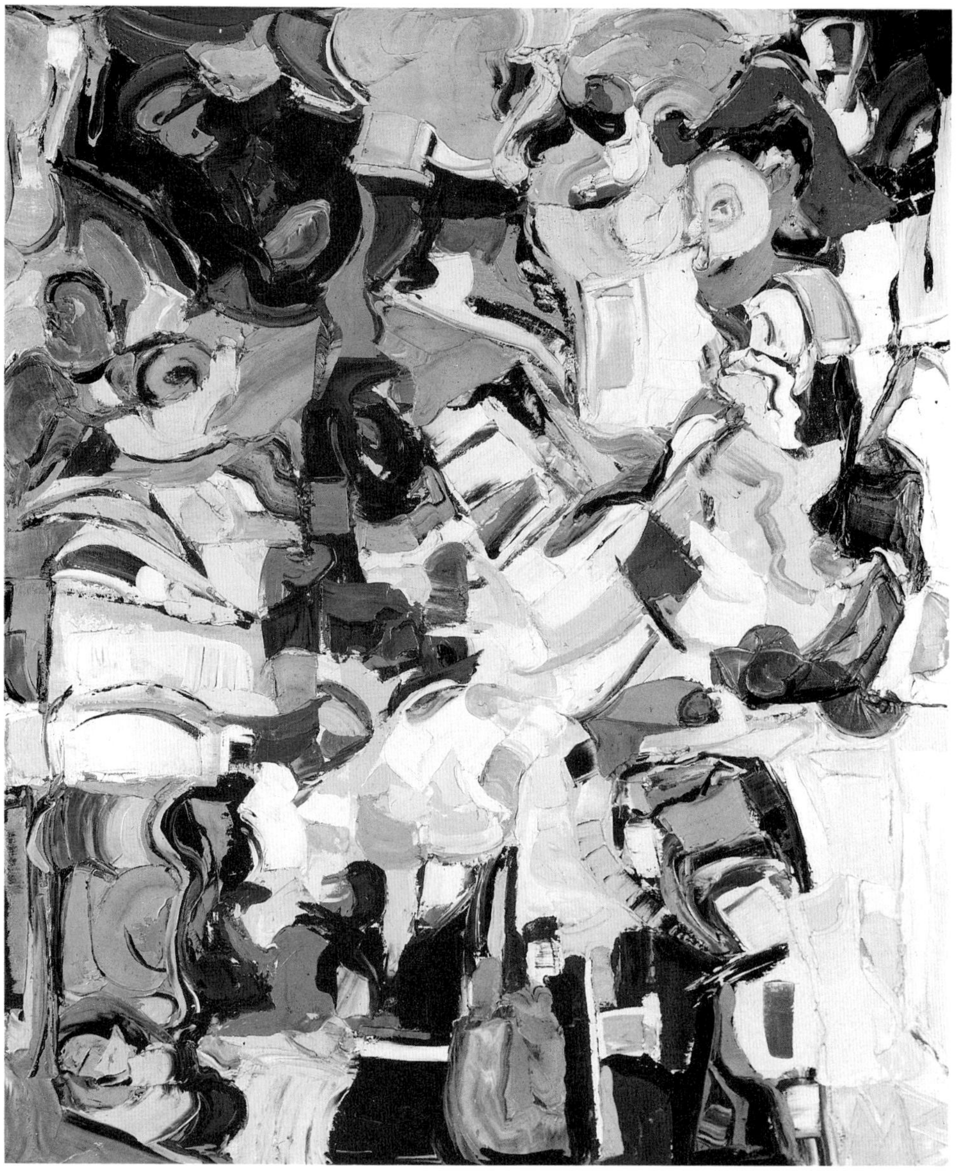

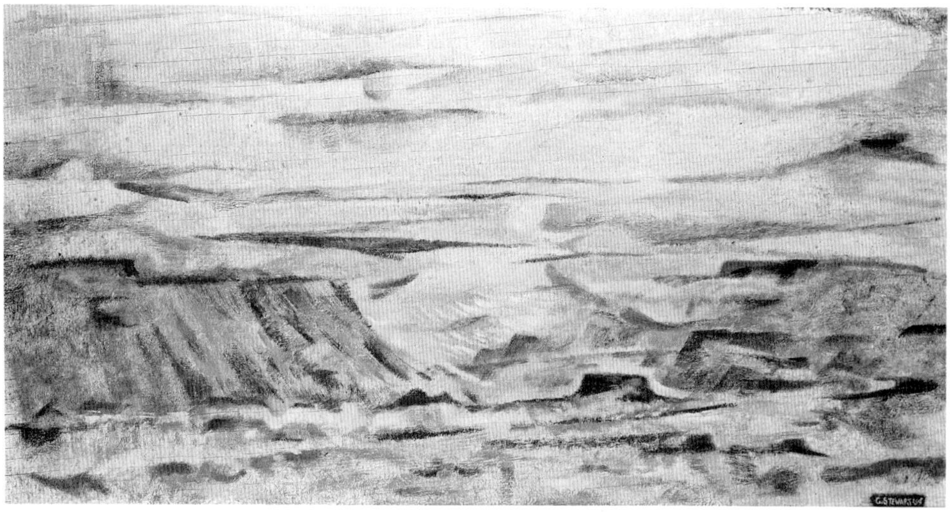

adobe fireplaces house design painting

51. (TOP)
MALCOLM BROWN
Olafs Dream, 1960
116 x 95 cm
oil on canvas
Harwood Foundation

52. (BOTTOM)
CHARLES STEWART
Sunset, Taos, 1959
60.7 x 111.5 cm
oil on board
Harwood Foundation

3-D

APPENDICES

Bisttram school of fine art

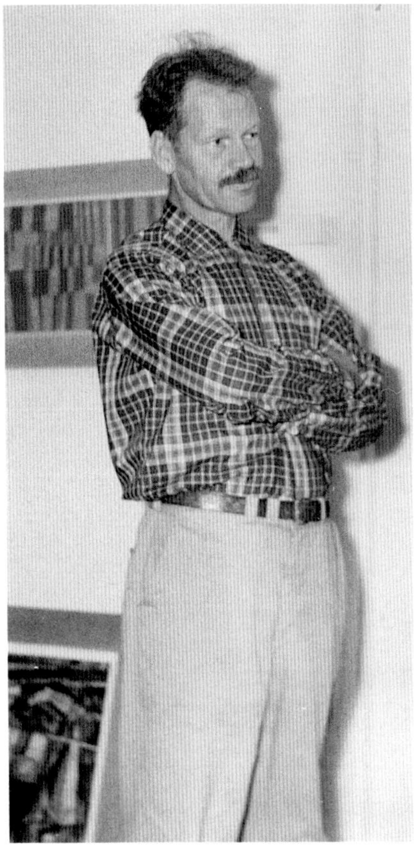

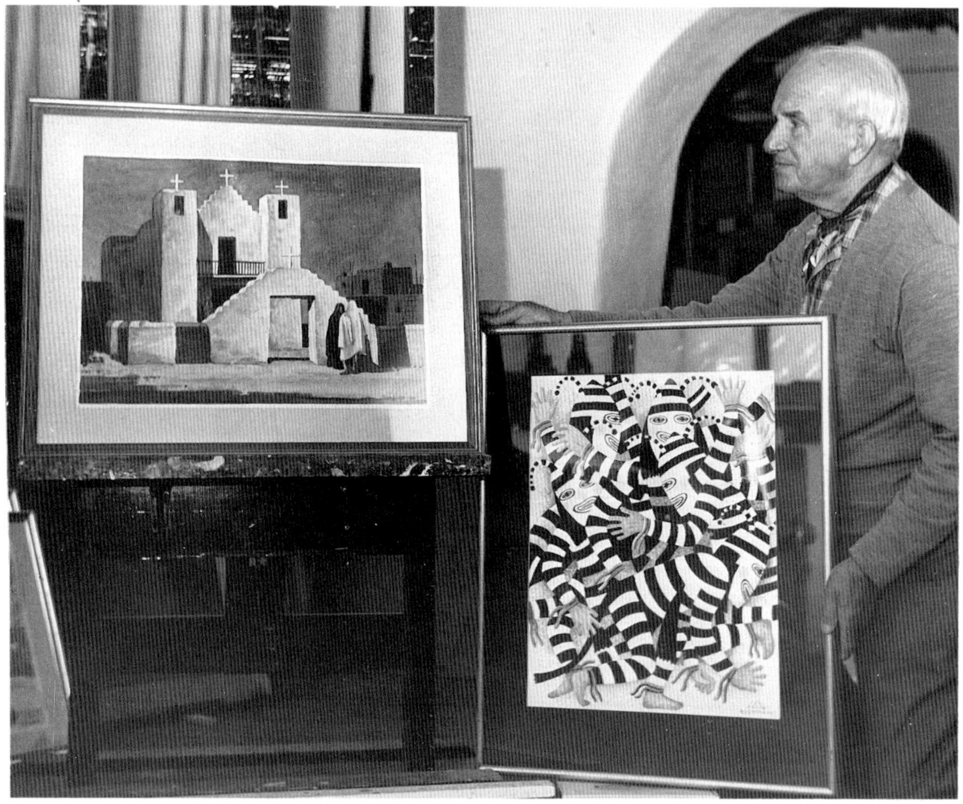

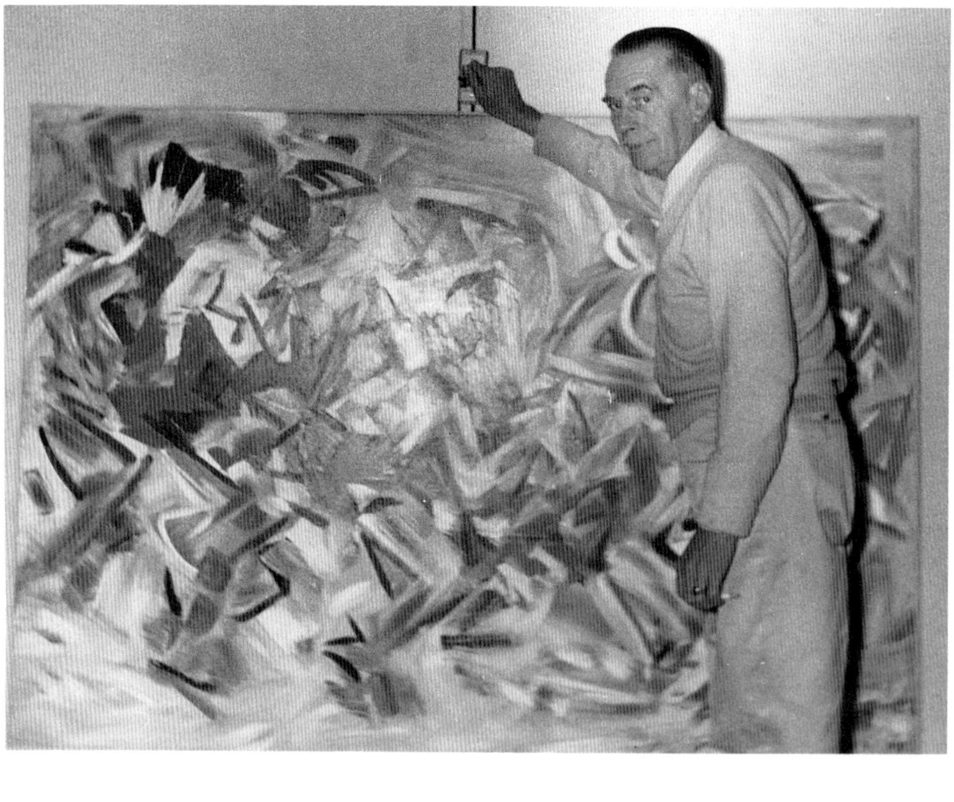

(TOP LEFT)
Howard Cook. ca. 1955.
Photographer: Regina Cooke

(TOP RIGHT)
Emil Bisttram. ca. 1959.
Photographer: Regina Cooke

(BOTTOM RIGHT)
Ward Lockwood. ca. 1962.
Photographer: Regina Cooke

APPENDIX A: Additional Artists

The "Contemporary American Painting and Sculpture" exhibition series was held seven times between 1951 and 1961 at the College of Fine and Applied Arts at the University of Illinois. The works of fourteen resident artists of Taos were included in those seven shows for a total of twenty-eight times: Thomas Benrimo, five; Ward Lockwood and Ted Egri, four each; Howard Cook, Alfred Rogoway, Robert D. Ray, and Cady Wells, two each; Clay Spohn, Dorothy Brett, Edward Corbett, Zalmar, Bernadette Wood, and William Heaton, once each.

■ ■ ■

The artists showing in the "Today" section of the Colorado Springs Fine Arts Center 1951 "Taos Painting, Yesterday and Today" exhibition were: Thomas Benrimo, Emil Bisttram, Kimball Blood, Malcolm Brown, Edward Corbett, Howard Cook, Andrew Dasburg, Ted Egri, Leo Garel, Ralph Grummet, Buff Haney, Cliff Harmon, Arthur R. Jacobson, Ward Lockwood, Beatrice Mandelman, Toni Mygatt, Louis Ribak, Alfred Rogoway, Clay Spohn, Charles Stewart, and Earl Stroh. The Taos Moderns included several dozen individuals. Some of those who continued on from this show to make careers for themselves are listed below.

Malcolm Brown (born 1925) first visited Taos in 1945, living in the art community part-time, including a stint at the University of New Mexico Summer Field School of Art. He became a permanent resident in 1955. He chose a pioneer-type lifestyle for himself, which proved so rugged that he gave up art for a time. He later returned to it through the creation of sculptural adobe fireplaces, house design, and finally, painting.

Cliff Harmon (born 1923) met Emil Bisttram in May 1946, just after leaving military service, and that summer traveled to Taos to enroll in the Bisttram School of Fine Art. This began a period of study which would also include work with Ribak and a stay at North Carolina's Black Mountain College. He met his future wife, Barbara, in 1947 in Los Angeles, where she also studied art, a natural pursuit for her as her father was an artist. The Harmons lived in Taos for part of the 1950s, returning again to remain as permanent residents in the early 1960s.

Arthur R. Jacobson (born 1924) lived in Taos from 1951 to 1956, for much of that time in the same compound of adobe apartments in which Agnes Martin and Ted Egri resided. He ran Ribak's Taos Valley Art School when Ribak left on his annual three-month trip to Mexico. Jacobson moved from Taos to teach at Philbrook Art Center in Tulsa, Oklahoma. He was named Professor Emeritus of Arizona State University in Tempe after his retirement from there in 1986.

Alfred Rogoway (1900–1990) visited Taos as early as 1941 and lived in the art community for much of the 1950s. He was a great iconoclast and eccentric who was unpredictable in everything but painting. Moved by an all-consuming passion for women and music, his painting mostly depicted those subjects, often within a mythological or fantasy framework.

Charles C. Stewart (born 1922) came to Taos in 1947 to study with Louis Ribak. Over decades in Taos, he sculpted and painted in a variety of forms, placing him among the small group of Taos Moderns who did three-dimensional work.

APPENDIX B: The Rise and Fall of the Stables Gallery

For artists such as Cliff Harmon, Charles C. Stewart, and Beatrice Mandelman, just to name a few, the Stables Gallery of the Taos Art Association would become central to their lives, a meeting ground for friends and a defining institution for the Taos Moderns.

The TAA actually borrowed its name from an earlier organization. In 1939, the Karavas brothers, local businessmen, founded the La Fonda Gallery at their La Fonda Hotel. Long a gathering place for artists, the lobby became well known for its ongoing chess games between artists and their friends. This gallery seems to have grown out of the first Taos Artists' Association of 1937, since the membership of both closely correspond. The first TAA dissolved prior to 1952, although the La Fonda Gallery continued well into the 1950s.

This left the TAA name free to be applied to the new organization formed in 1952. Charles Reynolds, president, and Perry Moore, treasurer, wrote the guiding philosophy of the organization, and in order to make sure these principles were followed, the credo was printed on membership cards and given to everyone who joined:

1. To work diligently, striving always to improve the quality of my work.
2. To aid and assist, whenever possible, other artists in developing their creative talents.
3. To aid the layman in the developing of a keener appreciation of the arts.
4. By no word or deed depreciate the efforts of fellow artists or craftsmen.
5. To maintain the dignity of art by physical, mental and moral conduct.

The tremendous artistic energy which characterized Taos in the early 1950s spilled over into the artists' new TAA, fueled in part by the desire many of them felt for reconciliation between Moderns and old-timers. Art lectures and social gatherings also contributed to the growth of the organization. By the early months of 1953, artist and lay membership had grown to well over one hundred. The sketch group drew as many as thirty-four to work from scantily clad models, often while listening to classical and jazz music. Out of this enthusiasm came the founding of the Stables Gallery, which allowed anyone to show but quickly became one of the centers for the Taos Moderns.

The Stables Gallery must have represented a particularly sweet success for Emil Bisttram, who seems to have been the Stables Gallery's prime booster, although he did not hold a bona fide office in the TAA until years after its founding. Among other events, he organized a group painting session that included teams of "aspen painters" and Moderns, then led them all in a group sing afterwards. It appears to have been his idea to display both modernist and "traditional" art together. This was appropriate, since he had an artistic foot in both of those worlds himself. A few months later, the gallery director hired to make the Stables a going concern, Leone Kahl, began hanging every sort of art produced in Taos at the time.

Naturally, the result was chaotic. Artists and would-be artists from throughout the Southwest took advantage of the opportunity to show at the Stables Gallery, which then charged only a twenty-five percent sales commission. In 1954, in an attempt to deal with the confusion, the number of exhibiting members was limited to one hundred from a six-state area. New members were elected by a three-person jury whose membership was apparently kept secret—possibly for the protection of the jury! In April 1956, all artists not living in Taos County lost exhibit privileges. The TAA expected the number of artists showing to level off at around eighty.

The TAA established that it could handle one major project (the gallery) and several lesser ones (the historical museum, the sketch group, the educational programs) successfully at one time. The era of the Taos Moderns had called for the creation of a new arts institution because the older art institution, the Harwood Foundation, was not in itself adequate to meet all the increasing needs of an ever-growing population of Taos artists. The expansion mood still upon them, the visual artists soon elected to take on a second major project—one which ultimately proved to be their undoing.

The artists, working with the Taos Little Theater and the Taos Chamber of Commerce, began planning development of an open-air summer theater on the grounds behind the Thorne House, the old Manby property where all TAA operations were located. Construction of the Encore Theater started in May 1955; the first play was produced in July. To the visual artists, many of them also amateur actors, the expansion of the TAA seemed like a logical development. They did not notice that the community's attention, and the focus of their own creative energy, began to shift slightly away from the Stables Gallery.

By June 1960, the number of artists showing at the Stables Gallery had dropped to forty-eight. In November, the gallery announced that membership would be further restricted. Among the new requirements were stipulations that an artist establish legal residence in Taos for one year before making application; that the applicant be a professional artist; that the applicant achieve recognition in the art field as determined by the screening committee; and that acceptance would be by majority vote of the art committee.

The TAA abolished its Historical Museum in 1957, but retained its interest in museums by renting the Thorne House to the Millicent Rogers Foundation for its museum the following year. With the Thorne House mortgage paid off in 1966, the TAA made a pledge to the community to become more active in promoting educational programs and theater, including renovation—and fire proofing—of its outdoor theater building. Fund-raising began in 1969 for improvements on the theater facility and $91,000 had been raised when the place burned to the ground in November. The TAA then began making plans to build a new permanent auditorium, an important asset to Taos but one which put the TAA deeply in debt and forced the organization to divert increasing amounts of emotional, creative, and financial energy away from the operation of the Stables Gallery. With this new obligation came the gradual displacement of visual artists from the TAA board.

The Millicent Rogers Foundation moved its museum from the Thorne House in 1968, and following a time of vacancy and a short-term occupancy by a group involved in a weaving project, the Stables Gallery moved from the old stable to the larger Thorne House in 1971, where the TAA's visual arts operation was to remain. The new auditorium was completed but not paid for during the following year. By this time, the character of the Taos art community had changed due to the influx of new immigrants and the boom in both commercial art galleries and real estate.

During the 1970s, the Stables Gallery admission process became so bogged down that the screening committee failed to reach consensus on which artists qualified for membership. Some local, full-time resident artists became alienated when nationally prominent artists who were only part-time residents, such as Lee Mullican and Larry Calcagno (from the same generation as most of the Taos Moderns) were admitted, while relatively unknown local artists were not. Gallery membership gradually drifted down to below forty, the Taos Moderns still hanging onto the last remnants of what had been their TAA. The Stables Gallery management began promoting some artists over others, thus factionalizing an already small group.

Concurrently, commercial art galleries increasingly became the most visible aspect of the art community. The atmosphere of a growing Taos, more integrated than ever with the economics of the rest of the art world, seemed to change from favoring the creation of art to favoring the selling of art. Most of the Taos Moderns remained in Taos, but their artistic dominance of the community had long since peaked, and their influence had waned. The TAA, now a reflector of change rather than a leader, was forced to sell its parking lot to the Town of Taos to raise funds, and would soon enter into an embarrassing deal with a real estate broker of questionable virtue in an attempt to capitalize on its remaining property holdings. Finally, in the 1980s, as if in a ritual of defeat and dementia, the TAA cut down most of the trees in its much-loved lilac garden. No longer meeting the needs of artists on a predictable basis, the TAA and its Stables Gallery were overshadowed by two successful arts festivals with which the TAA cooperated as a junior partner.

The TAA would survive, but the Stables Gallery as an artists' cooperative began to dissolve around 1980. In reality the old Stables was not merely dying, it was already dead, having outlived the era which spawned it by several years. Most of the artists did not even show up for the final, frantic effort to save what they had created. Only thirty-two members remained at the end. Those who attended the final save-the-Stables meetings (which I witnessed as an interested observer) exhibited emotions ranging from impotent anger to forthright despair. None of them knew what was happening, that a time still grasped, was lost. These meetings, in which the artists could do little more than voice complaints, seemed to be the wake for the era of the Taos Moderns.

There are various reasons for the cooperative's demise. Non-artists took control of the TAA and made it part of the social scene: they liked art far more than they liked artists. Commercial galleries wanted to see the demise of the Stables Gallery because they perceived the cooperative as representing unfair competition. The artists constantly bickered with management and with each other. Most importantly, during the 1970s the Stables Gallery moved into a position of no longer representing a cross section of community artists, thus ironically cutting off its own natural constituency. However, what was historically more important than any of these causes was that the old Stables was such an integral part of the 1950s that it could not survive in the colder, more impersonal environment which came to characterize the art community in the 1960s and later. An art community dominated by purely commercial concerns, and by artists paradoxically more isolated from each other than ever before, was one which was anathematized against the old ways. The cooperative had been an extremely personal kind of institution.

The Stables Gallery represented the very lifeblood of the era of the Taos Moderns, and it is remarkable that it held on to its old form for as long as it did. The artists could not have saved it. The final death knell came in December 1981, after all efforts by the artists to regain control of their organization had failed. In 1951, the Taos Moderns thought they had discovered new, significant answers to artistic problems, and thirty years later found themselves treated as harshly by newcomer artists as they themselves had treated the old Taos Society of Artists. There is neither justice nor a lack of it in this, only an inevitability. It is the peculiar fate of American artists to occasionally find themselves "buried alive" while they are still active and productive, victims of the larger, disposable-minded society over which they have no control. The inevitability of being buried under a subsequent layer of Taos is a sobering one, but this is a powerful valley, filled with romantic images and timeless legends. I believe that among the brightest of those legends will be that of the Taos Moderns, and the immensely creative era they originated. It has been my intent to use the plowshare of art history to dig into their layer of Taos so that it might be remembered.

NOTES

Part One: The Time and the Place

1. Arrell Morgan Gibson, *The Santa Fe and Taos Colonies, Age of the Muses, 1890–1942* (Norman: University of Oklahoma Press, 1983), 267. In his book, Professor Gibson proves the adage that a little bit of knowledge may be dangerous indeed: His statement that the art community ended, coupled with a significant number of other errors in his text, can only lead one to wonder if he ever visited the place he wrote about.

2. Clinton Adams, book review in *Artspace* (Fall 1986): 34–36.

3. Georgia O'Keeffe, *Georgia O'Keeffe* (New York: The Viking Press, 1976), text for Plate 64.

Part Two: The Newcomers and the Aspen Painters

1. Don Adams, "Taos Art Mart," *New Mexico* Magazine (September 1964). Although quoting Gaspard as if he were alive, the artist had died six months before the article was printed.

2. Interview with Earl Stroh, January 16, 1985.

3. For instance, Ribak and Mandelman traveled to Santa Fe on the advice of John Sloan and then independently found their way to Taos. Earl Stroh moved to Albuquerque because he liked the noncollegiate adobe architecture shown in the University of New Mexico catalog; he thereafter attended UNM's Summer Field School of Art in Taos. Cliff Harmon, a student of Emil Bisttram in Los Angeles, followed his teacher to Taos. Ted Egri and Charles Stewart independently heard of Ribak's Taos Valley Art School, while John DePuy learned of Ribak's school from Rothko and Hofmann.

4. Spud Johnson, "Galleries vs. Artists," *El Crepusculo* (undated clipping, ca. 1951).

5. Mabel Dodge Luhan, "Critic Lauds Seven Local Artists in Blue Door Exhibit," *Taoseno and the Taos Review* (July 17, 1947): 1. She praised Louis Ribak, who demonstrated "an uncanny sympathy with the various moods of time and place."

6. "Harwood, Blue Door Exhibits Give Taosenos Double Feature in Art," *Taoseno and the Taos Review* (August 7, 1947): 6.

7. Nan Sheets, "Lack of Exhibit Space Problem for Artists," *Taoseno and the Taos Review* (September 25, 1947): 3.

8. "Paintings of Great Taos Artists Shown," *The Houston Press* (April 2, 1957). Following Phillips's death, the newspaper wrote of him, "Bert Phillips often said he could never accept abstract art, but late in life remarked that, 'I believe these youngsters have something after all.' When he died he left one of his own."

9. Interview with Ted Egri, February 18, 1985. Time was their real enemy. Several of the Taos Society Artists had already died by the early 1950s.

10. It is probably impossible to find any two articles which agree on the number of galleries operating in Taos at any one time. They come and go rapidly, and the fine line between gallery and gift shop, like so much else in our time, is often obscure.

11. "Taos, N. Mex., Mixes Art and Credit, Gets Livelihood with a Lift," *Wall Street Journal* (July 27, 1956).

12. Much of the information on Eulalia Emetaz came from the dealer's own files, owned at the time of this study by her niece, Lalla Lepeschkin, who kindly gave me access to them.

13. Ibid.

14. Interview with Ted Egri, February 19, 1985.

15. Ibid.

16. Fred S. Bartlett, *Taos Painting, Yesterday and Today* (Colorado Springs: Colorado Springs Fine Arts Center, March 1952).

17. Allen S. Weller, C. V. Donovan et al., *Contemporary American Painting and Sculpture* [catalogs] (Urbana: University of Illinois, 1948–1963).

18. Letter from C.V. Donovan to Eulalia Emetaz, September 4, 1952, Emetaz's La Galeria Escondida files.

19. *The Ruins Group of Taos*, Group Representative: Oscar Salzer, Los Angeles (1951 or 1952).

20. Spud Johnson, "The Horsefly" column, *El Crepusculo* (June 19 and June 26, 1952).

21. Joan Evans, *Art Digest* (May 1952): 12.

22. Martin Tucker, "The End of an Era," *Coastlines* (Autumn 1958): 14–17.

23. Ibid.

24. Cliff Harmon's less publicized sketch group organized around 1949 worked with nude models; under various conveners, the group survived until about 1985.

25. Notes on the Stables were compiled from TAA archival records, Taos newspapers, and interviews with former Stables members.

26. *El Crepusculo* (April 23, 1953).

27. Kit Egri, "The Stables Gallery Opens," *El Crepusculo* (September 17, 1953).

28. Interview with Beatrice Mandelman, December 23, 1982.

29. Sanky Trimble, "Peace Finally Arrives at Art Colony in Taos," *Los Angeles Times* (September 21, 1954).

30. By then, the La Fonda group grew less conservative and came to include such moderns as Thomas Benrimo, Earl Stroh, and Cliff Harmon.

31. Interview with Dr. Henry Sauerwein, Jr., April 22, 1987. See also background on the foundation in "Helene Wurlitzer Foundation Marks Anniversary," *El Crepusculo* (November 24, 1955) and TAA *News Hound* 1, no. 7 (January 1957).

32. Background information is from Marvin Buckels's talk given at the Harwood Foundation in 1983; from *The Midland Federal Savings Art Collection* catalog from the early 1980s; and from an interview with Marvin Buckels, April 14, 1987.

33. On July 10, 1987, I filed a Freedom of Information Act Request to research FBI activities in relation to the Taos Moderns. The first information was released to me in the fall of 1989. Hundreds of pages of documents revealed that both Bisttram and Ribak were under surveillance for about two decades. However, no information was released on the other artists, and about eighty percent of the released documents were censored by the generous use of felt tip markers. The artist-subversives list (allegedly compiled by two Taos Anglos, a lawyer-businessman and a cowboy artist) did exist, but all names of both "subversives" and list compilers were withheld, therefore the most interesting aspects of this matter remain hidden for now. The thousands of dollars and thousands of hours spent spying on Ribak and Bisttram failed to turn up anything on either man.

34. Interview with Cliff Harmon, February 20, 1987.

35. This is based on my conversations with several of the Taos Moderns from the mid- to late 1980s.

Part Three: The Artists

1. Interview with Ted Egri, February 19, 1985.

2. Letter to Eulalia Emetaz, April 24, 1957, Emetaz's La Galeria Escondida archive. Dasburg showed in her gallery. The event referred to was a major retrospective of his work at the Dallas Museum of Fine Arts; Bywaters was its director.

3. Jonathan Scott, "Andrew Dasburg," *The Black Bear Review* (Winter 1975): 1–10.

4. Jerry Bywaters, *Andrew Dasburg*, exhibit catalog (Dallas: Dallas Museum of Fine Arts, March 1957).

5. Manuscript by Howard Cook, dated September 1959, from the Harwood Foundation archives.

6. After having spent fifteen years living mostly in Taos and Santa Fe, Dasburg settled permanently in Talpa (just south of Taos) in 1933.

7. Interview with Earl Stroh, January 16, 1985. Earl Stroh was in contact with all these artists and saw firsthand this particular Corbett-Dasburg-Benrimo interaction.

8. Andrew Dasburg, "Notes for a Criticism." The notes were for a talk delivered at the Harwood Foundation, July 31, 1953. Harwood Foundation archives.

9. *Cady Wells*, exhibit catalog, Museum of New Mexico (1956). The stylistic development of Wells's art was traced by Kate C. Duncan in a catalog, *Cady Wells, a Retrospective Exhibition*, for the University of New Mexico Art Museum (1967).

10. Ibid.

11. Donald Bear, *The Santa Barbara News-Press* (June 6, 1948) quoted in the Museum of New Mexico catalog (1956).

12. Allen S. Weller, "Truth and Vision in Contemporary Painting," in the exhibit catalog *Contemporary American Painting and Sculpture* (Urbana: University of Illinois, 1952), 19.

13. "Ariadne," *El Crepusculo* (March 8, 1951).

14. Personal notes on Benrimo were provided by Earl Stroh during several interviews from 1985 to 1987. According to Stroh, a committee led by Ernest Blumenschein called on Benrimo in 1939 to "inquire" about his reason for moving to Taos. Ribak told of similarly being interrogated by an old-timers' "intentions" committee. Such investigations were not confined to Taos. In the largest of provincial cities, New York, Edward Corbett and Stephanie Sonora (then his wife) were examined and questioned by a large visiting committee of black-suited, black-tied representatives of the New York School at the time of Corbett's major show at the Museum of Modern Art in 1952. Despite being scattered from San Francisco to Taos to New York, the cosmopolitan art world often exhibited the social traits of a small town.

15. Like other modern artists, Benrimo had gone through a cubist stage. Abraham Davidson noted that in 1916 Benrimo "entered the Marine Camouflage Service, where he disguised ships from detection—an appropriate sort of cubist activity." From Abraham A. Davidson's *Early*

American Modernist Painting 1910–1935 (New York: Harper & Row, 1981), 274.

16. *Exhibition of Contemporary American Painting and Sculpture* (Urbana: University of Illinois, 1951), 161–162. Benrimo quoted Charles Norman from the book *William Shakespeare.* Benrimo was also included in an important 1954 show at the Guggenheim, "Younger American Painters," a major recognition for him at the time. The title was a source of considerable amusement to the sixty-seven-year-old painter.

17. "From the Reviews," *New York Times* (May 16, 1954).

18. *Ribak*, catalog, Harry Salpeter Gallery, Inc., New York (1954). Salpeter's "well known" is a term of uncertain compliment, meaning perhaps well known to certain persons but not to everyone, or was better known formerly than currently.

19. The FBI had badgered Ribak in New York, following him around and interviewing him, his family, and friends about his alleged communist sympathies.

20. Harry Rand, *Louis Ribak—The Late Paintings* (Roswell, New Mexico: Roswell Museum and Art Center, 1984), 27.

21. Interview with Beatrice Mandelman, December 22, 1982.

22. "Together Separately, Separately Together," unattributed, *Taos Magazine* (September/October 1979): 18.

23. They went to New York prior to the May 1954 Salpeter show and returned permanently to Taos in 1956.

24. Ed Sasek, "Bea Mandelman: The Pulse of Contemporary Time," *Artspace* (Spring 1982): 25.

25. It would be interesting to speculate on the reasons for the mass public acceptance of abstract design in American Indian art at the same time that abstract painting on canvas meets with resistance. For example, the author of a 1953 article on Taos made appreciative comments of traditional Indian art, but admitted confusion about modernist art: "More recently the modernists have been putting onto canvas what they call 'abstractions,' which I don't understand, but some of them are lovely." From Rosemary Taylor, "Taos the Unspoiled," *Family Circle* (March 1953): 62.

26. Andrew Dasburg, *Earl Stroh*, exhibit catalog from the Mission Gallery, Taos (July 28, 1973).

27. Interview with Earl Stroh, January 16, 1985.

28. In the 1940s before coming to Taos, Stroh had learned lithography by mail. He was sent a small stone and instructions on how to use it. After he returned the completed stone, prints were run and mailed back to him. Interview with Earl Stroh, October 24, 1987.

29. "People," *International Herald Tribune* (November 7, 1980).

30. Interview with Agnes Martin, April 7, 1987.

31. Martin and Richard Diebenkorn were part of the thriving Albuquerque modernist art scene during the 1940s and 1950s. Modernism was less prominent in Santa Fe during that time where the modernist painters included Janet Lippincott and Alfred Morang, but few others.

32. Interview with Agnes Martin, April 7, 1987. Sources on dates for Martin, including the artist herself, are vague or contradictory. This frustrates researchers but is just a part of the Martin mystique.

33. Ibid.

34. The Taos Moderns interviewed about the 1950s generally agreed: 1) that they suffered financial hardship; 2) that they were artistically dedicated to the new; 3) that the Taos Valley is filled with a marvelous quality of light; 4) and that they threw some great parties.

35. Helene Wurlitzer Foundation archives, Martin letter of December 5, 1954.

36. Helene Wurlitzer Foundation archives, Martin letter of November 8, 1954. As a historical aside, it may be mentioned that Blumenschein and other Taos Society artists also said that they sought to create an identifiably American type of painting.

37. Reinhardt visited Corbett and Spohn in Taos around 1952, as did Clyfford Still. Mark Rothko visited Alfred and Marjorie Rogoway in Ranchos de Taos for about three weeks in 1952. While there is no evidence surviving locally that any of these visitors did any painting in Taos, their presence would not have gone unnoticed by the Taos Moderns.

38. Interview with Agnes Martin, April 7, 1987.

39. Why did Martin destroy almost the entire production of her period in Taos? This period with its biomorphic paintings was critical to her development as an artist. It established her use of elusive color, and most importantly, her overwhelming concern for proportion. Martin's work was derived from abstract expressionism.

Abstract expressionism came out of cubism and non-academic surrealism as represented by artists such as Miró and Andre Masson. Those artists worked to liberate their use of space from cubism and to create a more open architecture within the picture plane. From this lesson, Gorky and Rothko were able to take a next step into experimenting with biomorphic shapes in painting. Martin probably was familiar with their mid-1940s work as reflected in the images of her Taos period. Having passed through this stage, she also must have assimilated Mondrian cubist forms on the way to developing her grids. Were her biomorphic paintings influenced by the first abstract expressionists or was her work a case of parallel development from a common artistic ancestry? One could speculate that Martin had her Taos works destroyed out of her concern that they might be considered derivative. Very few works survive upon which to do analysis of that period of her work. Are the surviving works among her best of that time? At least for now, these questions cannot be given a definite answer. But these oils likely are representative, showing a well thought out artistic direction. They are also important for establishing that as early as 1953, Martin had come to an understanding of modernism and was poised to make contributions to American art.

40. Vivian Milford, "Oli Sihvonen—One of Our Own," *Artlines* (July 1983): 32.

41. Eliot Weinberger, "Grand Designs," *The Nation* (August 29, 1987): 167-170. The author reviewed a book, *The Arts of Black Mountain College*, by Mary Emma Harris that quotes Albers. Albers's teachings came out of the Bauhaus School of Design in Germany, which itself was an extension of Russian constructivism and Dutch neo-plasticism.

42. Interview with Oli Sihvonen, June 9, 1987. One could speculate that the monumentality of mountains could be a natural analog to bigness in modern painting. Earlier moderns and academic realists had popularized the idea of large canvases, but Sihvonen's immediate inspiration seems to have been the massive natural forms of the American West.

43. "Ted Egri, Sculptor of Symbols," *Southwest Art* (February 1976): 76.

44. Interview with Ted and Kit Egri, February 2, 1987. Ted Egri said that Taos businessmen took note of his socialist leanings and perceived him as being "a wild-haired, Jewish, modern painter—from New York, no less!"

45. *Contemporary American Painting and Sculpture* (Urbana: University of Illinois, 1952).

46. Alfred Morang, "Art in the News," *Santa Fe News* (March 14, 1952).

47. Ganthiers studied Hofmann's philosophy with Alice Kinzinger, who had come to Taos in 1947, but perhaps for reason of avoiding competition with her cubist-painter husband, Edmund, accomplished little work in Taos where she taught at the high school. Following up on work by Regina Cooke and Helen Blumenschein, she worked to establish the Taos Municipal Schools Art Collection in the 1950s. That collection contains a number of works by the Taos Moderns.

48. "The Artist Speaks for Herself," undated document (ca. 1960) written in conjunction with an exhibit of preliminary sketches at Gallery of Realities, Taos. Harwood Foundation archives.

49. Alfred Frankenstein, "Four Solo Art Exhibits Open Here—Each in Separate Place," *San Francisco Chronicle* (April 11, 1954).

50. *Contemporary American Painting and Sculpture*, exhibit catalog from the University of Illinois (1953),.224.

51. Conversation between Clay Spohn and Wesley Rusnell, winter 1971, relayed by Rusnell to the author September 1987.

52. Letter from Clay Spohn to Wolcott and Georgette Ely, November 14, 1959. Harwood Foundation archives.

53. Conversation between Clay Spohn and Wesley Rusnell, winter 1971, relayed by Rusnell to the author September 1987.

54. Hand-written statement from Spohn dated 1961. Harwood Foundation archives.

55. Conversation between Clay Spohn and Wesley Rusnell, winter 1971, relayed by Rusnell to the author September 1987.

56. Dorothy C. Miller, editor, *15 Americans*, catalog from The Museum of Modern Art (1952).

57. Mary McChesney, *A Period of Exploration: San Francisco 1945-1950*, catalog from The Oakland Museum Art Department (1973). This book is an important document on the significance of San Francisco as a center of postwar modernism.

58. Spohn had earlier recommended Clyfford Still for a teaching position at the school. Corbett matched Spohn's suggestion to Calder to use wire when, in 1950, he showed Ad Reinhardt the possibilities of black-colored painting.

59. A photograph of Corbett owned by Mildred Tolbert dated 1939 could have been taken in Taos; if so, he could have been a visitor to Taos when he was only twenty years old. Corbett spent most of his time in Taos until part way through 1953 although he also maintained an address in Sausalito, California, at least through August 1952 and possibly longer.

60. Interview with Joan Daw, May 13, 1986. Ms. Daw was an art student of Edward Corbett at Mount Holyoke College, Massachusetts, in the mid-1950s. She mentioned that Corbett told her about the significant visual impact which the snowy gorge made on him. Mildred Tolbert photographed two of the white paintings in Taos around 1953; the location of the paintings remains unknown.

61. Gerald Nordland, *Edward Corbett*, catalog from the San Francisco Museum of Art (March 1969).

62. Ibid.

63. Ibid.

64. Edward Abbey, "The Land of John DePuy," *Rocky Mountain News* (September 1981): 72.

65. Interview with John DePuy, October 31, 1985.

66. Ibid. The term "primitive(s) of a new art" has a long history—perhaps extending back to the prehistoric French cave painters. Within the history of modernism, the term comes from another Frenchman, Cézanne, who so labeled himself and his art.

67. David L. Witt, *Land of Clear Light: The Paintings of John DePuy and Polly Schaafsma*, exhibit catalog, The Harwood Foundation (January 1987).

68. *Robert Ray*, Colorado Springs Fine Arts Center catalog (March 1968).

69. Interview with Robert D. Ray, April 6, 1987.

70. Mary Fuller McChesney quoted Corbett, *Art Digest* (January 1954).

LIST OF PLATES

SELECT CRITICAL BIBLIOGRAPHY

The archives and special collections of the Harwood Foundation proved essential to this study, both for the primary sources it contains and for the ephemera (catalogs, periodicals, etc.) found nowhere else in one place. Much of the material in the archives was originally provided by the artists. Further primary documentation came from Georgette Ely (on Clay Spohn) and Lalla Lepeschkin (on Eulalia Emetaz and La Galeria Escondida); Mildred Tolbert and Regina Cooke each gave thousands of photographs to the Harwood which provided a meaningful visual understanding of the Taos of the 1950s. Other sources of information are located at the Fine Arts Libraries at the University of New Mexico (Albuquerque) and the Museum of New Mexico (Santa Fe).

A number of individuals were interviewed for their first-hand information concerning the second artistic era in Taos and its artists. Their cooperation and concern brought that era to life:

Mayrion Bisttram
Bill Bomar
Malcolm Brown
Marvin Buckels
Larry Calcagno
Regina Cooke
Gloria Corbett
Joan Daw
John DePuy
Kit Egri
Ted Egri
Barbara Harmon
Cliff Harmon
Georgette Ely
Wolcott Ely
Larry Hilburn
Arthur Jacobson
Lalla Lepeschkin
Beatrice Mandelman
Agnes Martin
Ila McAfee
Alfred Rogoway
Robert D. Ray
Henry A. Sauerwein, Jr.
Polly Schaafsma
Jonathan Scott
Oli Sihvonen
Stephanie Sonora
Charles C. Stewart
Earl Stroh
Mildred Tolbert

Books

Albright, Thomas. *Art in the San Francisco Bay Area, 1945–1980, An Illustrated History.* Berkeley and Los Angeles: University of California Press, 1985.

Ashton, Dore. *The New York School, a Cultural Reckoning.* New York: Viking Press, 1972.

Bickerstaff, Laura. *Pioneer Artists of Taos.* 2nd edition. Denver: Old West Publishing Company, 1984.

Canaday, John. *Mainstreams of Modern Art.* New York: Simon & Schuster, 1959.

Chip, Herschel B. *Theories of Modern Art—A Source Book by Artists and Critics.* Berkeley and Los Angeles: University of California Press, 1968.

Davidson, Abraham A. *Early American Modernist Painting 1910–1935.* New York: Harper & Row, 1981.

Eliade, Mircea. *The Sacred and the Profane—The Nature of Religion.* New York: Harcourt, Brace & World, Inc., 1958.

Goodrich, Lloyd. *Albert P. Ryder.* New York: George Braziller, Inc., 1959.

Guilbout, Serge. *How New York Stole the Idea of Modern Art, Abstract Expressionism, Freedom and the Cold War.* Chicago: University of Chicago Press, 1983.

Harris, Mary Emma. *The Arts at Black Mountain College.* Boston: MIT Press, 1987.

Homer, William Innes, general editor. *Avant-Garde Painting & Sculpture in America 1910–25.* Delaware Art Museum, 1975.

Isham, Samuel, and Royal Cortissoz. *The History of American Painting.* New York: Macmillan Company, 1936.

Loran, Erle, Weldon Kees, and Ernest Mundt. *Painting and Sculpture: The San Francisco Art Association.* Berkeley and Los Angeles: University of California Press, 1952.

Luhan, Mabel Dodge. *Taos and Its Artists.* New York: Duell, Sloan and Pearce, 1947.

Moore, Ethel, editor. *Contemporary Art 1942–72: Collection of the Albright-Knox Gallery.* New York: Praeger Publishers, 1972.

O'Neill, John P. *Clyfford Still.* New York: Metropolitan Museum of Art, 1979.

Plagens, Peter. *Sunshine Muse, Contemporary Art on the West Coast.* New York: Praeger Publishers, 1974.

Rickey, George. *Constructivism, Origins and Evolution.* New York: George Braziller, Inc., 1967.

Russell, John. *The Meanings of Modern Art.* New York: Harper & Row, 1974.

Schapiro, Meyer, editor. *Modern Art—19th & 20th Century, Selected Papers.* New York: George Braziller, Inc., 1973.

Seitz, William C. *Abstract Expressionist Painting in America.* Cambridge: National Gallery of Art/Harvard University Press, 1983.

Shepard, Paul. *Man in the Landscape.* New York: Alfred A. Knopf, 1967.

Udall, Sharyn Rohlfsen. *Modernist Painting in New Mexico 1913-1935.* Albuquerque: University of New Mexico Press, 1984.

Witt, David L. *The Taos Artists: A Historical Narrative and Biographical Dictionary.* Colorado Springs: Ewell Fine Art Publications, 1984.

Zigrosser, Carl. *The Expressionists.* New York: George Braziller, Inc., 1957.

Periodicals

Adams, Clinton. "Art in New Mexico 1900-1945, Paths to Taos and Santa Fe." *Artspace* (Fall 1986): 34-36.

Adams, Don. "Taos Art Mart." *New Mexico* Magazine (September 1964): 26-28.

Agee, William C. "Synchromist, the First American Movement." *Art News* (October 1965): 29-31, 62-64.

Banks, Marissa, Lorraine Glennon, and Jeffrey Schaire. "The 25 Most Undervalued American Artists." *Art & Antiques* (October 1986): 63-79.

Cassidy, Ina. "Art and Artists of New Mexico." *New Mexico* Magazine (January 1957): 33, 55.

"Clay Spohn." *Art in America* (December 1963).

De Kooning, Elaine. "New Mexico." *Art in America*, no. 4 (1961): 56-57.

Evans, Joan. "Albuquerque." *Art Digest* (May 15, 1952): 12.

Gruen, John. "Agnes Martin: Everything, everything is about feeling . . . feeling and recognition." *Art News* (September 1976).

Hewett, Edgar L. "On Opening the New Museum"; "On the Opening of the Art Galleries." *Art and Archaeology* 7, nos. 1-2 (January/February 1918): 9-13 and 50-52.

Hofstadter, Dan. "Profile—Richard Diebenkorn." *The New Yorker* (September 7, 1987): 54-73.

Loran, Erle. "Art News from the Southwest." *Art News* (October 1953).

McAgy, Douglas. "5 Rediscovered from the Lost Generation." *Art News* (Summer 1960): 38-51.

McChesney, Mary Fuller. "Edward Corbett." *Art Digest* (January 1954): 21-23.

Milford, Vivian. "Louis Ribak in Taos—Reminiscences of Bea Mandelman." *Artspace* (Fall 1983).

———. "Oli Sihvonen—One of Our Own." *Artlines* (July 1983): 32.

Monroe, Gerald M. "The American Artists' Congress and the Invasion of Finland." *Archives of American Art Journal* 15 (1975): 14-20.

"Out There in the Universe." *Newsweek* (November 1, 1965): 88.

Rogoway, Margorie. "Taos Artists Take Exception." *Art Digest* (August 1952): 4.

Sasek, Ed. "Bea Mandelman: The Pulse of Contemporary Time." *Artspace* (Spring 1982): 25.

Schapiro, Meyer. "Essentials in Art." *Art News* (Summer 1977).

Scott, Jonathan. "Andrew Dasburg." *The Black Bear Review* 1, no. 2 (Winter 1975): 1-10.

Sommers, John. "Earl Stroh—A Retrospective of Prints." *Artspace* (Fall 1982): 30-32.

———. "Tom Benrimo (1887-1958), An Appreciation." *Artspace* (Fall 1984): 29-33.

Stroh, Earl. "Andrew Dasburg—1887-1979." *Artspace* (June 1980): 56-59.

"Taos Contemporary." *Empire Magazine* (June 16, 1957).

"Ted Egri, Sculptor of Symbols." *Southwest Art* (February 1976): 76.

"Together Separately, Separately Together." *Taos Magazine* (September/October 1979): 18.

Tucker, Martin. "The End of an Era." *Coastlines* (Autumn 1958): 14-17.

Weinberger, Eliot. "Grand Designs." *The Nation* (August 29, 1987).

Winter, Amy. "Oli Sihvonen." *Artspace* (Fall 1983).

Catalogs

Agnes Martin. Philadelphia: Institute of Contemporary Art, University of Pennsylvania, 1973.

Andrew Dasburg. New York: American Federation of Arts, 1959.

Art and the Atom. Taos and Los Alamos: Stables Art Gallery and Los Alamos Scientific Laboratory, 1963.

Bartlett, Fred S. *Taos Painting, Yesterday and Today.* Colorado Springs: Colorado Springs Fine Arts Center, March 1952.

Bywaters, Jerry. *Andrew Dasburg.* Dallas: Dallas Museum of Fine Arts, 1957.

Dasburg, Andrew. *Earl Stroh.* Taos: Mission Gallery, 1973.

Duncan, Kate C. *Cady Wells, a Retrospective Exhibition.* Albuquerque: University of New Mexico Art Museum, 1967.

Ely, Georgette, and Leah Mingenbach. *The Taos Fire House Collection Presents the Taos Municipal Schools Collection.* Taos: Taos Arts Festival, September 1986.

Exhibiting Artists of the Stables Gallery. Taos: Stables Art Gallery, 1977.

Exhibition of Paintings and Sculpture. New York: The MacDowell Club, 1913.

Gallery of Realities Presents Taos Invitational. Taos: Gallery of Realities, 1960.

Jonson, Raymond. *Group 7.* Albuquerque: Jonson Gallery, University of New Mexico, October 1966.

Levin, Gail. *Synchromism and American Color Abstraction.* New York: Whitney Museum of Art/ George Braziller, Inc., 1978.

McChesney, Mary. *A Period of Exploration: San Francisco 1945–1950.* Oakland: Oakland Museum Art Department, 1973.

The Midland Federal Savings Art Collection. Denver: Midland Federal Savings, ca. 1979. As of 1988 the collection belonged to Western Capital Investment Corporation of Denver, Colorado.

Miller, Dorothy C., editor. *15 Americans.* New York: Museum of Modern Art, 1952.

Modern Painting in Taos: The 40's and 50's, A Selection . . . Taos: Stables Art Gallery, 1974.

Nordland, Gerald. *Edward Corbett.* San Francisco: San Francisco Museum of Art, March 1969.

Oklahoma Art Center, Inaugural Exhibition. Oklahoma City: Oklahoma Art Center, 1958.

Paintings & Sculpture from the Stables Gallery. Los Angeles: Esther Robles Gallery, 1959.

Rand, Harry. *Louis Ribak—The Late Paintings.* Roswell, New Mexico: Roswell Museum and Art Center, 1984.

Rebay, Hilla. *Solomon R. Guggenheim Collection of Non-Objective Paintings.* New York: Solomon R. Guggenheim Foundation, 1938.

Ribak. New York: Harry Salpeter Gallery, Inc., 1954.

Robert Ray. Colorado Springs: Colorado Springs Fine Arts Center, 1968.

St. John, Terry. *Clay Spohn.* Oakland: Oakland Museum Art Department, 1971.

Schooley, Elmer. *Louis Ribak.* Las Vegas, New Mexico: New Mexico Highlands University, 1963.

Sommers, John. *Earl Stroh.* Taos: Mission Gallery, 1982.

Strel, Donald O. *Louis Ribak Retrospective.* Santa Fe: Museum of New Mexico, 1975.

Stroh, Earl. *Tom Benrimo.* Santa Fe: Museum of New Mexico, 1973.

Taos Collects the Moderns Since 1900. Taos: Stables Art Gallery, 1973.

Taos Invitational 1960. Taos: Gallery of Realities, 1960.

Taos Moderns '59. Santa Fe: Museum of New Mexico, 1959.

Taos Moderns '60. Santa Fe: Museum of New Mexico, 1960.

Weller, Allen S., C.V. Donovan, et al. *Contemporary American Painting and Sculpture* (Urbana: University of Illinois, 1948–1963) [catalog series].

Western Painters' Annual Exhibition. Oakland: Oakland Municipal Art Museum, 1954.

Witt, David L. *Emil James Bisttram.* Taos: Harwood Foundation, 1983.

——. *Taos Modernist Art of the 1950s.* Taos: Harwood Foundation, 1985.

——. *Land of Clear Light: The Paintings of John DePuy and Polly Schaafsma.* Taos: Harwood Foundation, 1987.

Newspapers

The most important newspaper to report on the Taos Moderns was *El Crepusculo*, often referred to by Taoseños as "El Creeps." While only a few specific articles will be cited here from that paper, researchers looking into any aspect of the forties and fifties in Taos will find it invaluable.

Abbey, Edward. "The Land of John DePuy." *Rocky Mountain News,* September, 1981.

"Ariadne—Tom Benrimo." *El Crepusculo,* March 8, 1951.

"Artists Adopt Constitution." *Taos Review,* February 4, 1937. The article indicates that the Taos Artists' Association was extant by December 1936, or possibly earlier.

"Can Artists Control the Work They've Sold? For the Creative, Minimalist Wages." *New York Times,* November 23, 1986.

"Edward Corbett, Painter, 51, Dies." *New York Times,* June 8, 1971.

Egri, Kit. "The Stables Gallery Opens." *El Crepusculo,* September 17, 1953.

Frankenstein, Alfred. "Four Solo Art Exhibits Open Here—Each in Separate Place." *San Francisco Chronicle,* April 11, 1954.

"From the Reviews." *New York Times,* May 16, 1954.

"Harwood, Blue Door Exhibits Give Taoseños Double Feature in Art." *Taoseno and the Taos Review,* August 7, 1947.

Johnson, Spud. "Galleries vs. Artists." *El Crepusculo,* ca. 1951.

——. "The Horsefly." *El Crepusculo,* June 19, June 26, 1952.

"La Fonda Gallery Shows Stroh Paintings." *El Crepusculo,* July 26, 1951.

Luhan, Mabel Dodge. "Critic Lauds Seven Local Artists in Blue Door Exhibit." *Taoseno and the Taos Review,* July 17, 1947.

"Paintings of Great Taos Artists Shown." *Houston Press,* April 2, 1957.

"People." *International Herald Tribune,* November 7, 1980.

Sheets, Nan. "Lack of Exhibit Space Problem for Artists." *Taoseno and the Taos Review,* September 25, 1947.

"Taos, N. Mex., Mixes Art and Credit, Gets Livelihood with a Lift." *Wall Street Journal,* July 27, 1956.

"30 Artists Selected for Colorado Show." *El Crepusculo,* January 31, 1952.

Trimble, Sanky. "Peace Finally Arrives at Art Colony in Taos." *Los Angeles Times,* September 21, 1954.

INDEX

ABOUT THE AUTHOR

David L. Witt began his museum career in 1967 and has worked as a curator of art collections in the Southwest since 1972. He is a specialist in the art and art history of twentieth-century New Mexico. Curator of the University of New Mexico's Harwood Foundation in Taos since 1979, he is a leading scholar on the history of the Taos art community. In 1984, he published *The Taos Artists: A Historical Narrative and Biographical Dictionary.*

Mr. Witt lives in Taos, New Mexico, where he researches history, explores mountain ranges, and photographs wildflowers.